SOCIAL DEVELOPMENT IN SOCIAL WORK

Social work has always been concerned with the development of society as the basis for achieving the well-being of individuals, families and communities. Interest in this important aspect of social work is now seeing a resurgence, not only in the 'developing countries' of the global South but also in the global North. This innovative book provides an introduction to the area.

Using concrete examples taken from practice around the world, *Social Development in Social Work* addresses questions such as:

How should social development be understood as a core aspect of social work practice?

What is the significance of economics, politics and the environment for a developmental approach in social work?

How may a comparative understanding of social welfare practices, programmes and policies enhance social development in social work?

In what ways does social development contribute to international and domestic social work?

What skills, knowledge and theory do social workers need to practise in this field?

Arguing that social development should be at the centre of contemporary social work practice and theory, this book is ideal for social work students and academics with an interest in social development, international social work, social justice, social policy and community social work.

Richard Hugman is a professor of social work at the University of New South Wales, Australia. He has held positions in practice, teaching and research in Australia lished in social work and related fields. His recent t in Asia.

SOCIAL DEVELOPMENT IN SOCIAL WORK

Practices and principles

Richard Hugman

Routledge
Taylor & Francis Group

LONDON AND NEW YORK

First published 2016
by Routledge
2 Park Square, Milton Park, Abingdon, Oxon OX14 4RN
and by Routledge
711 Third Avenue, New York, NY 10017

Routledge is an imprint of the Taylor & Francis Group, an informa business

© 2016 R. Hugman

British Library Cataloguing in Publication Data
A catalogue record for this book is available from the British Library

Library of Congress Cataloging-in-Publication Data
Hugman, Richard, 1954– , author.
  Social development in social work : practices and principles / written by Richard Hugman.
    p. ; cm.
  Includes bibliographical references and index.
  1. Social service.   2. Social planning.   I. Title.
  [DNLM: 1. Social Work.   2. Global Health.   3. Social Change.   4. Social Welfare.   HV 40]
  HV40.H778 2016
  361.3—dc23
  2015004908

ISBN: 978-1-138-01763-4 (hbk)
ISBN: 978-1-138-01764-1 (pbk)
ISBN: 978-1-315-78033-7 (ebk)

Typeset in Bembo
by Apex CoVantage, LLC

Printed and bound in Great Britain by
TJ International Ltd, Padstow, Cornwall

CONTENTS

CONTENTS

PREFACE AND ACKNOWLEDGEMENTS

Although the concept of social development in many ways has grown out of social work, it often remains marginalised from the dominant perspectives in social work, especially in the countries of the global North. This has become apparent to me over a long involvement in international social work as a practitioner and academic. It has been highlighted both in the many debates that occur when people from different parts of the world meet and share their experience and their ideas and in the extent and types of research materials and educational resources that can be drawn on in practice and teaching. Thus the research into social development as practice and theory in social work that underpins this book began from both practical and theoretical concerns. For this reason, the analysis that is presented here likewise seeks to integrate practical and theoretical questions and to be relevant to the concerns of both practitioners and scholars in social work and beyond.

My own background in social work is that of a generalist practitioner. This has inevitably influenced the way in which the different dimensions of social development in social work are addressed. Nevertheless, as argued in the following chapters, this analysis concludes that the social development approach in many ways is most effectively examined from a generalist perspective. So although it has been drawn from questions that arose in international social work, this discussion is intended to inform social work in different national and local contexts as well as international practice.

Any analysis of this kind runs the risk of emphasising some aspects of the subject and ignoring others. However, throughout the discussion the central question has been 'what do these debates about social development tell us about its practice within a social work frame of reference?' In this way, the inevitable choices about what should be addressed in depth and what can be treated briefly was guided by a concern to connect the analysis with its practical implications at all times. This, I think, can be seen in the focus of Chapter 8, on skills and knowledge, on particular forms of practice – there are very few published studies of policy development as social work practice, for example.

It is also necessary for me to address a particular aspect of the way in which this book is structured. My own identity is that I am from the global North. So, even though my practice and research include working in global Southern contexts, I must be aware that I do so as a guest in international social work relationships. Given the importance of social development for social work in the global South, this is an important issue. For the discussion presented here it means that while I am able to address social development in international social work practice and for the so-called developed countries, reflected in the structure particularly of Chapters 6 and 7, I am not able to speak directly for global Southern perspectives and the extent to which I am able to address them is through the insights and inspiration of colleagues. In other respects, this is a task in which I must defer to colleagues from the global South.

A note on terminology – the vexed question of how to distinguish between the various parts of the world in relation to differences of social and economic development has no single agreed answer. Healy (2008) chooses the UNICEF terminology of 'developing' as against 'industrialised', while Payne (2014) prefers 'resource-poor' as against 'resource-rich'. In both cases they are seeking to avoid what they see as a confusion of the terms 'global South' and 'global North', illustrated by the location of Australia and New Zealand in the 'global North'. However, I regard all these terms as fraught with the same difficulty. Many of the 'developing' countries are rapidly industrialising and have parts that are now highly industrialised, in which major development issues centre on the unequal distribution of the benefits of development. Similarly, many of the so-called resource-poor countries are actually rich in natural and human resources, but face issues not only of internal inequality but also of international inequality and economic and political neocolonialism. Therefore, as these are questions that lie at the centre of the analysis of this book, I have chosen to stay with the 'South/North' distinction, which is widely used and understood in the development field and which is well defined by the Brandt Commission (1980), from which some critical approaches in development practice in the late twentieth century derived momentum.

I have been inspired by and learned much from colleagues from many different parts of the world, all of whom in various ways share an interest in social development in social work, from their practice and scholarship as well as through personal discussions. In alphabetical order, I would like to thank Margaret Alston, Eileen Baldry, Linda Bartolomei, Lena Dominelli, Mel Gray, Dorothee Hölscher, Nguyen Thi Thai Lan, Le Hong Loan, Jim Midgley, Mehmoona Mithi-Moosa, Otrude Moyo, Manohar Pawar, Eileen Pittaway, Vu Thi Le Thanh and Angie Yuen. Although we had never met, Leila Patel very kindly shared some ideas and materials by e-mail. While there may be aspects of the analysis presented here with which they may not agree, in various ways each has contributed in important ways to my engagement with and understanding of this important dimension of social work.

At Routledge I have been encouraged and supported by Grace McInnes, Louisa Vahtrick and James Watson. As always, it has been a great pleasure working with them.

Finally, I would like to acknowledge the many students with whom I have shared debates about many of the ideas that are presented here. I have been challenged and stimulated in my thinking by these encounters, and some may be surprised to know that education is a two-way process, in which the teacher learns as well, hopefully, as the student. This book is dedicated to all those who have gone on to put their learning into action in social development practice.

1

WHAT IS SOCIAL DEVELOPMENT AND WHAT IS ITS SIGNIFICANCE FOR SOCIAL WORK?

Introduction

Social development has emerged in recent decades as a distinctly defined approach to practice in social work. Yet the practice of social development often remains marginal to social work theory and debate. This book seeks to place social development more firmly in the mainstream of social work thinking by providing a clear account of the different issues and debates through which it is defined and understood. At the same time, this analysis offers a particular interpretation of the field. Thus, it not only explains the place social development has in the range of approaches to social work but also argues for a distinct understanding of social development theory, practices and values.

At the very beginning it is important to draw a careful distinction between social development and community development as complementary but separate approaches to practice in social work. Social development and community development are closely connected, but they are not synonymous. Their relationship is best understood by regarding social development as an overarching framework that brings together a range of practices, while community development is one of the practices that forms part of the social development perspective (Elliott, 1993). So the discussion that follows draws on what has come to be known as a 'generalist' approach to social work; although it clearly addresses community development, policy work and other 'macro' practices, it also includes 'micro' practices in social work with individuals, families and groups within a social development perspective.

This opening chapter examines the underlying definitions of development theories and practices and within that broad field the more specific area of *social* development. As it will be argued, this is important because the relationship between social work and development often rests on the claim that there is such a distinctive aspect, in which factors that cannot be seen simply as 'economics', 'politics' or 'technology' are recognised as crucial to the growing well-being of people, their families and communities and of countries as a whole. While social development is closely connected to these factors, and engages with them, it is also a separate area of theory and practice. Consequently, the way in which social development has been promoted as a necessary part of social work is to argue that social workers must become more aware of and able to work with economic, political and technological areas of social life, while bringing to such issues the knowledge, skills and values that are distinctive to all types of social work.

Material and structural need: a foundation and a debate

Many of the original proponents of social development as a distinct aspect of practice in social work argue it addresses a basic reality – namely that human life occurs in a material world (Midgley, 1984, 2014; Elliot, 1993; Lombard & Wairire, 2010). So for example at the most basic level the problems that people face in their lives may include access to water and food, and lack of shelter. As defined in the highly influential 'theory of need' (Maslow, 1954), these things are foundational to human life. In both an economic and a philosophical sense these are 'goods', because they enable people to live well (or simply to live) (Hölscher, 2008). One of the major points in Maslow's theory is that it is very hard to be able to focus on the higher-level achievements in human life if the satisfaction of necessities such as water and food cannot adequately be met.

Throughout human history a considerable amount of people's time has been occupied in activities to obtain these goods – that is in 'work' of a particular type. In the modern industrialised world, a great deal of work tends to be organised as 'employment', and so this also becomes a focus of concern for development as a basic need. Moreover, as societies become more complex there is an assumption that such work is increasingly specialised and dependent on technology. For example at least in general terms, the task of obtaining water can be compared between the countries of the global North and some rural parts of the global South. In cities such as Sydney, Paris, New York or London in order to obtain water most people expect simply to turn a tap in their home. Obtaining water thus becomes a transaction, in which the actual work performed is broken up between suppliers, those who construct and operate water supply systems (water catchment, purification, management of the pipework to deliver water to consumers, and so on), and consumers, who pay for the water supply. In contrast, in parts of Africa, Asia or Central America for example there are many places where individual members of the community, usually women and children, have to spend much of the day fetching and carrying water for each family's daily use. In this situation 'work' includes the activity of physically obtaining the water, rather than earning money in order to pay someone else to deliver the water, as is the case in more industrialised contexts.

Such differences between countries or between locations within countries were not always historically the case. For example the reticulated supply of water to homes is part of the development of the societies of the global North that has occurred within the last 150 years. Although reticulated water supply was achieved in some pre-industrial civilisations, it was usually available only to elites and in small geographical areas. In the industrialised countries of the twenty-first-century global North all but the most poor might expect to have access to this good. Indeed, not having such access has in itself become a measure of poverty. (In the global North, however, there are also other aspects of work focused on meeting needs in households that continue to be gendered in the same way as noted earlier regarding access to water [Kothari, 2002; Alston, 2013], a point that will be examined in more depth in later chapters of this book.)

Clearly, from this example, advanced water-engineering assists in the development of societies. Yet, although there is a technical dimension to meeting these needs, judgements about how these technologies are to be used are inherently social, political and economic. That is, decisions about how the provision of necessities, such as water, food and shelter, will be provided are made on the basis of human knowledge and skills, applied through values and relationships. They include questions about the decision-making structures of a society and the distribution of financial resources as well as technical dimensions. Thus, the way in which societies organise material provision for their populations is political and economic, as well as social and cultural. Indeed, in thinking about questions of development, politics and economics are often assumed to be the bodies of knowledge that will provide the solutions.

A field called 'development studies' now exists in a large number of universities (Haynes, 2008). In many cases these research and teaching programmes are grounded in political science, international relations, international studies or economics. Reflected in this is the current dominant focus on the eradication of poverty as the central goal of development. Indeed, if development is regarded in this way, then it is not surprising that the applied areas that derive from these disciplines are seen as the major contributors to development work. These include business, diplomacy, law, public policy and management, and more recently environmental science and engineering. Illustrative of this perspective, Kingsbury's (2008a, pp. 134–8) review of the key organisations involved in development at an international level is largely devoted to the World Trade Organization (WTO), the World Bank (WB), the International Monetary Fund (IMF), the Organisation for Economic Co-operation and Development (OECD) and the political, legal and economic role of the United Nations (UN), with mention only in passing of the UN High Commissioner for Refugees (UNHCR) and the UN Children's Fund (UNICEF). Agencies such as the UN Educational, Scientific and Cultural Organization (UNESCO) are not identified at all. This is despite a growing critique, summarised by McGillivray (2008, pp. 30–40), that material needs and solutions were overemphasised by development theorists in the late twentieth century. Nonetheless, McGillivray's own discussion of 'what is development?' continues to centre on income and wealth as the key indices of the way in which a better human life is to be pursued. Kingbury's (2008b) separate discussion of community development, while mentioning the importance of education, identifies this as an investment for economic growth and political change rather than as development seen in other ways, such as the foundation for greater human achievement in non-material aspects of life, such as gender equity. In this way, discussion of other factors, such as education, health and family and community life, appears to be seen in terms of the background conditions of development defined as material and structural improvements and not as development issues in themselves.

Of course, living in a stable society and having an adequate income are essential for being able to live a decent human life. While the detail of what makes a human life 'decent' varies between cultures (a point that is addressed further ahead in this chapter and in detail in Chapters 5 and 6), having the physical necessities to meet the basic level of need mentioned at the beginning of this section is a prerequisite across all cultures. Poverty eradication thus makes sense theoretically and practically as a starting point for development. So the contribution of Midgley (1984, 1995, 2014), Sherraden (1991), Mohan (1992), Elliot (1993) and Cox and Pawar (2013), among others, in their emphasis on structural and economic needs and responses can be seen as an important step in making the connection between social work and social development.

However, more recent advances in the field of development have grown from arguments that not all human needs can be understood in material terms. In particular, the concept of *social* development has emerged out of the realisation that although politics and economics are highly relevant, change in these areas does not necessarily lead to improvements in people's lives, which in many ways can be regarded as the goal of development (M. Green, 2002, p. 58). To put it in very simple terms, if human life does not 'get better' in some tangible way, then development cannot be said to have happened. This critique suggests that education, health, family relationships, community structures and cultural expression are all central aspects of human life that cannot be seen solely in material and structural terms (even though they have material and structural dimensions). These facets of what it is to be human are inescapably social.

Moreover, there is evidence that in some respects social achievements, such as improvements in education and health, are necessary precursors to economic and material gains, rather than consequential benefits of greater prosperity. A well-known and highly influential example of such research is Summers's (1994) report to the Economic Development Institute of the World Bank about the education of girls and young women. In brief, this careful analysis showed that increasing the years of schooling of girls and young women has demonstrable positive impacts on such phenomena as birth rates, child mortality, maternal mortality and HIV transmission. Summers justifies the policy and practice implications of his conclusions in economic terms, arguing that over a medium-term time frame the economic benefits to a country from these improvements in life experience are greater than the costs. Nevertheless, these findings have influenced the approach of social development practice in agencies such as UNICEF and UNESCO as well as more widely across the international non-government sector, precisely because they follow from changes in the way people live their lives and are seen as gains in the quality of life that they live.

Similarly, there is growing epidemiological evidence that health outcomes, like those of education, historically have not been produced as a consequence of economic growth, but have either preceded or occurred alongside increasing wealth. This understanding is now embedded as an assumption in arguments for planned health interventions in low-income countries, where people cannot afford the market costs of health services, as well as in higher-income countries (UNDP, 2013). The justification for this contains two parts. The first part is that health is a human right: without basic good health it is not possible to live a decent human life. The second is consequential: healthy people contribute more to their societies, both economically and in other ways. So although a developmental concern with health has close connections with economic concerns, the relationship is complex and cannot be taken as one based on economics as the necessary precursor to health developments or as the prime measure of the benefit of healthier lives.

Economics and social development

Yet we must begin by acknowledging that a major element in the promotion of social development as a distinct approach in social work comes from the claim that for much of the twentieth century social work had moved away from its origins of being concerned with material as well as psychosocial well-being. Midgley's original description of social development is very informative in this respect, stating that the approach has as its goal '[a] process of planned social change designed to promote the well-being of the population's whole in conjunction with a dynamic process of *economic* development' (Midgley, 1995, p. 25, emphasis added). The implication is that social work either has been ignorant of the way in which its professional concerns have an economic dimension, and so has failed to engage with economic issues, or has at least failed to understand that human need has a material basis.

Elliott (1993) also makes this critique. However, her analysis argues that although the development agenda has been set around questions of the economic causes of and solutions to poverty, there is also a clear recognition of the social aspects of the changes necessary for the improvement of human life. Elliott (1993, p. 23) uses the example of the USA to point out that high gross national income (GNI) or high expenditures on social provision, such as health and education, do not necessarily produce better human well-being (defined in terms of development measures, such as child and maternal mortality). What is required is that *social* gains accompany material growth and therefore should be seen as having at least equal priority. So Elliott revisits and affirms the earlier United Nations definition of development:

> [. . .] the greater capacity of the social system, social structure, institutions, services and policy to utilize resources to generate favourable changes in levels of living, interpreted in the broadest sense, as related to accepted social values and a better distribution of income, wealth and opportunities.
>
> *(UN, 1969, p. 2, as cited in Elliott, 1993, p. 24)*

Consequently, Elliot then considers ways in which economic, political and social questions of human well-being can be integrated, in which social issues are not seen solely in terms of economic investment or creating conditions for particular political changes, but as a distinct contributor to the whole of development.

Elliott also quotes other advocates of social development as saying either that it is too general and inclusive an idea (Khinduka, 1987) or that when it is theorised the ideas are expressed at an extremely high level of abstraction (Meinert & Kohn, 1987). In response, she argues that social development must be seen in terms of the actions in which practitioners working at all levels (from the 'macro' to the 'micro') can engage. In other words, it is not simply a philosophy, or an orientation, but a model of practice (Elliott, 1993, pp. 28–31).

More recently, Midgley (2014) has refined both his definition and the resulting model of social development. Social development, he states, is

> a process of planned social change designed to promote the well-being of a population as a whole within the context of a dynamic and multifaceted development process.
>
> *(Midgley, 2014, p. 13)*

From this subtly broader definition, Midgley goes on to spell out eight elements of social development that are integral to practice based on this definition. His goal is to create a general framework that at the same time manages to be sufficiently concrete, as it both creates an overall understanding of what is involved in social development practice and provides a way of thinking about what practice should look like in action. Social development, as defined by Midgley (2014, pp. 13–17), is

1 'a dynamic process', as compared to the 'static' response of ameliorating immediate need without addressing underlying causes;
2 'progressive', in that it is intended to produce 'steady improvements' in social conditions;
3 'multifaceted', integrating social, cultural, economic, political, environmental and other questions (notably gender) in its approach;
4 'interventionist', because it requires action in the form of various practices, such as 'projects, programmes, policies and plans' that are intended to accomplish the goals of development;
5 'productivist', in that it contributes to economic growth and development, for individuals, families and communities as well as the wider society;
6 'universalistic' in its focus on populations as a whole, although it may include affirmative action or 'targeting within universalism' in order to redress disadvantage;
7 'community focused' at the level of direct practice, even when it is engaged with individuals and families;
8 concerned with 'promoting people's social well-being'.

Midgley (2014, p. 17) acknowledges that there is no agreed definition of social development, whether among social workers or more widely, but argues that this summary of its scope is sufficiently broad to include many perspectives, while being bounded enough to provide a coherent model.

What is clear that from an earlier aim to encourage social workers to address and engage with the material dimensions of human need, specifically in practice that places economic and structural explanations of the causes of such need alongside solutions, is that the way social development is now conceptualised has become more 'multifaceted' (as in the third element of this model). This shift is important, as it enables the social development approach to be seen within the wider framework of social work, in which concerns with individuals and families are not necessarily anti-thetical to a grasp of the underlying structural dimensions of human well-being. As I have argued elsewhere (Hugman, 2009), there has been a tendency in social work to perpetuate a very long-standing opposition between 'macro' and 'micro' theories and practices. This polarised distinction is unhelpful, as it can lead social workers to ignore opportunities to promote effective change, by restricting both the way that issues are understood and the approaches that can be used to respond. In this respect, Midgley's recent model offers greater subtlety of conceptualisation that helps to rethink what is often a counterproductive binary divide in the way social work is understood and practised.

In Chapters 2 and 3, therefore, the questions of the 'macro' understanding of human well-being and of the engagement of social work with economics in social development will be explored in depth. In particular, the discussion will look at questions of the way in which a developmental perspective in social work is often seen as an alternative to 'micro' practices and theories, whether it represents a distinct terrain for the social welfare systems in which social work is located, or it provides ways in which economic concerns can be integrated with a *social* focus on 'living a better life'.

Environmental practice as social development

In the last decade there has been growing attention to the relationship between development and the environment (Woodhouse, 2002; Stern, 2007). The issues that concern social developmental practice are now seen to relate strongly to environmental concerns. The effects of climate change, the use and management of land, water and other natural resources, and the impact of natural disasters are all part of the problems faced by societies. Again, the predominant approach within the development field is to address the economic and political questions that these challenges present (e.g. see the collection edited by Helm & Hepburn, 2009; also, Stern, 2007)

Social work has begun to respond to the natural environment as a more central concern in the improvement of human life. Practice that addresses environmental concerns is shown increasingly to be a major aspect of social development (Alston, 2013; Dominelli, 2013; Pawar, 2012). This includes responding to the way in which developmental issues are always located in a geographical context where access to and use of natural resources are a key factor to be taken into account, as well as responding in more focused ways to the impact of natural disasters and other environmental emergencies and with long-term planned efforts to create more sustainable ways of living (Besthorn, 2012; Gray, 2013).

There are two implications of this intended shift in social work's focus. First, the knowledge and theory that informs social work practice have to be reconsidered in order to grasp the ways in which evidence concerning the relationship between the environment and social issues challenges more established perspectives. It is not that socio-economic class, gender, ethnicity, disability, sexuality and other dimensions in the construction of social life should be regarded as less relevant, but that these are seen to operate in and through the natural world. The physical environment is not separate from the social environment, but is both a medium through which social life is lived and a construct of social relationships and systems. As Besthorn (2012, p. 249) argues, the long-standing focus of social work on the concept of the 'person-in-environment' has until recently understood the idea of environment in social terms and ignored the connections between this and the natural world. From this perspective, it is not simply about locating human beings in the physical reality of nature, but understanding and responding to the realisation that human beings are part of the natural system.

Second, attention to the natural environment in social work requires new ways of practising. In some respects this can be seen in terms of rethinking the way in which established social work practices either ignore or make assumptions about the natural world. An underlying question in this regard is whether the goals of social work take for granted the use of natural resources in meeting human need without also grasping the capacity of humanity to harm this environment, whether through misuse or over-use. However, it goes much further in that 'ecological social work' (Besthorn, 2012), 'green social work' (Dominelli, 2012) or 'environmental social work' (Gray, 2013) calls on social workers also to develop more relevant practices. For example Dominelli argues that '[g]iven the professions' embeddedness in life-enhancing micro-practice in everyday routines, [. . .] contemporary social work has a vested interest in attending to environmental issues as an integral part of its daily routine' (2012, p. 3). A key aspect of this is the understanding that micro- and macro-level issues and practices should not be seen as separate but rather they can ultimately be successful only when they are combined, whether in programmes, teams or in the work of individual practitioners.

However, because some visions of development appear to assume that improvements in human life inevitably require additional consumption of natural resources, the challenges raised by considering this view of the relationship between social work and the natural environment pose significant questions for social development. Thus, in Chapter 4 the relationship between a critical approach to the natural environment, social work and social development is analysed. Furthermore, the chapter considers how these ideas and practices can lead to a more effective way of achieving sustainability in social development work.

International social work as social development

Much of the analysis of development in general and social development in particular reflects an assumption that these fields are international. Whether it concerns practices and projects, or planning and policy, there is a predominant sense that development is a matter of the issues and challenges faced by developing countries (e.g. Kothari & Minogue, 2002; Kingsbury, 2008a). By implication, the place of the (more highly) developed countries is to provide resources, expertise and other types of assistance. This understanding raises two critical questions. First, what is the relationship between the highly developed countries and those countries that may be considered to be developing? Second, is it plausible to see issues of development to be of concern only to those countries that are considered to be developing, or should concern with development, including social development, also be directed to the highly developed countries?

Before beginning to answer these questions, we need to consider an underlying issue of how to grasp what constitutes international practice. Healy (2008) offers a fourfold explanation of 'international' in international social work. These elements are

1   'internationally related domestic social work practice' (service users have crossed national borders);
2   'professional exchange' (ideas about social work have crossed national borders);
3   'international practice' (social workers cross national borders to practice);
4   'international policy development and advocacy' (social workers from two or more countries collaborate to act in relation to issues that are faced by two or more countries).

(Healy, 2008, pp. 10–16)

So, in summary, it may be social workers, service users, ideas or policy and advocacy that are international in the sense of something that bridges two or more countries.

Healy is also very clear that an international perspective does not have to embrace the whole world. It simply requires that practice or ideas have to involve more than one country. Healy (2008, p. 7) reserves the notion of 'global' for matters that concern the entire world. The reality of the working relationships of practice or of the social systems within which they are embedded is such that rarely does social work have a global character, other than at the highest levels of generality. Even the international social work bodies, such as the International Federation of Social Workers (IFSW) and the International Association of Schools of Social Work (IASSW), are usually best thought of in these terms as international and not global. Neither organisation has membership from every country of the world, while the perspectives of the member organisations or universities and colleges reflect a diverse range of positions. Only, perhaps, at the level of involvement at the United Nations is social work involved in global practice or policy.

There are distinct areas of social work practice that by their nature can be considered to be international (Lyons, 1999; Healy, 2008; Hugman, 2010; Cox & Pawar, 2013). These include refugee, asylum seeker and migrant support, aid and humanitarian relief, and interventions in the aftermath of disasters or conflicts, as well as more traditionally established actions involved in long-term social capacity building. These can all in some way be considered to have developmental aspects if not to be in every respect indisputably development issues. For this reason, certain types of international social work may not be part of a social development perspective, such as when social workers travel between global Northern countries simply 'to practice in another country' in micro-level interventions. What is of central concern here is the type of practice and the issues on which it is focused.

Healy also makes the point that international social work is more than simply comparing two or more countries. Comparative analysis of this kind is necessary as the basis for international practice and policy, but it does not in itself inform the connections between countries that the concept implies. In social development, likewise, a comparative understanding can be seen as necessary but not sufficient. This is the case whether social development is undertaken by national or international practitioners. Many of the concepts that underpin the idea of development are drawn from the historical experience of the more highly developed countries, so it is important to be able to articulate implications for new contexts. It is not that there are societies where the survival of more babies and their mothers is an unwelcome advance on past experience, for example, but that the ways of achieving such an improvement in health outcomes through changes to practice and policy have to be contextualised appropriately.

So in answer to the first of the two questions posed earlier concerning the relationship between 'developed' and 'developing' countries, there must be an awareness that social development cannot be based on an unproblematic notion of the transfer of knowledge and skills from those that are more highly developed to those that are regarded as developing. This requires a critical approach to both comparative and international dimensions of practice and policy. In this sense, 'critical' means that questions must be asked about the assumptions of past practice and policy and the goals that are held for social development now. Recent debates have focused on the neocolonial assumptions embedded in some developmental activity, in that in the past practices and systems in social welfare were transposed from global Northern countries to the global South in ways that were detrimental to the longer-term well-being of vulnerable parts of those populations. (It should be noted, though, that some of these practices and systems have also been heavily critiqued in the countries from which they originated.) Midgley (1981) in his classic analysis of international social work called this 'professional imperialism'. There are parallels here with the 'postcolonial' critique of economic and political development. As Kothari (2002, p. 38) points out, although it is possible to see development as a concern coinciding historically with decolonisation, power relations that perpetuate imbalances of the colonial era remain and the discourse of development tends to portray the global North as the model of development and the global South as unremittingly abject and in need of assistance.

In answer to the second question, as to whether the focus of development practice and policy should be directed only to countries designated as developing, we must consider the types of issues that they address. If factors such as child and maternal mortality, overall life expectancy and other measures of morbidity and mortality, levels of poverty, literacy and other related questions are considered, even the most highly developed countries have parts of their populations for whom these remain serious challenges. Across the countries of Europe, North America and Australasia there are communities in which it is clear that some people are not achieving the outcomes that are more widely seen among other groups in their society. For example in my own home country of Australia, the indices on these measures for Aboriginal and Torres Strait Islander people (taken as a population) remain significantly worse when compared to the non-Indigenous population (cf. AIHW, 2013). At the same time, the focus of development concern on global Southern countries also often fails to differentiate inequalities between different parts of populations. Developmental gains and continuing needs are segmented within as well as between countries and continents, on the basis of socio-economic class, gender, ethnicity and location (e.g. urban compared to rural populations, or between regions of countries) (Navarro, 2007; Kim, 2010). From this, it can be seen that when a comparative analysis informs international practice and policy, it challenges the view that that developmental concern and action are unidirectional. It also points to a key question about the way in which discussions of development tend to treat countries themselves in a unitary fashion, failing to distinguish the inequalities in the benefits resulting from the improvements in human living that are implied by the concept of development. What is known as 'uneven development' affects both the developing countries and those that are usually considered to be highly developed (Tomaskovic-Devey & Roscigno, 2007).

The questions that have been identified here form the basis for Chapters 5, 6, 7 and 8, examining in turn comparative welfare models, international social work, development as a domestic concern in so-called developed countries and the building of skills, knowledge and theory for social development. This focus also begins to raise a further question – namely that of the value base of social development, to which we now turn.

Values and ethics in social development

Underlying debates about social development are questions of the values that are used to determine what might be seen as the improvement of human life. Much of the existing debate identifies certain values as central to social development, as indeed they are to social work as a whole. These variously include social justice and equity, human rights and dignity, participation and democracy, and sustainability and peace (Khinduka, 1987; Elliott, 1993; Healy, 2008; Hugman, 2010; Ife, 2010; Midgley,

2014). Of course, in many ways such values do not distinguish social development from other approaches in social work, in that they reflect the broad statement of ethical principles that are claimed to be common to the profession globally and which are derived from international laws and agreements (IFSW/IASSW, 2004). Nevertheless, it can be argued that other approaches in social work, especially more 'micro' practices, may have these values embedded in them but they do not draw on these values as part of the skills, techniques or specific goals in the way in which social development seeks to, and which social development tends to share with 'macro' practices. In this discussion I want to avoid the binary construction of social work around which some value debates have occurred in the past. First, the following chapters argue that social development is a generalist approach, encompassing both macro and micro practices. Second, this analysis rejects the position taken by some early proponents of social development that micro practices are necessarily reactionary, victim-blaming or supportive of the status quo – or, indeed, that macro practices are necessarily the opposite. Some of these arguments come from a particular place and time, in which they were undoubtedly helpful, but it is now more constructive to move beyond a simple binary understanding in order to examine these values and the way that they are actually expressed in practice. This is the core purpose of 'critical reflection', which must be directed at all arguments, including (perhaps especially) one's own (Fook & Gardner, 2007).

Consequently, although the analysis presented in the following chapters embodies particular values and ethics, the goal is to open these up to scrutiny. In particular, there are often differences between social workers involved in social development that arise from the diverse national and cultural backgrounds from which they come (Hugman, 2013). Although some issues, such as human rights, are more frequently debated than others in this respect, it is the case that what constitutes justice, equity, dignity, participation and so on also is open to different interpretations according to who is considering them and where that person is located. This is not to suggest that values and ethics are entirely relative to culture and context so that there can be no common ground. Without a shared moral framework the very idea of a profession of social work, or of the social development approach within it as an international practice, could not make sense. Nevertheless, how skills, knowledge and values play out in any specific location will be affected by local customs, relationships, structures and beliefs. For these reasons the values and ethics of social development cannot be taken for granted but must be argued about and for. In as far as any particular values are regarded as necessary for the practice of social development in all contexts, then such a position must be established. This task is addressed in Chapter 9.

Summary

This introductory chapter has provided an overview of the central questions for the social development approach in social work. Having distinguished social development within the broader general field of development, and noted its relationship with the more dominant economic and political understandings of development, it has reviewed the key definitions of social development. These were seen to connect social work with economic and political dimensions of human need, redressing a tendency in the twentieth century for social work to ignore such factors in favour of other ways to understand and to respond.

The structure of this book has been set out. The following chapters in turn examine the idea of macro practices as part of social work (together with micro practices), and then consider the inclusion of an economic focus to social work. Social work is still gaining an appreciation of the natural environment as a professional concern, so the relevance of this for social development is explored in the following chapter. From there, the discussion looks at the relationship between social work and international social work, the place of social development in the national practice of the more highly developed countries and the skills, methods and theories of social development. Finally, the values and ethics of social development are examined in order to understand how these debates can help to create a more appropriate and effective practice.

Taken as a whole, this book presents both an analysis of social development as an approach in social work and an argument for its increasing importance in a profession that itself continues to grow to meet the challenges of a changing world. As we will see, it is not just that social development should seek to be 'effective' in ameliorating the problems of change, but, more than this, it should contribute to the wider achievement of a better human life by those people for whom this remains a goal.

2

THE 'MACRO PERSPECTIVE', SOCIAL DEVELOPMENT AND THE PERSON IN THE SOCIAL ENVIRONMENT

Introduction

Social work has long been understood as being concerned with 'the person in the social environment'. From the late 1800s, the founding generation of social workers identified the importance of seeing people they were committed to helping in the context of social structures and relationships. For example the work of Rathbone in the UK and Addams in the USA in the 'settlement house' movement focused attention on the conditions in which members of disadvantaged communities were living (Pierson, 2011). The settlement workers sought to effect change through interventions in such circumstances. Consequently, the settlement houses have been widely regarded as the forerunners of community work and community development, addressing the social structural nature of human need (Reisch & Andrews, 2014).

Although the casework model of the Charity Organization Societies (COS) and other comparable groups (Bransford, 2011, pp. 33–4), which was the other main strand of early social work, concentrated on helping individuals and families, early casework also helped people to engage with economic and other structural issues (Midgley, 1997, p. 183). However, their approach was different to the settlements, as it focused on helping people to respond differently to their circumstances rather than directly working to change the prevailing social structures. Consequently, most commentators argue that the settlement movement was politically radical, while the COS was conservative (Lundy, 2004; Olson, 2007; Reisch & Andrews, 2014). Others, such as Midgley (1997), see this as an oversimplification in that both approaches sought to provide the recipients of their work with means to improve their lives, materially and socially – what would now be termed 'capacity building'. Hansen (no date), writing about the settlement movement, suggests that the reality was more complex than either of these positions. In many instances the settlement house residents originally were interested in helping individuals and families to find ways to improve their capacities to respond to the surrounding society and overcome poverty and other issues. This largely differed from the COS in how capacity building was to be achieved. Nevertheless, he notes that it was through their experiences in these communities that many of the settlement workers became involved in overt challenges to policies and systems that caused or perpetuated conditions of poverty and disadvantage. Thus the greater engagement of the settlement houses with political action developed over time, through practice, having begun with more individually focused goals.

In this way, the distinction between the two main precursors to modern social work reveals the origins not only of casework and community work but also of debates about the causes of human need and the appropriate ways of intervening. As will be explored in more depth ahead, the question of conservatism against radicalism is more one of *how* practices such as capacity building are undertaken rather than one of necessarily the apparent techniques in themselves. So to understand the different legacies that these twin foundations of social work created we need to ask two questions. First, what assumptions did these approaches make about the causes of and solutions to human need? Second, what are the implications of these assumptions for the formation of particular skills and methods, and the practice theory that supports them?

In order to understand social development as a specific approach within social work, this chapter examines these questions in more depth. It does so by looking at three critiques of contemporary social work and the debates about social development that follow from them. First, it looks at the idea of the 'social' in social work. In particular, the long-standing concept of the 'person in the social environment' as the central concern of social work is explored. Second, this chapter considers the common division of social work into 'micro' and 'macro' concerns, which are often seen in terms of a split between 'direct' and 'indirect' practices. The argument here is that these distinctions are sometimes misconceived and so are often unhelpful ways of looking at social work, especially when taking an international perspective. Third, the distinction between 'residual', 'institutional' and 'developmental' models of social welfare and their implications for social work practices and theories is examined. As a whole, the discussion is concerned with understanding the potential of social work as a profession contributing to social development, in the sense of the betterment of human life and the relationship of this goal to the systems within which social work operates.

The person in the (social) environment: an abiding concept

Early social workers identified the distinctive contribution of social work as its focus on the connections between people (whether as individuals, members of families or groups, or of communities) and the wider social environment within which they live. For example both COS and settlement workers appear to have used this approach to understand the lives of those they sought to assist and to structure their practices, while in the later twentieth century the concept of person-in-environment became known simply by its initials as 'PIE' (D. Green & McDermott, 2010; Nilsson et al., 2013). Most recently, this concept continues to inform questions about practices as diverse as hospital social work (Nilsson et al., 2013), community health practice with migrant gay men (van Sluytman et al., 2013), disaster response and community development (Mason, 2011), forced migration and post-traumatic stress (Nuttman-Schwartz et al., 2011), community development responding to the social pressures faced by disadvantaged ethnic minority young people (Cleaveland, 2011) and citizen participation and community capacity building (Ohmer, 2010).

Despite this enduring presence in social work thinking, however, it is important to disentangle the way in which the concept is being used. As D. Green and McDermott (2010) point out, it can suggest practice and theory that integrates macro, meso and micro perspectives. Nevertheless, when the continuing discussions of the concept of 'person in environment' are examined, it becomes apparent that the meaning shifts according to the balance being struck between 'person' and 'environment' as the focus of social work, and in particular the role of 'environment' in this conceptualisation. In this way, these discussions can be divided into three groups. These groups divide according to the way they portray the goals of social work, the causes of social need and the objects of social work action. (See e.g. recent critical analyses of the historic 'mission' of social work, such as Reisch, 2002, Olson, 2007, and Reisch & Andrews, 2014.)

First, there is a construction of 'environment' as an external force (perhaps seen as a 'variable') acting on the person who is the primary focus of social work. In this way of understanding the concept, the goals of social work are to assist individual people and families to achieve better lives through increasing their resilience and capacities to act differently towards the world around them. While such actions may be to seek to change that world, the role of social work is to attend to the person. This constructs the origins of the needs to which social workers respond in the person and hence the person as the object of practice. In broad terms, this is the dominant view of micro practice.

Second, at the other end of a spectrum, is the opposite position. Here the primary goal of social work is to change social structures, as the causation of social need is seen to lie in this aspect of the world. From this, the objects of social work action are social systems, including institutions and their policies, as well as the political and economic relationships of a community or the wider society. This approach to social work constructs the origins of need in the (social) environment and so targets that as its object of practice. In broad terms this is a common view of macro social work.

Between these two somewhat sweeping generalisations there are a number of more complex ways to approach the relationship between the person and the environment. This is not simply the domain of 'meso' practice, as that term has come to refer to organisational work or in some situations to activities such as research; nor is it to be understood only as 'middle ground' in which practitioners engage sometimes in micro and sometimes in macro interventions. Rather, this third position understands social relationships in a more complex way, constructing the person and the environment as an interwoven whole. Such an approach can be seen in areas as diverse as assisting marginalised young people (C. Kirk *et al.*, 2011), local government case management (Schulze-Boing, 2010), responding to drug use among marginalised ethnic communities (Van Hout, 2010), gender-focused micro-credit programmes (Drolet, 2009) and community mental health projects (Gulcur *et al.*, 2007). The common element of all these programmes is that people and environments are seen and responded to in an integrated practice.

There are several theoretical approaches that underpin this position. For example in her development of the concept of 'radical casework' Fook (1993) argues for a form of practice with individuals and families that is grounded in a structural understanding of the causes of social and personal needs, which therefore should also address the 'environment' of people's lives as it also assists people to understand and respond more effectively to their situations (also see Fook, 2002). In a comparable attempt to integrate insights from both generalised extremes, Saleebey's (1996, 2002, 2004, 2006) work on resilience and strengths began from a focus on community development, while seeking also to recognise that such practice concerns people and so must attend at the same time, in an integrated way, to the 'person' who lives (or persons plural, in relationship together, who live) in this environment. Although they originate from theoretical concerns that are often considered to be in opposition, Fook's and Saleebey's concepts are complementary in the way in which they seek to integrate personal and structural dimensions of the issues faced by service users.

D. Green and McDermott (2010) acknowledge that this multi-level approach to the concept of the 'person in environment' has been subject to a variety of critiques, ranging from feminism (Kemp, 2001), through critical theory (Kondrat, 2002), deep ecology (Besthorn, 2003), culture/ethnicity (Robinson, 2007) to late life (Thompson, 1998) (all cited in D. Green & McDermott, 2010, p. 2417). Each of these critiques questions the extent to which the use of the idea has been able to embrace particular understandings of the social environment. This is important, as any concept that is too broad will not be useful in practice. However, as D. Green and McDermott argue, if these critiques are taken together, the way forward is to recognise that the social environment is a very complex system and to build social work practice and theory on this.

> [P]erson-in-environment is not a metaphor, but rather provides a compelling understanding of the ways in which phenomena evolve into more and more complex, interacting and interdependent systems. [. . .] We might envisage, for example, that students begin to think about social problems through the 'eyes' of complexity, identifying the apparent as well as less visible influences of interwoven systems and elements that create the problematic situations they confront.
>
> *(2010, p. 2427)*

That their preferred response to this is for social work to become more 'scientific' by drawing on neuroscience and other recent developments, and to abandon 'practice theory', is unlikely to resolve the critical debates about theories. Rather, it adds another dimension to the already multifaceted range of positions, although it potentially has greater accord with some, such as certain perspectives within ecologically committed social work, than a critical postmodern perspective, for instance.

All of these critiques must be listened to. It is possible to agree with D. Green and McDermott on the importance of addressing the complexity of the social environment and the way in which people develop and live within it, without necessarily agreeing with their wish to favour a particular view of 'evidence-based practice' as the solution. We will return to aspects of this in Chapter 4, in a more detailed examination of ecological perspectives and 'environmental' or 'green' social work (Dominelli, 2012; Gray, 2013). At this point, the complexity of 'person-in-environment' and its significance for social work practice in social development can be explored more closely through a detailed example of practice.

Practice example: rights, justice, public housing and gardening

To flesh out the issues raised by a 'person-in-environment' understanding of social work, the following example of social development practice is used to illustrate these concepts.

> Irene is a public housing tenant, who has lived in an apartment in a high-rise building, which is located in a relatively disadvantaged area of a large city in a global Northern country. She arrived in the country 35 years ago as a refugee, and although she did not anticipate growing old in a 'foreign land', she has long since abandoned thoughts of returning to her country of origin. Irene considers herself fortunate in living in this area because of the support the community has received from a non-government organisation (NGO), which has provided various forms of developmental input in the last 20 years. When Irene was first settled in this housing area she faced numerous challenges: language; separation from family; the death of her husband not long after they arrived in the country; lack of employment and low income. Several of her neighbours faced the same type of issues, but for many years there was little opportunity for them to develop any sense of community. In addition, when Irene first moved into the apartment, the housing authority was unresponsive to problems with building maintenance or the social issues that grew around the high-rise blocks.
>
> Lucy is a social worker employed by the NGO that provides support to Irene's area. Lucy took the position because she was very keen to work with structural issues rather than what she saw as the 'individualising' of problems. In the six years that she has worked in this NGO she has helped the tenants to organise representation with the housing authority, using a rights-based approach. After some initial reluctance, the authority has now become much more responsive and many previous issues have been resolved. Recently, the tenants' action group are now facing a political debate about the privatisation

of public housing in the area, which means that most existing tenants will be required to move further from the city centre to areas that are also disadvantaged. Another reason that the tenants are reluctant to accept this move is that Lucy and her colleagues have also assisted them over the years to campaign for and obtain various community facilities, including a community centre and communal gardens in which those residents who wish to are able to grow vegetables. In fact, the success of the gardens is recognised beyond the community and has been copied in other nearby areas.

Irene considers that she has benefitted not only from the much more responsive approach of the housing authority as her landlord but also from her enjoyment of gardening as well as participating in a multicultural women's group at the centre (which often focuses on cooking and shared celebrations, such as personal and cultural events). Irene's earlier isolation, bereavement and sense of powerlessness had led to depression, but she has not experienced this problem now for many years. Irene sees the benefit of all aspects of the changes that Lucy and her colleagues have helped to create as having helped in this way as well: she also thinks of them as things that the community has achieved together, not only as having been done by the NGO.

This example (which is drawn from suitably anonymised observations of a range of actual projects) raises three particular questions about social development as social work, as well as of the arguments identified earlier about the concept of 'person-in-environment':

1   What is the difference between 'rights-based' campaigning work and activities such as gardening and women's groups understood as critical practice?
2   How does this example relate to the debates about gender, culture/ethnicity, age, ecology and so on that have been identified as critical issues?
3   In what ways do the different parts of this narrative relate to the idea of social development as a distinctive focus of social work practice?

First, is it plausible to regard both rights-based campaigning on issues such as housing and employment and support for the creation and running of services such as a community centre or communal gardens as critical development practice? The situation described in the example of Irene illustrates that interventions at different levels can each contribute to improvements in people's lives. Irene and her neighbours have gained from both the improved relationship with the housing authority and the provision of the community facilities. Neither they nor the social workers such as Lucy separate these different interventions in their experience of social development. All are part of the overall assistance that has been provided by this NGO. From Lucy's perspective, it is not that one part of these actions has been central and the other peripheral, or that one element is more important than the other. Addressing issues of structured power and creating increased opportunities to engage in ordinary everyday activities that have meaning are equally important aspects of critical practice in this sense.

Second, in social work theory the notion of 'critical' is often seen as an explicit understanding of and response to inequalities and disadvantages that are created by existing social and cultural structures (Pease & Fook, 1999; Fook & Gardner, 2007; Bay & Macfarlane, 2011; Reisch & Andrews, 2014). So for social development practice to be seen in these terms it must be seen to address these challenges. In the detailed earlier example there are several points at which this concept can be seen in practice: questions of socio-economic class, the position of public housing tenants, gender, ethnicity and age are all responded to explicitly in different relevant ways. For example the activities that Irene values include a women's group. From some perspectives this might be seen as an 'uncritical' understanding of gender, one that does not address patriarchy as such because it appears to be based on a traditional idea of 'women's work'. Yet for Irene the opportunity to meet with other women and to be able to engage safely in things that she enjoys is in itself a valuable part of her life. More than this, because the group is multicultural and includes other women who share her experiences of forced migration, isolation and building a life in a new country, many different facets of her identity are affirmed and sustained. The crucial issue here for social workers such as Lucy and her colleagues is that the decisions about what is valued in life and how these relate to people's identities in their social context are made by the service users themselves. (In Chapter 9 the discussion will return to the connections between this point and Nussbaum's [2000] concept of 'human capabilities'.)

Third, how does this scenario demonstrate social development practice? In other words, what is 'developmental' about the situation of Irene and Lucy, as it has been described? If social development is seen as change that is planned, that benefits the community as a whole and that embodies positive differences in structural relationships (cf. Midgley, 2014, p. 13), then it is reasonable to see the work of Lucy and her colleagues in these terms. The practice that led to these outcomes was planned by the social workers together with the residents of this area. In this sense, planning is an incremental interactive process, not just a matter of one survey and analysis. More than this, looking back over time planning can be seen as a series of stages, with different 'projects' contributing to the larger developmental process. Although the discussion has used the example of one person to illustrate key aspects, overall the process has benefitted all the residents of this housing area in different ways. In addition, the residents and others recognise that the community (as more than the sum of each individual) has also gained, so that from being seen as a disadvantaged area it has become an area of choice for tenants of the housing authority. In addition, there have been positive changes in various structural relationships, including those between tenants and the housing authority, for women who have gained a space to develop their own interests, between members of different ethnic groups and between age cohorts. This discussion has avoided using the term 'transformation', because in social work theory this has so often been seen in terms of more major shifts in such structural relations (Reisch & Jani, 2012). However, for Irene and her neighbours the changes that have taken place are significant and far-reaching. While Irene remains an older, ethnic minority woman living in a society where each of these aspects of her identity is still the basis of inequalities, she has gained opportunities to live in ways that she values. Lucy and her colleagues are also aware that the experience of this one area enabled the housing authority to develop wider practices that have led to more rights for tenants being achieved in other districts. Again, this is not a total transformation, but it is a major shift in a positive direction.

This practice example has deliberately not considered a key debate in social work practice and theory – that is the dichotomy that emerged over time from the influences of the early forms of social work between the focus on helping individuals and families and attention to systemic and structural change – the legacy of the COS and settlement house traditions. However, this is also an important issue for social development practice in social work, and so the next part of this chapter considers how this distinction affects our understanding of this approach.

'Direct' and 'indirect' practice: a useful distinction?

The definition of social development that is reviewed in Chapter 1 identifies it as a distinct approach in social work. In this perspective, social development is seen as concerning the issues, problems and needs that are addressed by social work at the level of the social environment. According to Midgley, it is concerned with the well-being of the population as whole (Midgley, 2014, p. 13; also see Midgley, 1995). That is it begins by asking critical questions concerning social structures and relationships, systems, institutions, policies and other common factors that affect people's lives. In the earlier iteration of his definition, Midgley emphasises economic aspects of social systems and encourages social workers to address this aspect of needs and rights. In particular, Midgley is concerned that social workers either do not consider the material aspects of social problems or else engage with these in a political sense, in ways that are often conceptual rather than practical. He is mindful in this of the importance of promoting models of social work that address the needs of the global South as well as the North (Midgley, 1981, 1995, 2014). The two sets of questions raised by this analysis, regarding the place of economics in social work and of international social work, are addressed in several ways in the following chapters (and specifically in Chapters 3 and 6).

Elliott (1993) draws attention to a contentious point that lies at the centre of Midgley's argument – namely that while social work has evolved out of traditions that recognised the importance of the material dimension to human well-being, there is a clearly identifiable reason why this focus has been lost. Elliott asserts that a concern with the professionalisation of social work has led to an emphasis on 'empiricism and quantitative methods in research and the medical or curative model or therapy as a means to improve the credibility and status of the profession (Elliott, 1993, p. 22). So by the 1980s concern about social justice as a primary objective of social work had been overshadowed by the pursuit of 'efficiency', and attention to the social environment as the target of intervention was largely lost to concentration on intra- and interpersonal functioning.

This conclusion is endorsed by others. Olson (2007) agrees that empiricism and the pursuit of a particular form of professionalism have defined social work in the late twentieth century. He goes on to argue that the social and political context of this process is also relevant – namely that it has occurred in conditions of globalising neo-liberalism. Olson points out (2007, pp. 49–50) that this ideology promotes a highly individualistic world view, in which there are only persons and the idea of a 'social' environment becomes implausible. In these circumstances the authority of any practice that addresses the social elements of the 'person-in-environment' is weakened (cf. Hugman, 1998). The outcome, therefore, is that individualised forms of social work, such as those that are therapeutic or clinical, come to the fore while concerns with social systems and structures are shifted to the background. For Olson (2007), as well as for others, such as Elliot (1993), Solas (2008) and Reisch and Andrews (2014), the historical social justice concerns of social work thus become obscured. The language of social justice may remain, but in both practice and theory the core project becomes that of professionalisation (Olson, 2007, pp. 59–60).

In terms of approaches to social work practice, the processes of professionalisation in the late twentieth century therefore have tended to emphasise clinical practices and others that are focused on individuals, families and small groups. Counselling, casework, case management and focused groupwork all fit this particular vision of professionalism (Payne, 2014). All concentrate on 'the person' as the principal focus of concern. In many discussions of such practices, these practices are often referred to as 'direct', derived from the sense that they intervene directly with the person who is the intended beneficiary (Johnson, 1999; Allen-Meares & Garvin, 2000; Furman *et al.*, 2004; Murdach, 2006; Weiss-Gal *et al.*, 2014). Against this construct is set the characterisation of practices that concentrate on social environmental factors as 'indirect'. The distinction here is clearly that 'the person' should be the tangible focus of practice, and this binary distinction simply separates those actions that impact immediately on the person and those that achieve this end by way of an intermediary object. As Johnson puts it (1999, p. 330), the linguistic construction of 'person-in-environment' appears to reflect its dominant social construction, in that the person precedes the environment.

As I have argued elsewhere (Hugman, 2009), a serious problem emerging from this way of distinguishing between types of practice is that social workers and the wider community may come to see 'direct' practice as 'real' social work, while by implication 'indirect' practice is regarded as 'not real', or at least a limited and subsidiary approach that has value only insofar as it supports the real thing. One example of this can be seen in Claiborne's (2004) study of social work in international non-government humanitarian organisations, in which most of her sample said that they did not employ social workers because the organisation was not engaged in counselling or casework activities. To the extent that this might be accepted as a reasonable description of social work practice and theory, the implication for social development, community development and similar interventions is that because they are 'indirect' they are, at best, subsidiary or even marginal to the core purposes of social work; at the extreme they are not regarded as parts of social work at all. That this perception follows from the success of social work in pursuing the status of a profession is highly plausible, especially as much of the evidence for this comes from the global North, where social work has become established over a long period.

Yet this position does not address the realities of social work, either within the countries of the global North or internationally. It ignores the many ways in which social workers practise in community development, service administration and management, research and policy. It also fails to recognise that these ways of practising necessarily involve social workers in relationships with members of communities, and families, even in working with individuals. Indeed, it is a very unhelpful construction as it leads to the implication that such practices do not involve working with people. It also appears to suggest that those whose practice is focused on individuals and families are not also engaged in actions such as administration, policy and research. In this sense, community work is also 'direct' in that it involves interactions between service users and social workers at its core.

Some approaches to social development emphasise service systems, policy and research. For example one of the central concerns of Midgley's work has been to remind social work of its historic use of these practices. In addition, he encourages social workers to become more familiar with economics as part of their theory base (Midgley, 1995, 2014). Yet, although his own contribution has not usually addressed the interpersonal aspects of practice, Midgley (2010, p. 19) acknowledges that social development must be able to incorporate personal relationship skills, counselling and other related practices in its range of responses to social issues. Others have more explicitly argued that social development is generalist practice and must bring together attention to the needs of individuals, families, small groups, communities and whole societies. Elliott (1993) and Elliott and Mayadas (1996, 2001) have built up an approach to social development that brings these different practices together. For example Elliott (1993, p. 29) lists 'therapy' along with 'community development, social education (conscientization) and social action (empowerment)' as methods appropriate to social development, with relevant processes, skills and knowledge also identified. Elliott and Mayadas (2001, p. 11) identify practices such as focused groupwork as a way of achieving conscientisation, thus both promoting developmental goals and overcoming the macro/micro dichotomy. What matters particularly in these constructions is that when working with individuals and families, social development in social work seeks to avoid a 'pathology' focus. Although Elliot's first iteration of this model (1993) predates Saleebey's (1996) work on practices that emphasise strengths, it is consistent with the strengths-based approach and practice that supports empowerment, whether of individuals, families or collectively in groups or communities (Elliott & Mayadas, 2000).

Weil (2000) proposes a model of community-based social work, which she calls 'integrated' practice. Drawing on a structural understanding of the causation of need and the explicit use of social justice values, Weil places interventions with individuals and families in the social environment. So, although her approach also includes counselling and other clinical practices, it emphasises the use of social networks, 'natural helping systems' and community building as strategies for interventions with a wider range of issues and problems (Weil, 2000, pp. 387–91). Thus, Weil advocates a community-based social work approach in areas such as child protection, mental health, physical disability, general health, old age services and family violence, as well as community development (2000, p. 383). Usefully, she offers the term 'direct community practice' as a way of constructing this focus so that it remains clear that much of community work involves interactions with people and is still focused on the 'person-in-environment' as its broad objective. Community practice of this kind seeks to help people to improve their lives and not simply to produce good research or policy. Part of Weil's argument still includes a 'direct/indirect' divide, but she places this between any work that involves interaction with people and practice that actually focuses on data, ideas and argument with decision makers. To make this clear she refers to those areas that do not intervene in some way with the end users of social work as 'macro' practices, creating a 'direct/macro' distinction and a developmental orientation.

In one example of how this approach can apply to a contentious area of practice, Conley (2010) argues that these principles can be applied in particular to child protection and related family work. She notes that the service systems of the global North are reactive and institutional, with an emphasis on a culturally specific view of the family that is taken out of its social context (Conley, 2010, p. 32). For Conley, a social developmental approach offers an alternative model that places the family within the context of the social environment, including the variety of family structures and relationships that exists in multicultural societies (p. 39). While still concerned to ensure that children are not harmed, this approach takes into account that family poverty, wider community problems and other such factors create social environments in which child maltreatment issues are more prevalent (see Parton *et al.*, 1997; Barth *et al.*, 2005). The use of existing family and community networks as a resource is suggested as an alternative source of strength, in which social work engages with wider family and community members as partners in providing safe and nurturing environments for children (Conley, 2010, pp. 44–5).

This perspective is particularly influenced by the creation of 'developmental social work' in South Africa (Patel, 2005; Hölscher, 2008; Lombard & Wairire, 2010). Patel defines social development as practices and policies that

> meet needs, promote rights, manage social problems, and facilitate the maximisation of opportunities to achieve social well-being and the promotion of human empowerment and social inclusion.
>
> *(Patel, 2005, p. 203)*

Particular challenges faced by social work in South Africa, as well as across other parts of Africa, Asia and South America and the Caribbean, followed from the impact of colonialism. Under colonial rule various social welfare systems had been imposed. While these often originated from the humanitarian concerns of non-government organisations, such as religious and philanthropic bodies, they often buttressed colonial rule and in the twentieth century were slowly augmented by the colonial powers. In the late twentieth and early twenty-first centuries, having achieved independence, these countries were then usually left with social welfare systems and practices that were still grounded in the previous oppressive regimes. One aspect of this, which Patel (2005) and other have sought to challenge, is the very limited charitable relief model of most provisions. In its place, they seek to create approaches to social welfare that are developmental while still meeting immediate needs. Patel (2005, p. 27) ascribes the start of this shift to the influence of the United Nations in the 1960s. Thus, social development is seen not simply as a type of social work practice but rather as the way in which all social work practice should be conducted, whether with communities, groups, families or individuals. Yet it clearly locates the origins of social need in social structures and relationships — it does not ignore individual or family experiences of need, but addresses them in the social context in which they occur. So it always includes the wider society within its understanding and the practices through which social workers intervene.

At the same time, social development requires not only that practitioners engage directly with people in communities, institutions, organisations and so on, but also that clinical practitioners are involved in the development of policy, creating appropriate structures and institutions and also undertaking research. Effective policy and service systems depend on detailed knowledge of the issues faced by service users and of the ways in which social workers can intervene. Research in social work skills and techniques also clearly is a matter of great concern for practitioners working with individuals, families and groups as well as communities. In addition to this, it is clear that all levels of practice experience can inform policy-focused research — indeed, without the insights that practitioners bring to the formulation of research questions, policy that does not take these into account lacks a significant dimension (Alston & Bowles, 2003).

An alternative understanding is necessary to avoid the misconception that social work practice is related either 'directly' to interventions with people or 'indirectly' with social systems. As has been noted, not only does this binary construction inappropriately place community work and social development on the side of being impersonal, but also it excludes the possibility of practice with individuals, families and groups being located in structural context. In recent years the notions of 'macro' and 'micro' (with 'meso' between them) have started to replace the older distinction (Weil, 2000; Burghardt, 2014). This is not a simple panacea, as for some theorists who are critical of the reality behind this change in language these terms only replace the earlier use of concepts, when what is required is a shift in thinking. A more fruitful view is to regard these differences as a continuum or range of levels, in which various 'lenses' might be used appropriately to focus on the particular questions that social work is addressing in each particular situation. Regarded in this way, the different focus between various interventions can be understood as matters of degree, rather than as exclusive.

Moreover, this implies that within a social development approach we might expect to find either generalist practitioners (who are expected to be skilled across a range of practice modalities) (Poulin, 2005; Lavitt, 2009), or else an approach in which close working relationships between social workers with a relevant range of skills and knowledge are considered the norm. Thus it is often more appropriate to ask about the mix of skills and knowledge that are required to respond effectively to social problems and issues rather than looking for a single definitive way of understanding social work. It is also reasonable to expect practitioners to be more or less skilled in different modalities, and this way of looking at the range of social work practices is not a demand for everyone to have expertise in everything. Lavitt (2009, p. 464) suggests that generalist practice is actually the norm of social work. For Lavitt (pp. 466ff.), it must be seen as having three parts: multidimensional problem setting, leadership and ethical advocacy.

Multidimensional problem setting refers to the capacity to consider the micro, meso and macro dimensions of social issues and problems. This is necessary, Lavitt argues, because of the tendency for practitioners to understand needs in terms of the skills that they possess: to the person with a hammer, every problem looks like a nail (Lavitt, 2009, p. 467). Leadership is grounded in the capacities for reflection and innovative responses to problems and challenges (p. 468). In particular, Lavitt identifies the importance of avoiding routine solutions to the problems and challenges faced in practice (also see Schön, 1983; Poulin, 2005). What is often required in generalist practice is a creative response that finds new ways to intervene in apparently intractable situations. Third is the capacity for ethical advocacy, in which the practitioner actively engages with values of social justice, human rights and the tensions they may pose for working in agency settings (Lavitt, 2009, p. 470). It is not that specialist practitioners lack appropriate ethical responses, but that the organisational dynamics often encountered in generalist practice tend to obscure or even block these values and their centrality to social work's goals, so their pursuit must be deliberate.

Of course, agencies that employ social workers also tend to have particular mandates. Some are highly specialised and call for skills and knowledge that enable them to achieve their primary goals. The argument presented here is not a call for uniformity. Yet, it concerns the social work profession as a whole. At the same time it also takes account of the many practice contexts in which social workers need to be flexible and sufficiently skilful across a range of modalities. The point is that degrees of flexibility and multi-skilling are required among practitioners and that, as a profession, all levels of intervention and analysis are to be regarded as central to social work. Thus the idea of 'lenses' to understand distinctions between 'macro', 'meso' and 'micro' levels of practice is to be understood as vantage points, between which practice and theory can vary, and not as rigidly defined domains that constrain analysis and action.

As we have noted, the critique offered by Olson (2007), Solas (2008) and Reisch and Andrews (2014) is that in pursuing professionalism macro (and at times meso) orientations have been either downplayed or abandoned and, consequently, social work has lost its original commitment to the goal of social justice. Greater integration of these levels of practice as 'lenses' through which to focus analysis and action provides an opportunity to challenge this loss and to identify the way in which the core value of social justice is relevant to counselling and therapy, casework and case management and other work with individuals, families and groups as much as to community work, policy and research (Mendes, 2007). We will return to this point in more detail in Chapter 9.

From the point of view of Irene and Lucy in the practice example above, the way in which the NGO has adopted a developmental approach to its work has meant that it responded at several of these different levels. For example much of Lucy's work can be considered in Weil's (2000) terms as 'direct community practice'. The community as a whole has benefitted from changes in some of the policies and practices of the housing authority and from specific projects, such as the community centre and the communal gardens. So have individuals such as Irene. In addition, Irene's personal well-being and mental health have improved. On occasions she has been able to talk at an individual level with Lucy and other workers, and they supported her in accessing appropriate health services. While none of the NGO staff are themselves specialised counsellors, they were sufficiently skilled to know how to respond to Irene's situation; had Irene needed more intensive help, they have the professional networks to help her to access it. This illustrates the integrated way in which different aspects of social need can be responded to, with different 'lenses' used at appropriate times.

Social welfare systems and their impact on models of social work

The third critique of contemporary social work from a social development perspective concerns the way in which it either conforms to or challenges the social welfare regime in which it is being practised. Here again, Midgley has been a pioneer in distinguishing 'residual' and 'institutional' social service provision from a social development approach (Midgley, 1981, 1995). Using a typology that was first proposed by Wilensky and Lebeaux (1965), Midgley (1981) identifies 'residual' social services as the dominant mode through which social work was introduced into global Southern countries through policies set by colonial administrations. While Midgley's main example is that of southern and eastern Africa, his analysis is also pertinent to northern Africa, Asia, Latin America and the Pacific Islands (Walton & El Nasr, 1988; Mafile'o, 2004; Osei-Hwedie et al., 2006; Yan & Cheung, 2006). In this context, 'residual' refers to social work and services that are focused only on the most serious of social needs. It describes policies and practices that are reactive to problems that already exist and attempt only to limit and perhaps ameliorate such needs. The example Midgley (1981, pp. 52) particularly uses is that of large-scale residential children's homes as a means to address widespread child poverty and the fragmentation of African families in conditions of colonial rule. These approaches caused further disruption to traditional childcare practices and did nothing to resolve the causes of poverty, distress and other related issues. They were based on the policies and practices of the colonising country (the UK), which in fact by the start of the twentieth century were already starting to be questioned in that country. A similar pattern of importing inappropriate and damaging policies and practices occurred in other parts of the world, such as Australia, Canada and New Zealand (Trocmé *et al.*, 2004; Ban, 2005; Worrall, 2006; S. Green & Baldry, 2008).

More broadly, residual social welfare regimes are also characterised by a restrictive approach to social security, such as in the form of unemployment support payments and state old age pensions, an emphasis on private health care and other comparable policies. In a residual model, only those who are deemed unable to provide for themselves receive public support; to discourage reliance on such assistance access is restricted, and at the same time services are often deliberately provided in such a way so as to be the least attractive option. (In the older traditions of the UK this was referred to as 'the principle of less eligibility', first introduced in 1834 and only [officially] ended in 1929, meaning that ensuring such help was a last resort was inbuilt by making it difficult to access or explicitly unpleasant and stigmatising [Thane, 1996].) A central feature of this social welfare model is that it effectively treats social problems and needs as aberrations from social norms and not as indications of systemic issues. At the individual level it emphasises deficits and pathology, with assistance often dependent on the philanthropic or charitable efforts of those who are wealthier.

Elliott (1993, p. 25) picks up Midgley's differentiation of three forms of social welfare regime to distinguish some key features of the 'institutional' model. Where the 'residual' model relies on philanthropy and charity, the 'institutional' approach is founded on a human rights perspective. Thus there is less stigma attached to being in need, which is perceived to be more a normal life experience. In addition, there may be an element of proactive intervention to prevent problems occurring or at early stages. Yet although this approach to social welfare represents significant gains over the 'residual' model, it still does not address the systemic aspects of social need. Eligibility for assistance remains targeted at specific social groups, and as with 'residual' social welfare, a concern with limiting costs remains one of the key policy principles.

In contrast, the 'developmental' approach to social welfare both extends the 'institutional' model and has important differences (Elliott, 1993; Patel, 2005; Midgley, 2010). It is rights-based, but also seeks social justice. Unlike the other models, it is universal in coverage and not only is proactive in addressing potential needs and problems but also seeks to anticipate future needs through planning and systemic change. Moreover, the 'developmental' model regards social welfare expenditure as an investment in the well-being of a society and not simply as a net cost. Examples of countries that have sought to introduce some of these principles into their social welfare regimes include those in Scandinavia and also more recently South Africa (Kautto *et al.*, 1999; Patel, 2005; Rush & Keenan, 2014). While in the early years of the twenty-first century this model has been under severe pressure from the international financial policies of institutions such as the International Monetary Fund (e.g. see Hölscher, 2008), this approach most clearly embodies the values of social work (cf. IFSW/IASSW, 2004).

The question for social development in social work, therefore, is whether it depends on a 'developmental' social welfare regime. This appears to be one of the implications of the experience in South Africa (Hölscher, 2008). As Midgley (2010, p. 12) notes, there are many debates remaining about whether social development in social work is the same thing as 'developmental social work' and whether such practices can occur only within specific social welfare regimes or they can be part of the way in which such regimes are created. It is also the case that arguments for such changes may have had unintended consequences, such as the closing of residential care homes for children in southern Africa before viable alternative programmes were implemented (Midgley, 1984). This is a serious misunderstanding of the implications of this approach, and, to the extent that such decisions are justified on the basis of promoting a 'developmental' perspective, they are a misuse of the concept. A 'developmental' strategy would have been to create alternatives first and reduce the 'residual' provision only as they were put in place.

The discussions of the following chapters show that there are many examples of social development practice that have been achieved in social work. It is also the case that ideas such as Saleebey's (1996, 2002) concept of strengths-based practice, which originated in social development–oriented community work, have had a much wider impact and created possibilities for progressive practice in more individual- and family-focused social work. Saleebey's concept is one example of a practical concept that has generalist impact. More than this, the elements of social development in social work can be seen historically to be part of the profession's traditions both in terms of the practices it involves and the values that it expresses. In that sense, social development may even be seen as the rediscovery of a vital dimension of the identity and purpose of social work in the present day.

3

ECONOMICS, SOCIAL STRUCTURES AND SOCIAL WORK PRACTICE

Introduction

Many of the key proponents of social development in social work have emphasised the importance of economics and other structural issues for understanding the needs faced by service users and wider populations (Mohan, 1988, 2007; Sherraden, 1991; Elliott, 1993; Midgley, 1995, 2014; Sherraden & Ninacs, 1998; Sherraden & Sherraden, 2000; Elliott & Mayadas, 2001; Patel, 2005; Pawar, 2012; Cox & Pawar, 2013). Throughout the literature there are many different perspectives on both the nature and causes of poverty and the possible ways in which social workers can and should be involved in poverty alleviation measures. However, at the outset, it is necessary to recognise that despite all the other differences, the various advocates of a more material focus to social work theory and practice share the view that poverty is a major issue faced by many recipients of social work and, indeed, is one of the chief barriers to achieving a good human life. Yet there are differences of perspective within this overall concern with material and structural need, and these too must be addressed.

This chapter examines the way in which economic considerations, and related aspects of social structural concerns, have been recognised in social work practice and theory. In particular, it considers the way in which a social developmental approach requires both an awareness of and a response to the economic issues faced by many people. The chapter begins by examining the broad area and then looks in greater depth at particular concepts or programmes that have grown out of social work action in social development. At the global level these include major contributions made to the World Summit on Social Development (WSSD) in 1995, followed by the Millennium Development Goals in 2000 (Correll, 2008, 2011) and now the planning of post-MDG goals (Healy & Wairire, 2014). More detailed practices and programmes concerning economic and structural interventions include assets-based programmes (Sherraden, 1991; Sherraden & Sherraden,

2000), microfinance (Larance, 2001; Drolet, 2011a) and promoting access to education, health and other services (Cox & Pawar, 2013). Drawing the discussion together, the chapter concludes by examining the ways in which the different perspectives offered in responding to material and structural needs may be in conflict, such that each must be understood critically in order to recognise its strengths and weaknesses.

A global focus on poverty and other structural needs

In 1995 the World Summit on Social Development was held in Copenhagen. In total, 117 countries took part and signed the Copenhagen Declaration on Social Development (UN, 1995). The Declaration contains ten commitments for all of the participating nations to engage in social development action. These are:

1   create an economic, political, social cultural and legal environment that will enable people to achieve social development;
2   eradicate absolute poverty by a target date to be set by each country;
3   support full employment as a basic policy goal;
4   promote social integration based on the enhancement and protection of all human rights;
5   achieve equality and equity between women and men;
6   attain universal and equitable access to education and primary health care;
7   accelerate the development of Africa and the least developed countries;
8   ensure that structural adjustment programmes include social development goals;
9   increase resources allocated to social development;
10 strengthen co-operation for social development through the United Nations.

(UN, 1995, section 29)

There are then subsidiary commitments at national, regional and international levels, spelling out how each country will contribute to implementing these intentions.

Social workers made a significant contribution to enabling the summit to take place, largely through the activities of the international social work organisations (Correll, 2008). In fact, the International Council on Social Welfare (ICSW) in particular played a central role through the general reporting status that it holds at the UN. While now more widely representing peak bodies in the non-government sector in social welfare in over 70 nations, ICSW carries the legacy (and initials) of the first International Conference on Social Work that took place in Paris in 1928 (Healy, 2008; also see http://icsw.org/). Over several decades, its work (discussed in more depth in Chapters 6 and 9) has led the sector at the UN, especially in relation to the Economic and Social Council (ECOSOC) and the agencies and programmes that it covers, including the UN Commission on Social Development, the UN Research Institute for Social Development (UNRISD), the International Labour Organization (ILO) and the UN Education, Scientific and Cultural Organization

(UNESCO). Throughout these actions, ICSW has maintained a clear position that social development is not simply a matter of poverty reduction (although that is part of it) but a matter of addressing the ways in which all aspects of human life are affected by wider challenges to social integration and participation in various aspects of society, which includes (but is not confined to) the economic and political spheres.

Having agreed in the Copenhagen Declaration in 1995 to wide-ranging objectives to promote social development, by 2000 the government of the world refocused its attention to development issues in the Millennium Development Goals (MDGs) (UN, 2000). The goals of the MDGs are that, by 2015, each country should:

1 eradicate extreme poverty and hunger;
2 achieve universal primary education;
3 promote gender equality and empower women;
4 reduce child mortality;
5 improve maternal health;
6 combat HIV/AIDS, malaria and other major diseases;
7 ensure environmental sustainability;
8 develop a global partnership for development.

Each of these goals is spelled out in one or more specific targets. These targets provide some measurable benchmarks against which success or failure can be gauged. For example, within Goal 1 target 1A sets the aim to 'halve, between 1990 and 2015, the proportion of people whose income is less than $1.25 a day'. (The figures used in this statement are based on 'parity purchasing power', so that variations between levels of wealth, prices and other such factors can be equalised.) Recent figures suggest that this target was achieved in 2010 (http://www.un.org/millenniumgoals/poverty.shtml).

Especially given the increases in the world population in that period, this might be seen as a positive outcome. Yet there are several reasons to question that conclusion. First, the point at which agreement was reached in setting this goal and target occurred halfway through the period of counting. Figures were already available for the first ten out of 25 years. Thus, to the sceptical observer this raises the possibility that the figure was set to a level that appears to be known in advance to be relatively easy to reach, but in fact is very difficult actually to measure (Saith, 2006, p. 1173). Indeed, much of the necessary effort in establishing and evaluating such benchmarks assumes that they can be seen as objective, but as Saith goes on to elaborate, this is something that is known to be fraught with hazards of accuracy in reporting at local and national levels (2006, pp. 1174–6). More than that, Saith's critique points out that many genuinely *social* development goals, such as total abolition of child labour, or those with major impact, such as universal secondary school provision or universal access to health care, are missing from the goals and targets (p. 1189).

From a different angle Correll (2008) agrees that the MDGs are, at best, very limited. He castigates the global community for a lost opportunity, describing the

MDGs as 'a mediocre, minimalist, disjointed selection of left-overs' from the vision that has emerged only five years previously in the Copenhagen Declaration (Correll, 2008, p. 460). For Correll there are two particular aspects to this retreat from the ten commitments of the WSSD. The first of these is that in the MDGs social development becomes reduced to 'poverty alleviation'. Within that, the idea of alleviating poverty is itself minimised to the *reduction* of *absolute poverty*, without any recognition that the previous commitment of the WSSD was to 'eradication' of poverty and the creation of opportunities, including full employment, social integration and the inclusion of social goals in structural adjustment programmes. It is not that social development is separated from economic goals, but rather that economic objectives should be to serve the ends of *social* gains (including education, health, environment, participation and human rights). Instead, what the MDGs offer is a residual 'safety net' approach that is not capable of securing more than the minimum targets, which then in effect become maximum attainments (Correll, 2011).

The critiques from Saith (2006), Correll (2008) and others (e.g. Deacon et al., 2007; Deacon & Cohen, 2011) regard the prevailing ideology of neo-liberalism as the key problem in the links between social development goals and global social policy. The neo-liberal approach to policy argues that the necessary material gain is achievable only if the market is enabled to operate freely. This view is accompanied by the associated conviction that such freedom should extend also to the actions of individuals, so that matters such as education, health, and so on are all most effectively resolved by each person and family for themselves (e.g. see Girdwood, 2007). This ideology has influenced the actions of many social development actors since the 1980s, including the World Bank, the International Monetary Fund and some national governments, as well as some major non-government organisations. However, Ortiz (2007) identifies a primary problem for social development in the core idea of neo-liberalism – namely that market liberalisation necessarily leads to benefits for everyone in a society – what is often referred to as the 'trickle-down effect', in which increased wealth among the most affluent sections of a society automatically produces increased investment and economic activity that in turn produce jobs and other benefits for all. Such a view conjures up a 'rising tide floats all boats' image of shared benefits from a single cause, which in this case takes the form of an exclusively economic focus on growth. As all of these critics point out, empirical evidence that this is actually the case is lacking. Indeed, there are also indications that despite economic growth, disparities between the wealthier and poorer sections of populations in many countries are getting wider; in some cases this is partly because the poor are becoming poorer in real terms, including in wealthy countries, such as the USA (Deacon & Cohen, 2011; Midgley, 2014, p. 51).

Elsewhere (Hugman, 2010, p. 59) I have observed that although the MDGs represent a considerable diminution of the aims set out in the Copenhagen Declaration, and even with the obstacles faced in implementing them, some commentators note that limited gains have been made from them (Deacon, 2007; Mathbor & Ferdinand, 2008). Moreover, at the global level the policies that underpin social development have largely been set in terms of the MDGs since 2000. Thus any critiques of social development goals and achievements have to be understood in the light of the eight goals and their subsidiary targets. That these include education, health, employment and other factors points to the possibility of maintaining attention to the connections between these social aspects of human well-being and a more economic focus on poverty. In other words, despite the failures of neo-liberalism's exclusive attention to economic growth as the defining feature of development, it remains relevant to consider questions about levels of poverty and opportunities for employment, access to and control over assets and other indicators of the ways in which poorer sections of populations can achieve improvements in the material aspects of their lives.

Case study: poverty alleviation in social development

In order to examine the practice and policy implications for social workers in social development, the following depiction of a poverty alleviation project provides a concrete example of these issues.

Imara and Aziza are a married couple living in a small regional town in an East African country. They have three children, girls aged 11 and 4 and a boy aged 8. Although historically in this region many families have gained their livelihood from agriculture, with population growth land is less available than in the past. After several years of drought Imara and Aziza had to give up their smallholding and seek other sources of income. Because neither of them had any skills outside small-scale agriculture they had to rely on the money they got for their land, and although they have lived very simply this did not last long. Imara was able to get some work labouring in the town, but this work is casual and so it is never very certain. As their extended family is also affected by these problems they have not been able to provide material support.

About two years ago Harambee, a national NGO, established a poverty alleviation project in the town. This project is supported by international donors. In order to promote sustainable development, the project does not give money directly to families but focuses on three community-based initiatives to help families to increase their capacities to earn their living. These are: a skills training programme, a 'savings club' and a microcredit scheme for women in the community. Both Imara and Aziza have joined the activities of the project and have begun to gain some benefits from it. Imara has learned skills in building and domestic maintenance work, while Aziza has been able to improve her skills in working with fabric so that she can now make clothes that are of retail quality. With the work that they have both been able to do, about a year ago they were able to join the 'savings club'. Although they do not yet have much money saved, they have been able to begin to plan for their future.

Imara and Aziza's immediate plans are for Aziza to establish her own small business making clothes that she can sell in the market. To do this she will need to buy a better sewing machine (the one that she has is very old and is unlikely to last much longer). Aziza is optimistic about the possibility of this opportunity, for two reasons. First, she has discussed the plan with the community worker from the Harambee project who supervises the micro-credit scheme and she has helped Aziza to review the prospects of being able to make a living from this work. Second, the microcredit scheme is run as a community group, with loans made through the group, which then takes responsibility for encouraging the women in making their repayments. Aziza has good relationships with women in her local group, so she thinks that she will be trusted and can trust others.

Although the national government has a policy of universal free education, in reality there are still costs for a child to go to school, so Imara and Aziza faced the prospect of their children not being able to attend. In fact, when she was ten years old, they considered their older daughter leaving school to undertake domestic work for a wealthy family in the town. Because of the help of the Harambee programme, both Imara and Aziza now think that they will be able to keep their children at school. Although their income will not be large, there is now a good opportunity for them to at least sustain their lives well enough to give their children opportunities through education. Furthermore, at the school where both their older daughter and their son attend, this year UNICEF has also introduced a Girls Education Movement (GEM) project. Although the direct help this programme provides is for those girls who are at risk of leaving school early because one or both of their parents has died, it also has enabled the school to strengthen the opportunities for all the girls who attend. In turn, this also has a positive impact for the boys.

The situation described here is unusual in several ways. First, in the countries of East Africa the impact of HIV/AIDS has been such that in many families such as this family one or both parents have died (Laird, 2008, pp. 144). The scale of the impact of this pandemic has meant that the capacities of extended families and whole communities to provide traditional forms of care for orphaned children have been severely disrupted (Laird, 2008, pp. 145).

Second, this is a family in which the gender dynamics are relatively positive, in that the woman concerned is shown as having the capability of exercising agency and there is no evidence of financial exploitation by her husband or of violence (Swart, 2012; cf. Nussbaum, 2000). As is the case in many communities, this must not be taken for granted. Moreover, both economic and cultural factors affect the rate of school attendance by girls, making this a continuing challenge to realisation of MDGs 2 and 3 in many parts of the world (Healy & Wairire, 2014, pp. 237–8).

Third, although the community portrayed here faces economic challenges, there are also opportunities and the decline of agriculture has not forced this family (or apparently many others) to move into the capital city and join the many thousands of internal migrants who are mostly swelling the numbers of slum dwellers (Jorgensen & Rice, 2010; Swart, 2012). As is evident in the following discussion, there are wide variations in such experiences and none of the realities depicted here can be assumed. At the same time, this (hypothetical) situation is modelled on research and reports of practice from many parts of the world.

Assets-based social development

One of the key factors in the positive outcome for the family portrayed in the for-going case study is that they were able to accumulate some material assets. Having lost their smallholding, part of their move away from poverty was based on financial savings and the gradual accumulation of things, such as a sewing machine or tools, to engage in income-generating work. Without access to these means of earning a livelihood, Imara and Aziza would probably have faced migration to the slums of the capital city, with the potential loss of educational opportunities for their children, or even the breakup of their family.

A highly influential concept in social development practice in social work is that of 'assets-based development' (Sherraden, 1991). The foundation of Sherraden's concept of assets as a focus for developmental social work is that poverty and levels of income are not the same phenomenon. In his approach, poverty consists of the lack of wealth and opportunity, because these are factors that give people the capacity to engage actively in addressing the challenges faced in their lives. As Sherraden and his colleagues have repeatedly noted, the social advantages exercised by those who they call the 'non-poor' are underpinned by the accumulation of basic assets that include home ownership, education, retirement accounts and small businesses (e.g. see Sherraden & Sherraden, 2000, pp. 62–3). Moreover, these assets are accumulated through the support of taxation policies that treat such gains favourably, either by ignoring them in the calculation of income or wealth taxes or even by positive returns to individuals through tax rebates (Deacon & Cohen, 2011). In contrast, they argue, policies that are intended to address poverty tend to focus on income for immediate consumption – that is through income maintenance policies that are simply direct cash transfers (Sherraden, 1991). Such payments are residual, in that they are structured to meet only the most immediate survival needs. Thus they have no developmental goal, and as they are set at the minimum possible level to achieve survival they do not provide the basis for people to help themselves to move out of poverty.

Based on this analysis, Sherraden (1988, 1991) has long been an advocate of creating opportunities for people in poverty to receive the same level of social support to accumulate assets as do those who are already better off. In particular, the main practical mechanism that has been promoted by the Center for Social Development (CSD) at George Warren Brown School of Social Work, Washington University, in the USA, is that of individual development accounts (IDAs). The principle of this mechanism is that a person can hold a bank account in which they commit to make regular savings, with the funds that accumulate matched by tax-funded payments so that the gains made by saving are accelerated. This also creates greater equity within the taxation system in that the matched payments achieve the same outcome as any tax breaks that are provided to support home ownership, retirement saving and so on (which tend to be enjoyed by those who already have other assets). Indeed, the purpose of these accounts is not only to create a pattern of asset accumulation (although financial education is part of it) but also to support home ownership, education for children or adults and other changes in life opportunities.

One example of a scheme using this model is that of the 'Saver Plus' programme in Australia. Originally founded by the Brotherhood of St Laurence (a faith-based, non-government social welfare organisation), the programme is offered in partnership with several other social work and social welfare NGOs and one of the large Australian commercial retail banks (http://www.bsl.org.au/Services/Money-matters). This programme offers matched savings as developed in the CSD model, in combination with financial education and advice. Criteria for people to join the programme include having a low income (including casual or seasonal work), being eligible for subsidised health care and either having children in education or being in full-time education or training as an adult. The programme lasts only for one year, in which time it is expected that the IDA recipient will have been able to support her or his own efforts to 'invest' in asset accumulation. In these terms, education and health are seen as forms of investment in potential for future material well-being.

In practical terms, this type of programme requires particular approaches from social workers. For the most part the focus of research has been on the detailed working of these schemes and of the needs of service users (Lombe & Ssewamala, 2007; Lombe *et al.*, 2007; Han *et al.*, 2009; Huang, 2010; Rothwell, 2011). The evidence is that the reasons why people who are in paid employment remain poor are complex. However, some common features are identified. For example, the costs of housing, transport, health care and the education of children all present major financial challenges for the participants in IDA programmes (Shobe & Christy-McMullin, 2005). One of the findings across several studies is that people earning at the lower end of the low-income scale that is a criterion of IDAs appear to gain the most from asset accumulation that is fostered in this way (Huang, 2010, p. 589). This suggests that those who are running such programmes might appropriately focus financial advice and support among these service users towards developing savings patterns. With broader implications, there is also evidence that the IDA programmes help people to develop new assets and not simply to transfer wealth from other sources (Han *et al.*, 2009; Huang, 2010). Beyond this, there is support for the assumption that financial education and wider social supports have a positive impact on how people make use of the schemes. Thus, at the micro and meso levels the role of social workers and other community-based practitioners appears to be important in the success of IDA programmes (Zhan *et al.*, 2006; Sherraden *et al.*, 2007; Huang, 2010).

Some researchers in this area argue for social workers to use their knowledge of service users' lives and struggles as the basis for policy advocacy and development (Shobe & Christy-McMullin, 2005; Rothwell, 2011; Rothwell & Sultana, 2013). As Shobe and Christy-McMullin observe, '[o]ne of the great injustices of this country [the USA] is that many of the working poor hold more than one job yet still have difficulty in meeting their basic needs' (2005, p. 234). This leads them to identify policies about the affordability of housing, minimum wage levels and access to post-secondary education as aspects of wider social policy that can be informed by such professional knowledge. In Australia the Brotherhood of St Laurence has long combined practical programmes to support people in moving out of poverty while at the same time engaging in policy advocacy concerning the causes of poverty (Brotherhood of St Laurence, 2014). In a recent submission to an Australian government review of the social welfare system, it raises precisely these areas as major barriers to people on low incomes improving their participation in the society. This not only is an example of macro-level practice but also represents the connections between levels and the integration of social work encountered in social development, as discussed in Chapter 2.

The assets approach: critiques and debates

Although the assets approach to poverty alleviation has provided a way of engaging social work with economic and other material needs, and it has assisted many participants in programmes such as IDAs, at the same time there are several aspects that are questioned by proponents of the concept as well as by those who are more clearly identified as critics. To gauge the potential contribution of this approach to social development in social work, it is necessary to address these points.

First, the research that supports assets-based approaches, including IDAs, raises some concerns about limitations. Several studies point to the way in which external forces, such as broader social welfare policy, shifts in the economy and their impact, such as the global financial crisis (GFC) of 2007–8, as well as personal life events, can create unanticipated barriers to success (Shobe & Christy-McMullin, 2005; Han *et al.*, 2009; Huang, 2010). For this reason, it would be inappropriate to regard such approaches as an alternative to research and policy development in the area of poverty and its causes. This is not to suggest that detailed studies on the way in which these approaches operate are misleading, but rather that their findings need to be located in a broader economic and political framework.

Second, although the data from all the studies that have been undertaken on IDAs as a specific form of asset-based programme show that the majority of participants are women, this is largely ignored as a point for discussion. A few studies have looked specifically at issues faced by women on low incomes, such as Zhan and Sherraden (2003) and Shobe and Christy-McMullin (2005). For example, recent data suggest that in the USA households headed by single mothers are five times more likely to be poor than households headed by a couple (Zhan & Sherraden, 2003, p. 191). Among single mothers, there are also effects of ethnicity (negative for women of ethnic minority background) and location (negative for women in rural areas). However, having identified that women head the vast majority of low-income households, there is very little attention to other implications of gender in causes of and possible solutions to poverty. While Shobe and Christy-McMullin (2005) argue that African American women gained considerably from their participation in such projects, and they also identify ways in which programmes could be more flexible to assist those on the lowest incomes, there is no recognition of the ways in which programmes might help women to address the gendered nature of poverty. For example part of their sample worked in what might be seen as 'middle-class' jobs, as nurses, as a dietician and in an office (Shobe and Christy-McMullin, 2005, p. 226); the policy implication of the gendered nature of low pay is a crucial factor in these women being among the working poor. Issues of racism also tend to remain implicit in these discussions.

Third, almost all of the information on the assets-based approach and IDAs in particular comes from the USA and, to a lesser extent, other global Northern countries. However, social work researchers associated with the CSD have also worked with similar programmes in Africa and identified comparable results (Chowa *et al.*, 2010, 2014; Ssewamala *et al.*, 2010). In these analyses there is greater attention to contextual factors, such as the impact of HIV/AIDS, as well as cultural differences in the way in which individuals and families are embedded in community relationships. So, for example, the way in which being cared for by grandparents can have a negative effect on asset accumulation by orphaned adolescents is seen as a complex factor and not simply as a barrier to avoiding poverty (Ssewamala *et al.*, 2010). In addition, both Chowa *et al.* (2014) and Lombe *et al.* (2014) show that community relations are important in sub-Saharan Africa, so that informal savings programmes (such as that portrayed in the forgoing case study) are as important as formal projects. Thus it is vital that when concepts such as assets-based development are transferred to other parts of the world careful thought is given to questions of culture and national context. For example, Lombe *et al.* (2014) also make the tentative suggestion that there may be value in this setting of linking assets approaches more specifically to microfinance programmes, which is not a feature of the global Northern application of the concept.

Fourth, for some social workers there may be a more political or value-based objection to approaches that explicitly use mechanisms that are grounded in the very social structures that cause poverty and other inequalities in the first place. As Ferguson and Lavalette (2005) argue, there is the potential to strengthen the *status quo* in approaches to 'empowerment' based uncritically on increasing people's capacities to engage as consumers in neo-liberal economies. Should social workers therefore devote their attention to helping people accumulate assets on these terms, or should the profession's focus be on how people in poverty might secure social justice (Ferguson, 2007; Reisch & Jani, 2012)? For example, the health professionals, such as the nurses or dieticians identified by Shobe and Christy-McMullin (2005), who despite their employment status are on very low incomes, would be better served by ensuring that their work is appropriately remunerated. That these particular people living in poverty are also Black women shows that issues of racism and sexism are part of the struggle that they face. Similarly, there is little attention in these debates to the specific situations of Indigenous peoples (Rothwell, 2011).

These criticisms point to an underlying issue that must be addressed in developing strategies to help people get out of poverty. For Imara and Aziza in the forgoing case example a 'savings club' that supports them in accumulating some personal assets may be very helpful in their immediate situation, as may IDA programmes in other countries. That the former are in a 'developing' country in East Africa while IDAs were originally designed for people on low incomes in (at least relatively) 'developed' countries of the global North does not create a vast difference in this respect. Indeed, there has been some limited introduction of this idea to African cities (Chowa *et al.*, 2010, 2014; Ssewamala *et al.*, 2010; Lombe *et al.*, 2014). Both for Imara and Aziza and for the recipients of IDAs, greater social justice is necessary in education, employment, health, housing and other social policies in the longer term. Without attention to these macro concerns there is a risk that responding to economic issues in practice of this kind draws social work back into individualised solutions to structural issues.

Microcredit in social development

Another highly influential approach to poverty alleviation is that of 'microfinance' (Drolet, 2009). Ahmed (2012, p. 358) identifies the origins of this approach in the 1970s, with the beginnings of 'microcredit', but states that it now includes savings facilities, transfer payments, insurance and pensions. The benefits of microfinance include asset building, access to education and the strengthening of social networks to support entrepreneurial activity. Ahmed also summarises the available evidence that microfinance has helped people in poverty to improve nutrition levels, achieve higher immunisation rates and to reduce vulnerability to unforeseeable challenges (2012, pp. 358–9).

This present discussion focuses on the form of microfinance developed in the concept of 'microcredit' that was originally pioneered by Yunus in Bangladesh through the creation of the Grameen Bank (Yunus & Jolis, 1998). The way in which microcredit programmes operate is to provide very small loans to individuals in order to provide the basis for developing small-scale income-earning activities. Examples include the purchase of chickens for egg production, the purchase of equipment, such as a sewing machine, in order to set up a garment manufacture or repair business, or the purchase of utensils and commodities to establish a business selling food in a local market.

Yunus's original concept has very important aspects. First, it seeks to address the poverty of people in rural areas – Grameen means 'rural' in Bengali. Second, one of the original motivating forces for the model that Grameen developed was that people living in poverty were often prevented from improving their situations because their only access to money was through informal, high-interest money lenders (often referred to as 'loan sharks'). So it was based on making banking available at standard rates. Third, the Grameen Bank focuses specifically on lending to women (Larance, 2001; Ahmed, 2012).

There are important reasons for Grameen's focus on women, as summarised by Drolet (2009). In general, women are the majority of the impoverished members of all communities, and in the countries in which microcredit was pioneered women often are unable to obtain loans from commercial banks (Kabeer, 1991). Research has also demonstrated that in many situations women tend to use their income to increase the well-being of their family as a whole, as compared to the effects of increased income for men. Adding to this, women are also perceived through research evidence and practice wisdom to be more likely to work co-operatively in group programmes, which have greater efficiencies and are therefore more sustainable.

As indicated by Drolet (2009, p. 56), the early model developed by the Grameen Bank introduced some key elements to the ways in which the microcredit programme operates. Loans are granted and managed through local groups, in which women meet on a weekly basis to make repayments and to support each other in their income-generating activities. For example, in a detailed study of a local Grameen Bank 'centre' (i.e. the weekly meeting of the women who are part of a local group with a district representative of the bank at which repayments are made), Larance (2001) found that members had been able to build supportive relationships outside their homes in ways that had not previously been open to them. In turn, many of these relationships benefitted the women not only socially and psychologically but also in being able to improve their economic situation. Similar findings have been reported in other studies (Rajouria, 2008; Ahmed, 2012).

The operating rules of Grameen include an expectation that loans are tied to what might be called micro-business planning. That is in order to get a loan it is necessary to show that it is to be used to support income-generating activity. This is vital, as the person receiving the loan must make a commitment to regular repayments. Thus, use for dowry in particular was intended to be excluded as the purpose of taking a microcredit loan (Yunus & Jolis, 1998). (This exclusion was also linked to an objection to child marriage of girls, against which the members of the Grameen Bank projects were supposed to commit themselves.) The Grameen Bank claims a very high rate of loan repayment as a measure of the success of its programme (Larance, 2001; Ahmed, 2012). This is a measure both of the success achieved by individual women and their families and of the success of the programme as a whole. In particular, it is an indicator of sustainability. For the women it means that their community relationships are strengthened along with their financial situation. For the overall programme it means that funds are available for further loans.

Microcredit: critiques and debates

Although this model of microfinance has become well regarded internationally (Yunus and the Grameen Bank together received a Nobel Prize in 2006 for this work), there have also been many concerns raised about the impact of particular programmes as well as of the underlying concepts on which the model is based. In order to consider the contribution of microcredit to social development in social work, these must be addressed.

The first key question about microcredit programmes is to what extent they achieve the goal of alleviating poverty. Here evidence is mixed. Insofar as this is measured by improvements in the economic situation of individual women and specific households, then some success can be claimed for this approach. The studies undertaken by Larance (2001), Rajouria (2008), Drolet (2009, 2011a, 2011b), Vijayalakshmi *et al.* (2010), Aideyan (2011), Ahmed (2012) and Gökavali (2013) all show gains for the majority of participants at the household level. This evidence draws on diverse countries, including Bangladesh, Egypt, Nepal, India, Nigeria and Turkey. In each case those who benefitted saw gains both in their available income for immediate expenditure needs and in their ability to repay loans and to accumulate some assets. At the same time, there are also risks and weaknesses that are clear across studies. In some cases gains are sustainable only with continued loans, which some participants see as trapping them in a cycle of debt. This challenges the extent to which the activities that the microcredit is supporting are sustainable (although these data differ in the way in which they portray the reasons why participants take further loans, many of which are for expanding their business activities). In other cases, debt comes from a lack of attention to capacity to plan economic activity, from the use of loans for purposes other than income generation and from unforeseen crises, such as personal ill health (Rajouria, 2008, p. 126). Considered in this way, it is important to recognise that microcredit is not a concept that can be implemented without careful planning and integration with local social structures and cultural expectations.

Beyond the immediate alleviation of poverty, a further achievement often claimed for microcredit is that it supports the empowerment of women. (Kabeer, 2001; Larance, 2001; Gao & Hu, 2005; Vijayalakshmi *et al.*, 2010; Drolet, 2011a; Gökavali, 2013). Again, the origins of the Grameen Bank in rural Bangladesh have a strong influence on this notion, as participation in the programme there gave women a culturally acceptable reason to engage with the wider community (Larance, 2001). At the same time this programme has also provided many women with access to education, which the large majority had not received past the most basic levels (Ahmed, 2012). A similar impact was observed, although to a lesser extent, in China (Gao & Hu, 2005), in Nepal (Rajouria, 2008), in India (Vijayalakshmi *et al.*, 2010) and in Turkey (Gökavali, 2013).

However, other studies are much more cautionary or actually negative about the impact of microcredit on women's empowerment. For example from her studies in Egypt Drolet (2011a, 2011b) states that although there is potential in the concept of microcredit to support women's empowerment, the reality of social and institutional pressures means that where such gains are experienced they are confined to the personal level. That is there is no clear impact on wider social relationships or structures, such as the wider social position of women. Similarly, in a discussion of programmes in Nigeria, Campbell (2005) argues that although there were some modest gains for women at the individual level, more broadly nothing changed in relation to women's overall social status. Indeed, she concludes that any apparent gains are, in fact, illusory. In part this apparent failure can be explained by reference to different cultural contexts (Bagati, 2003). The question must be asked whether it is reasonable to expect a method to address poverty designed in one country or culture to be transferable to others without major adaptation. There appears to be no detailed debate within the field on this point. However, insofar as the gain experienced by women in countries such as Bangladesh and Nepal might also be seen only at the level of individuals, the wider question of the capacity of microcredit as a vehicle for women to challenge oppression is at best still open to debate.

At the most general level, many critics of microcredit argue that, as with critiques of assets-based programmes, the failures of microcredit to promote women's empowerment effectively lie in the way that it supports the neo-liberal ethos of the global economy (Campbell, 2005; Drolet, 2011a). At best it may provide a means for women and their families to mitigate the impact of wider economic factors, while at worst it may prepare women simply to be appropriately behaved consumers (cf. Girdwood, 2007, p. 421). This critique points to a wider issue – namely that whether microcredit of the type derived from the Grameen Bank model can be a basis for promoting women's empowerment depends as much on how we understand empowerment as it does on any other aspect. In this regard Campbell's largely negative assessment is based on the view that the objectives of the programmes she studied were to promote the goals of the donor organisations and programme staff, which left unchallenged 'the social construction of production and reproduction – the basis of women's oppression' (Campbell, 2005, p. 115). Drolet is more nuanced in her conclusion that microcredit programmes have the potential to contribute to changes in women's lives, while at the same time they have been severely limited in their attention to individualistic notions of financial outcomes at the cost of the wider social issues that structure women's lives (Drolet, 2011a, p. 642). However, for Drolet this potential can be achieved only if social structural issues are also addressed, and in this she is in agreement with Campbell.

This central problem is addressed by Kabeer (2012) in terms of a struggle between different views of feminism that are inescapably encultured. That is it must be asked to what extent the critiques of microcredit programmes as capable of promoting women's empowerment are based on challenges to the liberal conception of rights born by individuals as citizens (Kabeer, 2012, p. 222). If this is the measure, but it is being applied to a context in which rights are grounded in relationship, then it may miss important features of the situation. Citing Benhabib's (1992) notion of relational justice, Kabeer (2012, p. 223) is very careful to distinguish this from an uncritical relativism that amounts to support for an oppressive status quo. The point is that how gender injustice is to be understood and challenged must come from within any given context. She examines this idea through the way in which microcredit programmes contributed to, but were not the only factor for, change in the lives of women in Afghanistan and Bangladesh (cf. Drolet, 2009; Vijayalakshmi et al., 2010). Two particular responses to the opportunities provided by microcredit can be observed. One is that many of the women included in Kabeer's studies focused on enhancing the rights and opportunities of their daughters, rather than their own (2012, p. 227). That is they took an intergenerational view of the achievement of gender justice. For these women, this is not a goal that will necessarily be accomplished in the short time frame of an international donor-funded NGO project.

This cross-cultural observation is represented in the forgoing case study of Imara and Aziza as a widely recognised value held in low-income communities. Kabeer also emphasises that there was a very wide range of views held by women about cultural norms and social relations, which tends to be obscured in the generalisations of formal studies. She notes that rather than a completely radical questioning of patriarchal relationships and structures, the majority of women are more likely 'to renegotiate [familial] roles in ways that respected their contribution to the family, gave them a voice in family affairs, expanded options beyond the family and challenged men's arbitrary use of violence' (Kabeer, 2012, p. 229). In addition, these processes were taking place in specific political and cultural contexts that shaped the possibilities open to women, and men who contributed positively to the processes.

The challenge for social development practice in social work that seeks to use the microcredit model is to recognise that, as with any practice, it is important to retain a critical awareness of context and meaning. Some social work proponents have emphasised the positive potential of this approach, without necessarily looking in depth at structural, cultural and historical issues (e.g. see Jansen & Pippard, 1998). As part of a more critical orientation to economic and structural concerns, one that is informed by the goal of social justice, microcredit programmes can be a helpful approach.

Education and health as structural social development

Closely linked to poverty alleviation and gender parity, the Millennium Development Goals also focus particularly on education and health as major developmental concerns. Together with programmes and practices to address poverty, these are key social development issues for social work. Mathbor and Ferdinand (2008) suggest that education and health are interconnected. However, to examine them this discussion focuses separately on specific examples of each, from which some general points are drawn.

Education programmes in development contexts have a range of objectives. The most basic of these is that of increasing the proportions of populations that are functionally literate. A wide variety of strategies are used, focusing on both children and adults. Again, there is a particular concern about the access of girls and women to education in general as well as to literacy in particular (Heidemann & Ferguson, 2009). This follows from the influential World Bank report by Summers (1994), which argues that literacy education for girls is demonstrably the most significant investment a country can make in economic as well as social development. In a meta-analysis of social work and related research concerning girls and education, Heidemann and Ferguson (2009) observe that there is agreement that girls are often ignored or even actively excluded from education due to ignorance or to cultural and religious traditions as well as the effects of poverty. This then appears to be associated with girls being socialised to expect violence and harassment, linked to issues such as early marriage and pregnancy, child labour for girls and also vulnerability to human trafficking. Similar patterns of marginalisation of young women, especially from lower income levels, can be observed in countries at various overall levels of economic prosperity (George, 2011; Terrazas *et al.*, 2011; Çelik & Lüküslü, 2012).

Acharya *et al.* (2007) discuss a community development project in Nepal in which a literacy programme for women was a central component. The goal was to enable women to achieve more active participation in a microcredit-based poverty alleviation project. They conclude that the literacy programme succeeded as evaluated by the way in which women were able to participate more effectively and also by the creation of a self-help group among women in the community (Acharya *et al.*, 2007, pp. 43–4). The key practice of this programme is based on a participatory approach to education, drawing on a combination of 'progressive', humanistic' and 'critical pedagogy' models of learning (p. 37).

Similarly, Terrazas *et al.* (2011) describe a project in California that is part of a national American youth programme called 'Girls Incorporated'. Here, too, literacy education forms part of the overall agenda in supporting a range of activities for girls and young women that focus on various aspects of education, including not only health and personal development but also areas that are often problematic for girls in the school system by comparison to boys, such as science and maths (Terrazas *et al.*, 2011, pp. 67–8). In what is overall a wealthy part of the world, the focus is also on low-income communities, where issues of racism in access to education, housing, health and other human services are prevalent.

In Africa UNICEF sponsors the Girls Education Movement (GEM), which was launched in Uganda in 2001 (J. Kirk & Garrow, 2003). This programme has now been adopted across southern Africa as well as in Egypt (Mlama, 2005). J. Kirk and Garrow describe GEM in the following terms.

> GEM is a major effort to transform African schools, education systems and societies into environments where girls can achieve and have equal opportunities. It is an experiment in how to actively engage young people, particularly girls, in the identification of policy problems and development of solutions for the problems.
>
> *(J. Kirk & Garrow, 2003, p. 5)*

Thus, this programme operates in an integrated way at macro, meso and micro levels. J. Kirk and Garrow also note that its title is gender-specific because the focus is on redressing the exclusion of girls. In practice the programme seeks to involve boys also (2003, p. 13). So, for example, GEM provides ways in which gender equity can be addressed in educational policy and school organisation. This might lead to changes in classroom practice, but also in the provision of segregated toilets. In addition, it helps individual girls through provision of material assistance where poverty keeps girls away from school. Again, the benefit of this project for all children is represented in the case study of Imara and Aziza. In that sort of situation, however, it must be acknowledged that the greatest benefit is seen for girls because they are much more likely to be disadvantaged in educational opportunities than boys.

As I have noted elsewhere (Hugman, 2010, p. 64) there is a major difference between the global South and North in terms of the focus of social work practice in this area; in the South there is a broader focus on programmes that address education at the community level, while in the North attention often tends to be more on individuals and families. However, these are trends and not absolute positions. The same broad difference can also be seen in the area of health.

Laird (2008) identifies the way in which traditional African family and community strategies for coping with health needs in situations of poverty have been severely impacted by the HIV/AIDS pandemic. In particular, family structures have been negatively impacted so that many children are either completely orphaned or cared for by grandparents. While this has led to the formation of new self-help approaches, it also raises the question of how future care for older people and other associated health impacts will be provided. Laird also suggests that both the current challenge of HIV/AIDS and its future effects will further compound difficulties in achieving poverty reduction and the development of livelihoods. For Laird, participatory community development models provide the most potential for social work responses to these issues.

Participatory and community-based practice is also identified by Juliá and Kondrat (2005) as the basis for effective practice in health-related social development in El Salvador. In the projects they describe, all aspects of health development activity were shared between women in the communities and the professionals, including definition of problems and assessment of health needs and the strengths of the communities. These projects also incorporated the use of Indigenous health knowledge alongside 'scientific' health knowledge, and local women were trained as 'barefoot' health workers to provide care in their own areas. As a consequence, there were improvements in both the general levels of health and the sense of self-reliance in these communities (Juliá & Kondrat, 2005, p. 545).

In relation to health, the MDGs have been criticised for focusing specifically on maternal health (apparently both reducing women's lives to childbearing and excluding men's health issues), with the exception of priority given to HIV/AIDS (Mathbor & Ferdinand, 2008; Kvernflaten, 2013). Kvernflaten also argues that they have been used to create very narrow targets instead of promoting wider health development (also see Gover, 2013). While HIV/AIDS remains a major challenge for health practices and policies, especially in sub-Saharan Africa, it is also the case that malaria is responsible for more deaths annually, especially among children (Mweru, 2008; Lordan et al., 2011). This suggests that here is a need to ensure that priorities in health development remain balanced.

Zimmer (2008) points out that there is a close connection between levels of health and poverty. Looking specifically at the health needs of older people in Cambodia, Zimmer concludes that the relationship is complex but that the capacity of those with even a little wealth to cope with ill health far exceeds that of people who have nothing at all (2008, p. 68). Similarly, Austin and Mbewu (2009) show that in a nutrition programme, run by the NGO 'Philani', it was necessary to integrate poverty alleviation and health measures in order to achieve sustainable outcomes.

This included micro-enterprise support and skills training alongside health education strategies so that families were able to challenge the underlying oppression of poverty as the basis for improving health care of children. (This example is discussed further in Chapter 6.)

Towards balanced development

One of the implications of the neo-liberal concern with economic growth as the primary solution to development challenges is that resources are taken away from important structural concerns, such as education and health (Mathbor & Ferdinand, 2008; Austin & Mbewu, 2009; Lordan et al., 2011). There are two consequential risks for social development practice arising from this. The first is that poverty alleviation approaches look only at the question of how to assist communities to enhance their livelihoods. The second is that attention to education and health issues is taken out of the content of the material well-being of communities. There may be some grounds for arguing that social development, such as in education and health provision, is a necessary precursor to sustained economic growth, at least in low-income countries (Summer, 1994; Schell et al., 2007). However, it is also the case that this does not hold so true for 'middle-income' countries (countries in transition), while in the high-GNI countries wealth becomes a more significant factor, affecting access to these important human rights.

Where parts of a society benefit more than others from economic growth, this is usually referred to as 'distorted development'. Although this notion is often applied to the way in which the gains of elites in developing countries are disproportionately large compared to those of the rest of the population, it can also be used to describe very wealthy countries, such as the USA, Canada, New Zealand or Australia, where minorities can fare very badly. One example that is common to these specific countries is the economic status and access to education and health for Indigenous peoples (Trocmé et al., 2004; S. Green & Baldry, 2008).

So, this suggests that some of the strategies that might be adopted to address economic development, such as asset-building or microcredit programmes, are unlikely to be of identical value in countries at different levels of wealth. In each country the communities in which such approaches are relevant, and how they are structured and implemented, will differ according to specific circumstances. What is shared is the recognition that social workers need to address these material and structural issues and to develop appropriate approaches as part of a more holistic framework that combines macro and meso levels with the micro level of practice.

4

ENVIRONMENT, SOCIAL DEVELOPMENT AND SOCIAL WORK PRACTICE

Introduction

Perhaps surprisingly, given the very long-standing adoption of the person-in-environment approach to practice, as discussed in previous chapters, social work has only recently started to address the physical environment (Alston, 1990, 2007, 2012; Besthorn, 2002, 2012; J. Coates, 2003, 2005; McKinnon, 2008; Dominelli, 2012; Miller *et al.*, 2012; Gray, 2013; Pawar, 2014a). That this is the case points to the implicit focus on an understanding of this concept as referring specifically to the social environment (Besthorn & Saleebey, 2003; McKinnon, 2008; Miller *et al.*, 2012). In contrast, the late twentieth century has seen a general growth of awareness of the way in which human life is part of the natural world, and not simply 'linked with' or 'connected to' it. Social work theory and practice are increasingly becoming more responsive to the questions that such awareness raises. Moreover, many of the issues that are faced in social developmental practice are either interwoven with or even caused by events in the physical environment, whether these are understood as 'natural' or 'human created'. Indeed, this shifting awareness raises questions about the extent to which it is appropriate to separate 'physical' and 'social' conceptions of the environment as both the ground and part of the focus of social work. For the purposes of this discussion, however, the notions of 'ecological social work' (Besthorn, 2002, 2012), 'green social work' (Dominelli, 2012) or 'environmental social work' (Gray, 2013) will be taken to apply to the incorporation of the recognition of the physical environment in social work theory and practice.

Ecological social work

Issues of the 'natural' environment and its relationships with social work have been explored by J. Coates (2003, 2005), who concludes that social work often remains part of the dominant paradigm that, mostly, sees the physical world simply as a resource. Thus, because the core values of social work are those of *human* rights and *social* justice, the goal of greater equality is seen only in terms of the way in which the benefits of continued economic growth are shared more fairly. In contrast, Coates argues for social workers to become more explicit in their attention to the links between the issues they face in their practice and the crisis facing the natural environment. For Coates (2003), the implications are that social workers need to be more focused on collective forms of practice, including community work, social action, policy and advocacy and research. At the same time, he does not ignore the ways in which working at the micro level also involves an ecological dimension. For example Coates discusses the way in which health problems faced by low-income families often have environmental dimensions, such as exposure to hazardous materials or pollution of their locality (2005, p. 39). Moreover, he notes that such problems often disproportionately affect Indigenous peoples, migrants and refugees, ethnic minorities and other marginalised groups (p. 40). From this Coates argues that practitioners at the micro level can work in alliance with their macro-focused colleagues to ensure that ecological information and insights inform structural change.

Deep ecology and social work

Besthorn (2002, 2003, 2012) draws particularly on the work of Naess (1989), who proposed the approach that has become known as 'deep ecology'. This is a stance that makes a distinction between attention to immediate adaptations in the existing pattern of life (sources and use of energy, recycling material goods, improved agricultural practices, such as organic farming, and so on) and a more radical attention to the underlying organisation of human life. The deep ecology approach therefore is long-term and challenges both the global consumer-led and profit-oriented economy and anthropocentric views of the place of humanity in the world, thus challenging the reduction of the physical word merely to a resource for meeting human needs (Besthorn, 2012). For Besthorn, this understanding leads to a new way for social work to consider the core value of social justice. In summary, this is an argument that social justice must be seen not simply as about the balance between 'members of the human community' but as about requiring that balance to include non-members, such as plant and animal species and natural habitat, as well as future generations of all living things (including humans) (Besthorn, 2012, p. 255). As for J. Coates, for Besthorn also the implications of this analysis for social work practice should be integrated with practice at the micro as well as the macro level (Besthorn, 2002, p. 62). Further, he asserts that it must also be embedded in social work ethics and the ways in which practice is conceptualised (pp. 63–4). In other words, it should be part of all aspects of the profession.

Green social work

For Dominelli (2012), green social work draws not only on deep ecology but also on explicitly critical perspectives concerning human society. Thus, green social work is defined as that which intervenes to protect the environment, and enhance people's well-being by integrating the interdependencies between people and their socio-cultural, economic and physical environments, and among peoples within an egalitarian framework that addresses prevailing structural inequalities and unequal distributions of power and resources.

(Dominelli, 2012, p. 8)

Moreover, Dominelli is concerned that attention to these questions and their implications for social work practice, at all levels, tends to be missing from current debates within the profession and in its supporting academic disciplines. Specifically, the problem is seen as a lack of overt attention to the political dimension of social work and of ecological issues, as well as the connections between them. To address this, Dominelli argues that social work should rethink all aspects of practice, integrating political, social, cultural, spiritual and psychological analyses with awareness of environmental concerns. In the area of social development this includes attention to the impacts of disasters and environmental crises, social conflict and the challenges of both urban and rural living, especially as these affect people in poverty, Indigenous peoples, migrants and refugees and others who are excluded or marginalised.

Ecology and social development

There are several ways in which the physical environment must be considered as part of the focus of social development in social work. How people live is dependent on water and food, and beyond these survival needs livelihoods considered more broadly also often are connected in some way with the physical world. This is true not only for rural communities but also for urban life. In recent years the attention of social work has also become focused on particular environmental events, those that are understood as 'disasters'. Often seen in the popular media as 'natural', such events can also be understood as 'human created'. Ironically, the role of human action in the origins of such occurrences can be the consequence of pursuing livelihoods in ways that have failed to take account of the interconnectedness of humanity and nature. Thus the very development that has been pursued in achieving a better human life raises questions about whether particular practices and policies can be sustained over time.

To address these questions, this chapter first considers the way in which economic and related structural needs, as discussed in the previous chapter, are also environmental. It then examines the recent growth of concern with the role of social work in disasters and environmental crises, both in responses to their immediate impact and in longer-term planning. Finally, it explores the implications of these questions for the principle of sustainability as a central concern for social work practice and theory, not only in relation to disaster-related social development but also in terms of the wider profession. In doing so the connections between these issues and other practice areas identified by Dominelli, such as working with migrants and refugees, are linked to discussions in later chapters.

Environment, economy, technology and livelihoods

A common thread running through discussions of the connections between the environment and social development in social work is the way in which, in aggregate terms, human life has benefitted enormously from the technological advances that have flowed from the rise of science and the processes of industrialisation. The total levels of wealth, as defined by annual gross national income per person (GNI), have risen in real terms in the last 200 years, so that the majority of countries now have a GNI higher than that of the wealthiest country in 1800 CE (Gapminder, 2014). Yet, wealth is not distributed equitably in any country, or between countries, as in 2012 CE of the 193 full members of the United Nations there were 43 states with GNI lower than US$2,750 (which was the approximate highest level in 1800 in terms of parity purchasing power). Moreover, at the same time these very changes have caused major problems that can cause harm directly to those presently living as well as potentially to future generations (Besthorn, 2002; Coates, 2003). In other words, it can be seen that the improvement in the overall levels of material prosperity has come at the cost of the impact this has had on the natural world from which people derive the physical resources that are part of the foundations of this broad economic development (Beck, 1992).

As Beck and others have argued, there is also a deep irony in the way in which modern material prosperity has been built on industrialised development and technology, in that this growth in wealth has failed to remove the risks of life but rather has changed the way in which people think about them. There may be a sense of the natural world being under human control, but as industrial and technological changes have solved earlier problems of living they have created new ones at the same time. The irony comes from the fact that, as a consequence, the very expertise that has created these increased risks to the natural and social worlds is required simultaneously to resolve the new problems that humanity now faces.

Furthermore, it is now claimed that the level of material consumption in the most highly industrialised countries is at a level that cannot be achieved by other countries. For example it has been calculated that if all countries were to live at the levels of consumption in North America, Europe and Australasia, the resulting impact on the physical world would be to completely deplete all known energy and mineral sources in considerably less than another century (WWF, 2014). In addition, the pressures on arable land, fish stocks and drinkable water mean that continued improvements in health and nutrition are under threat (Kingsbury, 2008b, p. 283). As Kingsbury goes on to note, the possible consequences of these changes in terms of climate, loss of habitable land and rising sea levels are now recognised as having the potential to create conflicts within and between countries as communities increasingly struggle simply to maintain their existence (2008b, p. 288).

There are several implications of this situation for social workers in social development. First, it means that an assumption of economic growth as the measure of development is problematic. For this reason, over the last three decades the concept of 'sustainable development' has become a more central focus, following the Brundtland Commission Report (WCED, 1987). This report defines sustainability as 'the development that meets the needs of the present without compromising the ability of future generations to meet their needs' (p. 43). It goes on to argue that this must require a bias favouring the needs of the poorest communities and that the limits of the natural environment to support technological change must be accepted. For a global economy that is built on the assumption of constant growth, this is a challenging argument. However, the perspective of sustainability points to the necessity for all development practice to be based on goals and methods that make this a central principle. Thus all these areas of peoples' lives, including livelihoods, housing, access to water and fuel and so on, have to be based on sustainable approaches. It also means that other social development concerns, such as education, health, family and child well-being and so on, must be grounded in sustainable principles.

Next, sustainability requires that social workers and other social development practitioners are involved in policy and research work. In the economic sphere, the dominant perspective in the last 30 years has been derived from the 'Washington consensus' of neo-liberal economic policy. This has come to mean free trade, production for export (which in poorer countries is often mono-commodity based, with negative environmental impact), privatisation of government services, and reduced taxation with an emphasis on flat rates and a broadened base (McKay, 2008). This model has been criticised as a failure, as not only has it not clearly produced the intended benefits but also it has led to increasing inequality in all countries and declines in gains that had been made in education and health in some countries, and also was the cause of the Asian financial crisis of 1997 (e.g. Stiglitz, 2002, 2006). The principles of the Brundtland Report and the core social work value of social justice together support a stance that is contrary to this prevailing approach. The challenge that these principles present to social workers is that policy and research work must therefore be from this critical standpoint, requiring strong advocacy as a central aspect of practice.

Then, third, sustainability principles may well go against the taken-for-granted cultural norms in communities where practitioners are involved. This includes businesses as well as those who are employed. However, it is important to recognise that it covers all areas of the way in which livelihoods can be developed, including both rural and urban forms of work. According to the context, social workers and other social development practitioners need to be working directly in multidisciplinary structures with economists, agricultural scientists, marine scientists, engineers of various types and others who have relevant technical expertise. Understanding and acceptance of the sustainability principles such as those outlined by the Brundtland Commission cannot be assumed among colleagues, and so the role of social workers may include advocacy with such colleagues as well as in communities and with political leaders.

Example: fishing in Kerala

So for social workers in these contexts, what might such practice look like? One example is provided by Kuruvilla (2005) in her discussion of a long-term project to enhance fishing in the Indian state of Kerala. It involved the modernisation of fishing by introducing new technologies from Norway to increase the productivity of fishing, in effect by industrialising what had been a craft-based economic activity. However, because of the top-down approach that was taken, the fishing communities became excluded from the very livelihoods that they had previously had (Kuruvilla, 2005, pp. 47–8). These communities were not participants in development but rather were 'being developed' by the actions of others. However, the actual beneficiaries were foreign-owned companies who were able to harvest fish on an industrial scale. In turn, the fish stocks have been rapidly depleted and the physical environment of the fishing grounds severely damaged. The result for the fishing communities themselves was that they became excluded, demoralised and often unable to afford to eat the fish that had previously been their livelihood. In response, social workers in the non-government sector engaged in community work with community members to assist them to gain confidence and skills to oppose harmful changes and to advocate with government and external organisations for access to education for children and the creation of community-based microfinance (with a focus on women) (Kuruvilla, 2005, p. 49). Kuruvilla recognises that these actions are part of the somewhat forced transition of the fishing communities into modernist society, but that this had become inevitable. So, in the broadest terms, in pursuing social justice in this situation achieving rights for these communities and achieving protection of the marine ecology were inextricably joined together. In the longer term the achievements of environmental sustainability and the empowerment of low-caste, poor communities are also integrated.

Example: drought in rural Australia

Similar issues are faced by people in the industrialised countries. One example is that of rural communities in Australia. Alston (2007) describes how a severe drought which lasted for several years created poverty among farming communities, which in turn caused problems for the already inadequate social welfare services. Given the large distances between small centres of population in rural Australia that result in services being provided by federal government agencies from outside communities, the forms of assistance provided frequently fail to attend to rural social contexts (Alston, 2007, pp. 424–5). Previous social welfare support structures have been reduced significantly as a consequence of privatisation, the 'workfare' approach to income support and targeting of interventions. For example the many secondary businesses on which agricultural communities depend are not eligible for many types of support that are available specifically only for farmers (Alston, 2007, p. 423). Thus, livelihoods are threatened and social workers are often faced with supporting families and communities in which isolation is increased alongside other financial issues. As a consequence there are increases in rates of mental ill-health, including the incidence of suicide, family violence and other problems.

One scheme that sought to provide assistance involved social workers providing short-term support for rural families and communities. From the community base these interventions were able to be more culturally appropriate and less stigmatising for families to access. Alston provides a specific example within the scheme of a social worker co-ordinating an outreach service that was based on these principles, combining medical, social and financial assistance by using local pubs as a base; the result was that men found it much easier to seek help, and so it was more effective than it might otherwise have been (Alston, 2007, pp. 432–3). However, this scheme and similar projects were short-term, which reduced the extent to which the social workers could engage in longer-term community capacity building. At the same time, they provide a potential model for a social developmental approach to interventions in rural communities.

Both of these examples are from rural or regional contexts and primarily concern questions of livelihoods in agriculture and fishing in relation to environmental issues. In urban settings the problems people face may be somewhat different. Pollution of land and water by industries that at the same time are providing livelihoods is one such challenge that is mentioned in several studies (Coates, 2005; Ortiz, 2007; Jorgenson & Rice, 2010; Swart, 2012). This problem is distributed inequitably, as it impacts most on poorer communities as well as affecting less well-developed countries more than those that are highly industrialised. In some sense land and water pollution affects an entire country, but those who are wealthier have greater opportunity to avoid the implications through land ownership and through accessing alternative water supplies. Dominelli (2012) refers to a series of industrial pollution catastrophes in recent decades, such as at Bhopal in India and Seveso in Italy. Dominelli notes roles played by social workers in response to these situations include advocacy, personal and community support in compensation claims, and restoring community life, although she acknowledges that many social workers see themselves as constrained by policies and organisational protocols to providing psychosocial and material relief (i.e. micro-level) responses only (2012, pp. 72–3). However, Dominelli also points to the way in which industry initiatives, such as 'Responsible Care', which, although voluntary, now covers the vast majority of major chemical manufacturing businesses, can provide a basis for more collective action (2012, p. 71).

In the longer term it is also necessary to think of the creation of livelihoods that are not based on forms of work that deplete or otherwise damage the environment. Chambers (1983), among others, proposed the approach of 'sustainable livelihoods' that combines attention to five 'types of capital' – namely financial, human, social, physical and natural (Francis, 2002, p. 86). This is an integrated approach in that it looks at the way in which people are located in context, focuses on strengths and resources and also recognises that each type of 'capital' (i.e. the resources required to create livelihoods) is interlinked. An example of sustainable financial capital in this approach is that of asset building, as discussed in Chapter 3. Human capital includes personal capacities, enhanced for example by education and health, while social capital is the 'resource' of community relationships, which will be discussed further in Chapters 6 and 7. In relation to ecological or green social work, the inclusion of physical and natural resources here is very important, especially the latter as this recognises that ecology is part of the development of livelihoods.

Midgley (2014) is critical of what he sees as the livelihoods approach in social development, as he regards it as individualising the needs of poorer families and so running the risk of blaming poor people for poverty. However, when attention to livelihoods is integrated with participatory community work and with the ecological perspective, creating opportunities for people to engage in the development of sustainable work can be done in more collective ways (cf. Ferguson & Lavalette, 2005). Understood and practised in this way, an ecologically informed focus on livelihoods does not have to lead to highly individualised programmes that are based on 'rational choice theory', as tends to predominate in the livelihood approach attributed to Chambers (Midgley, 2014, p. 55). This theory is widely applied in orthodox economics. It assumes that each person acts to maximise his or her own gain, as if calculating the costs and benefits of each action, and that every person will always try to obtain more of whatever good he or she is seeking. Against this, others argue that people base their decisions more broadly in terms of overall ideas, dispositions, attachments, commitments and values, none of which are adequately grasped by orthodox or neoclassical economics (Bourdieu, 2005). Seen in this way, a sustainable approach to livelihoods represents an alternative to the orthodox position, because it allows for the possibility that people will seek 'enough', rather than always wanting 'more'. When people understand the impact of their decisions on the environment in which they live they can, and do, act for the good of the wider community and for long-term sustainability.

Understood in this way, the objective of promoting sustainable livelihoods as part of social development requires social workers to focus on local contexts. This includes local environmental conditions as a starting point, seen in the way that these interconnect with social relationships, cultural expectations, political structures and other aspects of human life (e.g. levels of education, health and so on). On the basis of this approach, social workers working with others can participate in promoting and supporting sustainable agriculture, manufacturing, trade and other forms of livelihood that are relevant in context. As has been seen from programmes such as the Grameen Bank and the work of non-government organisations, when undertaken from a community participatory approach, collective forms of intervention are more likely to provide a way of supporting such initiatives than are individualistic programmes (Kingsbury, 2008b). By working with civil society organisations, trade unions, professional associations, religious bodies, credit unions and other community groups, social workers can co-operate with others to support these goals (Coates, 2003; Dominelli, 2012; Gray, 2013).

Kingsbury (2008b) also points to another area of concern for social workers: that attempts to act collectively against the imposition of economic and other infrastructural changes that harm the environment and impact negatively on local livelihoods can lead to human rights abuses. Advocates and campaigners can at times even face violent attacks by those who have vested interests. As an example of positive human rights practice, Dominelli (2012, p. 155) describes how in post-apartheid South Africa there were struggles between competing Black organisations for scarce land, housing and jobs. In one situation, the School of Social Work at the University of Kwa-Zulu Natal initiated a community project that brought together members of the Africa National Congress (ANC), the ruling party, and the Inkatha Freedom Party (IFP), which was the ethnic Zulu party representing the Zulu communities of the province. As a result of a community mediation approach tensions between the ANC and IFP were reduced, and the school has further used this approach to mediate around issues of tension and violence against refugees, asylum seekers and other migrants who have come to South Africa in search of work. Through this project, the school also was able to involve the South African government and the South African Human Rights Commission (SAHRC) in creating a longer-term basis for resolving human rights concerns, by promoting anti-discriminatory practices and legislation, as well as providing more direct assistance to individuals, families and groups who had experienced violence or been discriminated against. The involvement of the SAHRC is another instance of social workers using skills in organising, negotiating and mediating with others to achieve development goals.

Indigenous peoples and the environment

Among disadvantaged, marginalised and poor communities, Indigenous peoples are often seriously affected by the impact of economic and structural development on the physical and natural environment. For Indigenous peoples, the harm done to the environment in the name of development carries major implications of harm also being done to ancient cultures. Article 25 of the *United Nations Declaration on the Rights of Indigenous Peoples* (UN, 2007), which by 2015 has been endorsed by 148 countries, recognises that the physical and natural environment is central to Indigenous world views. For the most part, at their centre the human rights of Indigenous peoples are 'land rights' and 'cultural rights'. In Indigenous terms, the right to land being expressed is not the right of individualistic ownership as this has come to be understood in modernist society. Rather, it is the right to the ongoing relationship between a people and the land, water and air, including all other living creatures and plants that share this environment. This is important for cultural rights, because this relationship with the environment is foundational to all aspects of culture. In many Indigenous cultures, for example, the relationships between people, whether as individuals, families or groups, are connected to the relationships between people, non-human animals, plants and physical places (S. Green & Baldry, 2008, p. 392). It is simply not possible to separate people's cultural identities from these other parts of the world.

Examples of the way in which orthodox approaches to economic development come into conflict with the rights of Indigenous peoples include the use of traditional territories for building large dams. While these may be able to provide both power (through hydroelectricity schemes), irrigation and drinking water, and in some places reducing flooding, they also destroy large areas of land and kill many living creatures, including in some instances destroying whole species, as well as displacing local populations (Roy, 1999; Kingsbury, 2008b, pp. 290–1; Pawar, 2014). In addition, in some schemes it has been questionable whether the economic gains have actually matched the intended goals, while the social and cultural costs are difficult to calculate as they play out over long periods of time. Finally, dams have a limited functional lifespan, due to silting and erosion, so in some cases they may not last even one generation – they certainly are not guaranteed to provide a sustainable benefit that can be accepted by Indigenous peoples when measured against the cultural expectation of holding the world in trust for future generations, as opposed to owning it as a resource to meet current ever-growing wants.

To illustrate how social development that addresses livelihoods can be related to Indigenous communities, two instances from Australia provide quite different stories. The first concerns the mining company Fortescue Metals, whose operations have included formally negotiated agreements with the recognised Aboriginal traditional custodians of the land in Western Australia on which the company operates, commitments to employing and training Aboriginal workers and provision of other economic and social returns to the local Indigenous communities. The chief executive of Fortescue Metals, Andrew Forrest, is publicly associated with this policy and is supported by some Aboriginal leaders, such as Noel Pearson, the director of the Cape York Institute for Policy and Leadership, an Aboriginal education and development organisation in northern Queensland, and Professor Marcia Langton, an Aboriginal academic and activist (Fortescue Metals, 2015). For its supporters, this approach is seen as valuing the land rights of local communities and respecting them as custodians of the environment, while also developing human and social capital. To its opponents, such an approach embodies all the faults that Midgley (2014) identifies with the orthodox 'livelihoods perspective', in that it is implicitly individualistic and neo-liberal, which can be seen as directly contrary to the collectivist cultures of Aboriginal Australians.

The second Australian instance is that of the Arnhem Human Enterprise Development (AHED) Program (Why Warriors, 2005). This programme operates on Elcho Island in Arnhem Land in the Northern Territory, working with Yolŋu (Yolngu) inhabitants who are the local Indigenous peoples. The project offers education and training, ongoing business advice, access to microfinance and cross-cultural support in dealing with mainstream Australian institutions. Most importantly, the goal of the project and its way of working embody local control by participants. The forms of small business that are being developed also reflect traditional forms of economic activity, such as sustainable agriculture and forest industries, with a particular emphasis on the local area and wildlife, as well as cultural consultancy and related services. External advisors are employed as consultants under local direction and within the local, clan-based social relationships. This external support is managed by a private company, Why Warriors Pty. Ltd., the name of which expresses the damage done to Yolŋu culture by two centuries of colonisation ('why warriors lie down and die') (Trudgen, 2000).

Both these examples are based on the goal of creating livelihoods, in contexts where for many years local Indigenous people have been excluded in their own country. Both use business models and in that sense promote the potential for integration into existing economic structures. Where they differ significantly is that the first brings Indigenous people into the mainstream, in large-scale industry, while the second is built on local cultural relationships and practices with an emphasis on promoting the empowerment of Aboriginal Australians, by their own action, in their own environment and under their own control. Where the first creates greater economic wealth, providing much greater financial resources for communities and individuals, the second sustains the culture and the communities in their own traditional terms; the second is also more sustaining of the physical and natural environment. For social workers in social development, choosing between involvement in and support for these different approaches is political, influenced both by values and by pragmatism. From a value perspective, the important questions are about the promotion of human rights and social justice and the way in which these relate to the traditional lands of the local people. In pragmatic terms, the north of Western Australia is already being mined and simply removing the mines may not be feasible or necessarily desirable, although social workers can join others in advocating for better environmental planning in new projects. In Arnhem Land small business is possible as there is no basis on which large industries might be invited into the area, although there are also good cultural reasons to suggest that as such businesses are not already there, bringing them in would have negative consequences that would not justify the financial return. Most of all, in both cases, the test of sustainable development must rest on whether local Indigenous people gain control over planning and decision making regarding their land.

Environmental disasters

Another growing area of ecological concern for social work is in the area of 'natural' disasters. These are catastrophic events in the physical world that cause loss of life and devastation of both natural and built environments. These include hurricanes and cyclones (typhoons), earthquakes, tsunamis, floods, droughts and bushfires. The qualification of 'natural' here comes from the way in which these events can be the result of human activity, not only naturally occurring geological or meteorological incidents. Indeed, the debate of the early twentieth century about climate change, global warming and the impact of human activity suggests that in a world dominated by high levels of industrial and technological activity the separation of 'natural' and 'human' in this way is no longer plausible (Besthorn, 2012; Alston, 2013; cf. Garnaut, 2008).

Because they occur suddenly, or the onset of specific events can be anticipated only very shortly before they happen, it is usually very difficult or actually impossible to take action to prevent or limit harm. Thus such incidents tend to be devastating, with loss of life and of the normal infrastructure of daily human existence. Infrastructure, such as buildings, water supply, roads and communications, is destroyed, while in agricultural areas livestock are killed and crops are lost and among fishing communities boats are wrecked. For those who survive there are both short- and long-term consequences. In the short term shock and grief are often combined with difficulties in meeting basic needs, such as water, food and shelter; there may well also be a threat of disease and problems in treating injuries. In the longer term, personal trauma at both individual and community levels is mixed with practical problems in the processes of rebuilding, which may be especially great when roads and other communication infrastructure have been damaged.

For all these reasons, environmental disasters present many challenges to social work (Gray, 2013). In these situations, psychosocial responses to care for the immediate needs of individuals and families who are affected by a disaster event cannot be separated from a social development focus on the longer-term issues of rebuilding communities. Three particular major disaster events of the last decade provide examples of the issues raised for social work and how practice may be improved: the Indian Ocean tsunami of 2004; Hurricane Katrina in 2005; and the Haiti earthquake of 2010. These examples are chosen here because they have been studied and debated from a social work perspective, and so provide considerations of the role of social work and the challenges that are faced by the profession in responding to such situations (Taubman & Weisz, 2011).

Example: Sri Lanka and the tsunami in the Indian Ocean, 2004

An earthquake under the Indian Ocean, on 26 December 2004, close to Indonesia, precipitated multiple tsunamis that affected at least ten countries in South-East Asia and as far away as East Africa. With more than 270,000 people killed directly by this event, the loss of life has been estimated as the largest from such an incident in over 500 years, with most of the devastation and loss of life in poor communities in India, Indonesia, Malaysia, Myanmar, Sri Lanka and Thailand (Taubman & Weisz, 2011, p. 38; Dominelli, 2013, p. 48). Low-lying coastal areas were particularly badly affected, although other locations also suffered from direct impact as water followed river courses and valleys. However, much of the available considered analysis of professional action focuses on Sri Lanka. Askeland (2007) ascribes this emphasis to the personal connections global Northern professionals have with the country, although it is also possible to understand this in terms of the state of civil war in Sri Lanka at that time and the attitude of the government about accepting foreign aid, compared to countries such as India, Indonesia, Malaysia, Thailand and especially Myanmar. It is also the case that these other countries were assisted by INGOs, many of whom employ social workers in humanitarian work, but who are not identified as social workers by job title (cf. Claiborne, 2004). Nonetheless, because of the emphasis within this evidence the following discussion concentrates on Sri Lanka.

Many professionals responded with immediate humanitarian aid, including medical practitioners, nurses, engineers and other technical experts, as well as social workers. Rowlands and Tan (2007) describe the Families and Survivors of Tsumani (FAST) Project, sponsored by the International Federation of Social

Workers (IFSW). This project co-ordinated support for work across several countries, including Sri Lanka, where it focused on a children and youth programme, a women's group and a 'home garden' project. In each case, this work has been conducted in partnership, both with the national social work professional association and with local community organisations.

Lešnik and Urek (2010) describe another project, in which staff from the Faculty of Social Work at the University of Ljubljana worked with colleagues from the Sri Lanka National Institute for Social Development (NISD), which at that time provided the only recognised local social work programme, together with sociologists from the University of Colombo. In another project, social workers and their colleagues from the Centre for Refugee Research at the University of New South Wales also were invited by women's groups to undertake immediate response work and participated in this together with the national office of the United Nations Development Programme (UNDP) (Pittaway et al., 2007). These were both participative action research projects, with the goal of assisting (in the former) a particular community and (in the latter) women's groups to identify needs and resources and to take some control for themselves in beginning the reconstruction process. As Dominelli (2013, p. 51) notes, there were, in fact, many schools of social work that responded actively in this way.

Dominelli (2013) adds to the evidence for social work intervention by looking at the more long-term co-ordinated activity of the International Association of Schools of Social Work (IASSW), which formed a project in partnership with groups described by Lešnik and Urek (2010). The IASSW project undertook several activities. First, by working with local people, they established that 'medicine, motors for boats and house repairs' were the priorities for the community (Dominelli, 2013, p. 55). From this, they supported advocacy with the government and NGOs for appropriate responses. Second, they continued to support local people in struggling for ongoing control and participation in reconstruction aid. Partnerships were further developed with other local organisations, including other universities and Sarvodaya, which is a Sri Lankan NGO founded on Ghandian principles and active in over 1,000 villages (Dominelli, 2013, p. 61). Third, recognising that the limitation set by the government on social work training meant that there was a lack of local trained social workers led to support for the extension of social work education to the university system. This was combined with ongoing partnership arrangements between foreign and local universities.

The implications for social work in disasters, from this experience, can be summarised by noting that compared with some other professions social work may appear to be secondary to disaster response. Social workers do not build roads, houses, clinics or schools, nor physically treat wounded people. However, social work is an essential part of the range of professional responses in these situations precisely because of the need for psychosocial support, combined with advocacy, negotiation, mediation, community mobilisation and community education, all undertaken with the goal of promoting local participation and control (Pittaway et al., 2007; Lešnik & Urek, 2010; Dominelli, 2013).

Example: Hurricane Katrina, 2005

On 29 August 2005 the city of New Orleans and the surrounding area of the US Gulf Coast were hit by a hurricane of up to 280 kilometres per hour (Category 5 storm). Approximately 80 per cent of the city was inundated by up to 25 feet of water. Approximately 1,800 people died as a direct result of the impact, with more deaths following, while homes, schools, hospitals and businesses were destroyed or damaged; the drinking water and electricity supplies that are now taken for granted in 'developed' countries were severely compromised (Park & Miller, 2006, pp. 11–12; Spence *et al.*, 2007, p. 540).

At one level, the debates about policy and practice that follow from this event are somewhat different from those stemming from the Indian Ocean tsunami. Partly they are predicated on a sense of 'scandal' that in one of the wealthiest countries on the planet the lack of preparedness, with the resulting loss of life and destruction, combined with delays and serious mistakes in responding, could have caused so much more human suffering than was strictly unavoidable (Park & Miller, 2006; Moyo & Moldovan, 2008). Moreover, as many studies have identified, the death, destruction and misery were not spread across the community, but were disproportionately experienced by Black and other ethnic minority communities, those on lower incomes or unemployed and other disadvantaged and marginalised groups (Park & Miller, 2006; Rivera & Miller, 2007; Spence *et al.*, 2007; Moyo & Moldovan, 2008). This leads Park and Miller (2006) to question the notion of Hurricane Katrina as a 'natural' disaster and to assert that it has to be understood as socially constructed. They cite a Brookings Institute study to note that in New Orleans 'hydrology and topography have long intersected with race, class and sociology' (Brookings Institute Metropolitan Policy Program, 2005, cited in Park & Miller, 2006, p. 15).

In the immediate situation of the hurricane, social workers were no more able to act than any other profession. In the short term, practitioners focused on survival needs, providing shelter, water, food and first aid (Pyles, 2006; Smith, 2012). Capacity to do this was severely limited as the areas that remained dry were also affected by the loss of infrastructure. In the longer term social workers have been involved in many aspects of the reconstruction of the city and its surrounding areas, and lessons for practice continue to be learned (Pyles, 2007; Smith, 2012). Notably, while there was a need for trauma counselling and associated interventions, research that has been undertaken in the years following the hurricane demonstrate that social work is positioned to play a much wider role. For example residents identify that they need assistance in rebuilding homes and communities, in restoring education and health services and in addressing other needs that can be understood as material and practical (Pyles, 2011). Smith (2012) records that directors of NGOs place trauma interventions lower than these more practical considerations in the priorities that they have learned from working with the affected communities, although they incorporate trauma counselling within other strategies. Pyles (2007, 2011) argues more forcefully that while social work in the USA is well focused on counselling and related interventions, alongside this it needs to rediscover the community revitalisation and empowerment traditions that it has lost over many years. This also points to the importance of human rights and future planning as part of the social work response to 'natural' disasters (Pyles, 2006).

Example: earthquake in Haiti, 2010

An earthquake of 7.0 magnitude hit Haiti on 12 January 2010, killing over 250,000 people and rendering well over 1 million homeless (Pierre-Louis, 2011, p. 187). One of the documented ways in which social workers responded was in a project from Fordham University, in New York, to provide on-site disaster relief (Taubman & Weisz, 2011, p. 42). This project also sought to enable social work students to learn from the experience of engaging in tangible assistance to survivors. A core element of the project also was to undertake a community-needs survey as the basis for generating further links and action by social workers and others from the USA. The Fordham group worked in partnership with KONPAY (Konbit Pou Ayiti), a local NGO, which was already involved in social development work in the town of Jacmel (south-west of Port-au-Prince) (Taubman & Weisz, 2011, p. 44). KONPAY is a not-for-profit community-based organisation that focuses on social, environmental and economic needs, through training and the creation of economic opportunities, including through the provision of microfinance (see http://www.konpay.weebly.com). In turn, this has led to a longer-term project to support the development of human capital in training and employment initiatives (Taubman & Weisz, 2011, pp. 45–6; also see http://www.socialtap.org/).

Less obviously (as discussed elsewhere in this book), social workers were also involved through major non-governmental and quasi-governmental organisations. For example in the UNICEF Haiti Child Protection Section response social workers looked after the interests of children separated from their parents, seeking to reunite them or to make appropriate arrangements for alternative care (UNICEF Haiti, 2011, p. 12). In the child protection section of UNICEF Haiti, by early 2011 over 90,000 children were assisted to find safe spaces to live, to receive psychosocial support, to access education and also to participate in recreational activities. For the longer term, one year after the earthquake UNICEF Haiti was already working with the Haitian government to develop child-focused policies, including those concerned with child protection and strengthening social work and related services (UNICEF Haiti, 2011, pp. 13, 20). Social workers in other major NGOs, such as the International Committee of the Red Cross, World Vision and Save the Children, were also involved in similar type of work as early responders and in longer-term social reconstruction.

Also less obviously, social workers found themselves caught up in debates about inter-country adoptions, especially those from disaster areas or countries in conflict (Selman, 2011). As Selman notes, there is a long history of inter-country adoption being used as a means of 'rescuing' children, but since the mid-twentieth century it has increasingly come to be questioned as a form of wealthy global Northern countries 'stealing' children from the impoverished countries of the South (cf. Davies, 2011). In post-earthquake Haiti, NGOs such as International Social Service (ISS) and Save the Children quickly became enmeshed in enforcing the Hague Convention expectations that adoptions must follow agreed legal protocols and be under the control of the national government of the child's country of origin. Nonetheless, those adoptions that were already in process were often accelerated and the total number of children adopted out of Haiti in 2010 exceeded the annual numbers for the preceding few years (Selman, 2011, p. 45). Although many of these were in accordance with the Hague Convention, there were also clear cases of child trafficking (Selman, 2011, pp. 41–2). As social work NGOs, ISS and Save the Children were very active in advocating for international law to prevail and for aid to focus on supporting the people of Haiti in the country and not by the removal of children.

Lessons for practice: developing preparedness

There are other examples of social work practice in response to environmental disasters, including earthquakes (Javadian, 2007; Wang & Lum, 2013; Maidment & Brook, 2014) and bushfires (Mason, 2011; Rowlands, 2013). Of all the implications that can be drawn from these many different situations, there are many similar lessons to be learned. The first of these is that disasters always have an element of social construction (Park & Miller, 2006, p. 11). That is the way in which similar events in the physical world can create different levels of devastation and have differing degrees of impact on people and communities is shaped by social forces, including intra- and international politics, economics and other related factors. For example Pierre-Louis (2011) is very critical of the long-term actions of NGOs in Haiti as undermining the government, causing duplication of effort, lacking co-ordination and at times even being more focused on competition for dominance in the provision of aid. Despite the many projects, the Haitian government was often unaware of what was being done, so in the context of a major earthquake the co-ordination of effective responses was impossible. Pierre-Louis attributes this situation to the long-standing effect of the neo-liberal development agenda, through which an emphasis on economic policies that benefitted industrialised countries, such as the USA and Canada, had caused an influx of Haitians to Port-au-Prince and an abandonment of land, leading to dependence on imported food. Consequently, over 220,000 people died directly as a result of the earthquake in Haiti, whereas by comparison in similar-level earthquakes in Chile in the same year only 1,000 were killed and in San Francisco in 1993 there were fewer than 100 deaths (Pierre-Louis, 2011, p. 187).

More widely, there are many countries that are prone to disaster events that have been unprepared in these major events. In a review of evidence from countries affected by the 2004 Indian Ocean tsunami, Mathbor (2007, p. 364) notes that although there was large-scale physical devastation in the Andaman Islands, no one was killed because of an effective early warning system and local understanding about evacuation procedures. In New Orleans in 2005, the stark divide between those communities where people died and those where they did not is structured around access to resources to leave, including transport and an understanding of the situation (Park & Miller, 2006).

For social workers, this means not only that development of disaster plans becomes an important part of community development but also that human services themselves have to be conscious of the risks and challenges that arise in disaster situations (Smith, 2012; Wang & Lum, 2013). This affects the capacity of services to respond to the needs of people who are impacted by an event. Other longer-term issues of social reconstruction, such as ensuring schools, the health system and other aspects of reconstruction are provided, also require planning and a commitment by social work services to be part of the process (Javadian, 2007). Moreover, attention must be given to ensuring that social workers engaged in post-disaster responses are appropriately supported and supervised (Cronin *et al.*, 2007).

A broader issue that runs through all the major environmental disaster situations of these kinds is that of gender (Pittaway *et al.*, 2007). As with many other aspects life, the gendered nature of human societies often means that women and children do not fare as well as men in survival. Moreover, Pittaway and her colleagues record that in the immediate post-disaster context women are subject to heightened levels of gender-related and sexual violence, both 'in the course of unsupervised rescue operations and during residence in temporary shelters' (2007, p. 309). Although perhaps 'unthinkable' for some people, planning that assumes such risks are very likely to occur would produce safer outcomes for women. Examples include practical steps, such as gender-segregated toilets and washrooms, lighting in public spaces and so on, as well as longer-term practice and policy approaches that would ensure that women are included in decisions making. Pittaway *et al.* (2007) call for social workers to develop a stronger sense of gender in their practice in disaster situations, as well as adopting more of a community participation approach that seeks to involve all parts of communities. They point to the ongoing work of the United Nations Population Fund (UNFPA), other NGOs and the Sri Lankan government in setting up and supporting 27 women's organisations across Sri Lanka to provide more gender-aware reconstruction (Pittaway *et al.*, 2007, p. 315). To make this happen involves social workers supporting women (and men) in advocacy at the local and the international levels.

At the international level, social workers can also contribute to sharing ideas, through research and policy work, advocacy and education and training. This must include countries of the global North learning from the South, as well as being seen as a source of ideas and practical assistance (Hugman, 2010). For example several schemes from schools of social work involved students and their teachers responding in the early post-event stages in Sri Lanka (Tang & Cheung, 2007; Lešnik & Urek, 2010; Dominelli, 2013) and in Haiti (Taubman & Weisz, 2011). A common important lesson in these projects is that ensuring a partnership with local communities is foundational to any intervention. Tang and Cheung (2007), in particular, note explicitly that programmes need to prepare students adequately concerning the realities of a post-disaster situation and to plan how they will support students undertaking this work. From this experience, Tang and Cheung (2007), like Taubman and Wiesz (2011), argue that disaster response practice should be included in appropriate parts of the social work curriculum.

A further way in which social work academics can be engaged in developing practice and policy in 'natural' disasters is to work in partnership with colleagues in the field. Much of the literature on these areas considers practitioners as research subjects, rather than as partners in the process. While considered research is necessary, there is also need to work with practitioners to record experiences and lessons. For example social workers in government and non-government organisations in Christchurch, New Zealand, developed considerable expertise over the period of responding to two earthquakes in 2010 and 2011; however, this practice knowledge is yet to be shared more widely (F. Robertson, personal communication, 7 July 2015). The study by Maidment and Brook (2014) is perhaps an exception, in a review of student learning related to participative community development after the earthquakes. The projects described by Lešnik and Urek (2010) and Dominelli (2013) also demonstrate learning from partnership work, in which local partners stand alongside those who contribute research expertise. The international social work organisations IFSW and IASSW have ongoing projects to draw together the learning from disaster response work that values practitioner as well as academic knowledge (Cronin *et al.*, 2007; IASSW, 2010).

Environment and social work practice

In this chapter we have discussed two major aspects of the way in which social development in social work must integrate environmental awareness. Whether practice concerns economic development, urban planning and community change, or responses to 'natural' disasters, the physical world is part of the range of factors of which social work must take account: not only is it where human beings live, but also people are themselves part of the natural world (IFSW, 2012). Although they differ in their theoretical approaches, J. Coates (2003, 2005), Besthorn (2002, 2012), Dominelli (2012) and Gray (2013) are in agreement that without this focus social work fails to address the whole picture of human life.

The range of ways in which social workers might do this is very broad. For instance, in the case study discussed in Chapter 2, Irene (a public housing tenant) benefitted not only from human rights–based advocacy but also from the provision of a community garden – both these achievements by the local community social work programme were of great significance for her (cf. Dominelli, 2012, pp. 80–1). Similarly, the case study of Imara and Aziza discussed in Chapter 3 shows how work focused on livelihoods also has a clear environmental element. The circumstances faced by this family and their community had an environmental origin, and so solutions have to be able to respond to this reality.

As Besthorn (2003, 2012), Dominelli (2012) and Gray (2013) all argue, the development of ecological or green social work does not require the abandonment of critical practice and theory in social work. Rather, it aims to extend social work by ensuring that the natural environment is integrated with the social environment as part of the 'person-in-the-environment' focus that distinguishes social work. Indeed, as we have seen in this chapter, environmental aspects of human need are part of a range of critical issues that interact with gender, socio-economic class, ethnicity and nationality and other structural factors. Understood in this way, ecological or green social work is a necessary part of social development practice.

5

COMPARATIVE SOCIAL WORK AND SOCIAL WELFARE

Welfare paradigms and social development

In her foundational discussion of a model of social development in social work, Elliott (1993) argues that it is inextricably part of a country's 'welfare paradigm'. Drawing on a range of descriptions of social work, Elliott (p. 24) takes Wilensky and Lebeaux's (1965) classic model of social welfare, distinguishing between residual and institutional welfare states, and adds the developmental paradigm as a new type of approach. By providing the ground on which social work practices achieve legitimacy, each of these social welfare paradigms creates the basis for different approaches to become dominant within an overall national social welfare framework.

The three paradigms of residual, institutional and developmental social welfare differ in terms of the understanding of human need, the causes of need, the goals of social workers and other practitioners in addressing need, the methods used to respond to need and the values that underpin practices, policies and institutions. Briefly, the major distinctions between the three reflect social and political values concerning the relationship between individual people and society (understood as acting through collectivities, such as communities or the state). Thus each paradigm supports a particular range of social welfare practices, organisations, policies and systems. Table 5.1 summarises the main elements of Elliott's (1993, p. 25) model.

In addition, Elliott (1993, p. 25) sketches out a continuum of other aspects of policy and practice that tend to distinguish these three paradigms. These include: safety net/planned development, selective/universal and cost containment/social investment.

Esping-Andersen's (1990) classic model of 'three worlds of welfare capitalism' also offers a potential comparative model of social welfare structures. Esping-Andersen compared welfare states in Europe and concluded that they tended towards one of three types: liberal, conservative and social democratic. These he calls 'welfare regimes'. Esping-Andersen's core criteria are the extent to which social welfare is

TABLE 5.1 Summary of Elliott's (1993) core elements of 'welfare regimes' related to social development

Human need	Residual	Institutional	Developmental
Focus	Individual	Humanitarian	Egalitarian
Causes	Human functioning	Mixed	Social inequality
Goals	Crisis intervention and promote independence	Proactive: anticipate and prevent crises	Planned structural change and empowerment
Methods	Clinical/micro	Mixed/meso	Social change/macro
Values	'Philanthropic'	Welfare rights	Social justice

subject to the market (commodification), the role of the state in challenging or supporting social stratification and the extent to which there is a public-private mix of social welfare provision. Broadly, the differences between these can be seen in terms of an interplay between individuals and families, government and civil society institutions (e.g. religious bodies, voluntary groups and so on).

On first consideration it might appear that the notion of welfare regimes complements the use of the idea of welfare paradigms to create a model for understanding social development. There are strong similarities between liberal regimes and the residual paradigm; similarly, social democratic regimes come closest to the developmental paradigm. Insofar as this might describe connections between social systems and ideologies then, it may be supposed, the type of regime in a country would be likely to determine the extent to which social development is possible. Yet there are several reasons why this is not actually the case. These include both theoretical and empirical objections to the welfare regimes as Esping-Andersen (1990) describes them.

First, from many points of view, the conclusions Esping-Andersen (1990) reaches about some countries have been challenged on methodological grounds. For example his analysis placed Ireland and the UK in the liberal regime type. As several critics have pointed out, slight adjustments in the methodology that was applied to the data, or in the criteria used to divide types of welfare states, could result in these countries being grouped quite differently. Bambra (2007) identifies that Ireland could more plausibly be seen as similar to countries such as France and Germany, which the model identifies as conservative. On the same basis, the UK is actually more complex and can variously be seen in a number of other ways. Other writers have identified different possible regime models, such as that which could be said to describe the Mediterranean European countries (the 'southern' model; Ferrera, 1996), or the countries of East and South-East Asia (Walker & Wong, 2005; Aspalter, 2006). In particular, assumptions about the roles of family and civil society institutions that distinguish the conservative from the liberal and social democratic regimes in this typology create even greater variations in these other possible regimes.

Second, Esping-Andersen (1990) effectively privileges social transfers (e.g. pensions and other financial payments) as the defining feature of social welfare and does not adequately address the many other ways in which societies provide for the needs of their populations. Much of the debate about social development and social work considers the provision of direct supportive services to families, education, health and housing, as well as the promotion of livelihoods and strengthening community (Elliott, 1993; Patel, 2005; Conley, 2010). Insofar as the goal of development is the improvement of human life, then these are all aspects of people's daily lives that matter, as well as being areas of practice and policy that create the framework for future possibilities.

A further critique, summarised by Bambra (2007), is that Esping-Andersen's model lacks any sense of social stratification other than socio-economic class – in particular, the lack of attention to gender has generated considerable debate, which is an aspect of stratification highly relevant to social welfare and to which this present discussion will return ahead (cf. Sainsbury, 1994). Given the debates about gender and social welfare provision seen more broadly, this missing dimension is surprising, especially because it was already widely debated in Europe prior to Esping-Andersen's work, including his native Scandinavia (e.g. see Wærness, 1990). From this and related debates it is also reasonable to question the extent to which other distinctions, such as that between ideas about the cause of human need, are as clear-cut.

A more flexible model of social welfare is also offered from European debates, in the idea of the 'welfare mix' (Evers & Svetlik, 1991; Huston, 1991). In this way of understanding social welfare structures and systems, each country is considered in terms of the balance ('mix') between the state, the family, civil society and the market as providers of support and care to people in need. This is not a typological model but rather a framework in which critical questions can be asked about each specific instance; in this sense it is heuristic. Subtle differences between countries can be identified and considered. Moreover, this idea allows for change over time, so that the shifts between approaches to social welfare can be understood in terms of the relationships between different aspects of the mix.

If read in a similar heuristic way to the welfare mix concept, Elliott's (1993) typology of welfare paradigms continues to be useful as a basis for considering a social development approach to social work. As with any 'ideal typology', it is important not to read this model as a concrete description of welfare paradigms historically; nor must it be seen as deterministic. That is if we consider any one particular country at a given point in time, it is very likely that the social welfare system and associated forms of social work will have characteristics that combine aspects of the different elements in this model. In this sense, an 'ideal typology' should be seen as a typology of ideas, not a statement of the 'pure' or 'best' relationship of social phenomena. What is important for social development in social work is the way in which the concepts in these paradigms form the foundations of particular structures and systems for social welfare provision.

Further, it must be recognised that the historical shape of social welfare in any particular country may incorporate different elements of this threefold model to different degrees. So, for example, it may be that in any specific context variations will be observed in the ways in which social welfare programmes are structured and implemented. For example there is a risk that if these paradigm distinctions are taken as blueprints, then decisions based on them can have unintended negative consequences. This point is well illustrated by Midgley's (1984) observation that that some apparently 'remedial' interventions continue to be necessary within a developmental system. Similarly, there is likely to be a range of social work values and practices, reflecting the contested nature of the profession. In this sense, here I am proposing that a notion of a 'welfare paradigm mix' may be more useful as the basis for investigating and understanding particular concrete systems, structures and relationships at any given point in time.

Seen in this way, when it comes to the way a social development approach can form a basis for social work, Elliott's discussion potentially reflects the more subtle and flexible ideas that are discussed in Chapter 2. For example she notes that such an approach can address practice with individuals and families as well as with communities, organisations and policies. Indeed, she refers to it as 'multilevel intervention' (Elliott, 1993, p. 29), suggesting a generalist practice perspective. In this sense, social development in social work includes clinical work, welfare services provision and community intervention, possibly sometimes within the same programmes (e.g. as was portrayed in Chapter 2 by the case example of Irene). The point is that underlying paradigmatic elements are reflected in the way in which it is possible to conduct these practices. The one aspect of a social development approach to social work that can be regarded as remaining very close to the typology of welfare paradigms is that of the value base, in that a developmental model embodies a combination of human rights and social justice as its basis and rejects notions of philanthropy as the normative basis for social welfare.

Developmental social work: South Africa

A more recent and concrete model of a social development approach to social work is provided by Patel (2005) in her detailed analysis of social welfare in South Africa (also see Lombard, 2008). In particular, because this is a description of the system that has been developing in South Africa since the collapse of apartheid and the creation of a democratic constitution, it provides an opportunity to see how social work can engage with these ideas. While there are some key areas of overlap with Elliott's model, there are also some important differences. For Patel, the central aspect of a social development paradigm is that it is still itself being developed. In that sense, some of the core ideas remain aspirational to an extent, while others are being realised.

In the South African model, the provision of social services remains a central role for social work. However, as we have already noted with other aspects of social developmental practice, within a social development approach both the structures and the practices are significantly different. So Patel identifies four key features of a social developmental welfare service model (2005, p. 156). These are:

1   a rights-based approach;
2   integrated family-centred and community-based services;
3   a generalist perspective;
4   community development together with developmental welfare services.

Each of these features refers to a core aspect of social welfare service delivery: values, system, practice and goals.

In order to consider the wider application of this approach, it is helpful to examine key aspects of Patel's description of developmental social welfare. First, that it is rights-based means that it is not sufficient simply to meet human needs, but that the system must also be established in such a way that 'the promotion, protection and defence of the rights of those who are vulnerable and at risk are an integral part of human development' (Patel, 2005, p. 156). Building the system on this value means that it should be evident at every level, including policies, organisations, strategies and practices. Taken as a whole it requires that the culture of social welfare as a whole reflects this. At the same time, it is consistent with the reality that the need for social welfare provision differs between sections of a society. The greatest need is experienced by those who are most disadvantaged or at risk. The point is that in a rights-based approach the society recognises that all aspects of the system must both safeguard the rights of those who are in need (e.g. against abuse, discrimination and exploitation) and be accessible to those people.

Second, family-centred and community-based services are those structured in ways that integrate with the lives of service users. It is in this respect that the notion of a 'welfare mix' may assist, as the combination of formal and informal services through which needs are met will vary between settings. The goal is to make the home and the community the location in which services are provided as much as possible. For South Africa, as for many countries, this means that the history of large institutions as the basis of welfare, with an assumption of people leaving their homes and communities to receive help, had to be dismantled. As with other countries too, a key challenge in this is to ensure that such changes do not simply shift the costs and responsibilities for care onto women and onto already poor and disadvantaged communities (Patel, 2005, p. 159).

Third, as already noted, the idea of a generalist approach to service delivery points to multi-level interventions used in an integrated fashion. As appropriate, attention maybe paid to individuals, families, groups and entire communities as the focus of services. All these levels are also expected to be active participants in the process, alongside professionals and other formal services, as well as voluntary contributions from civil society groups. In the South African context there was also the history of a system based entirely on the remediation of pathology, both individual and social, in addressing human needs. As already noted in previous chapters, the strengths perspective is part of the generalist approach, and this has been important in South Africa (Patel, 2005, p. 160). In turn, this creates a dynamic in which empowerment of individuals, groups and communities can be supported by social welfare, instead of being undermined.

Finally, community development is an integral aspect of developmental social welfare. For Patel (2005, p. 161) this includes a range of practices, including community education, the encouragement of civic engagement and volunteering, citizen advocacy, poverty reduction and the promotion of sustainable livelihoods. In particular, a community development approach tends to be associated with participatory models of social welfare and so integrates not only with community-based systems but also with the rights-based, family-centred and generalist aspects of the overall developmental agenda (cf. Larsen *et al.*, 2014).

South Africa is currently the only country in which the whole social welfare system is being rethought in terms of developmental principles in this way. Partly this follows from the historical struggles to end apartheid and the legacy of that period in the entrenchment of poverty and disadvantage among the majority of the population. Having been part of the problem, because it either supported the apartheid system or at the least did not challenge it, it has been vital for social welfare to be completely rethought (Lombard, 2008). Indeed, Gray (2006) argues that it is not possible to understand developmental social welfare outside the national framework of reconstruction. It might also plausibly be argued that in some other parts of the world, such as Northern Europe and Scandinavia, the different histories of social welfare have enabled developmental principles to become more implicitly integrated in overall structures. This would imply that a developmental perspective simply does not make sense in that different context.

Two particular notes of caution have been voiced concerning this model. Gray (2006) questions whether confusion has developed between the concepts of social development and developmental social work. How this is understood largely depends on whether social work is seen as direct provision of care services to individuals and families, child protection and the like or it involves structural practice focused on change in policies, systems and organisations (Gray, 2006, p. S63; cf. Mullaly, 2003). Taking this point further, Hölscher (2008) argues that without the necessary policy background social work is not able to become developmental. In particular, for South Africa, this requires a wider commitment to greater equality and structural poverty alleviation. Pointing to the wider international pressures on the South African government to adopt neo-liberal policies and so effectively to limit the extent to which greater equality is a tangible objective, Hölscher questions whether developmental practice in social work can have an impact in this current context. In other words, as the system implicitly resorts to a residual welfare paradigm, for reasons of cost reduction, the basis for developmental practice disappears (Hölscher, 2008, p. 116). This is not a matter simply of changes in the balance of a welfare mix, but rather the reduction of social welfare goals in favour of a particular approach to economic growth through acquisitive capitalism. Social work may be able to contribute to a developmental system working with others, but it is not possible for social work as a profession in itself to achieve this outcome in a political and economic environment that is shifting in a different direction.

East Asian social welfare models

Aspalter (2006, p. 290) suggest that in East Asia a different balance has been created between social welfare and economic goals in development policies and practices. Although at previous stages economic growth was prioritised, in recent decades there has been a shift to seeing social welfare provision as part of the ways in which countries might secure an overall development trajectory. This has meant that instead of treating education and health expenditures as 'costs', they have actually been supported as 'investments' in human capital in what has been termed a 'productivist' approach (Holliday, 2000). The same phenomenon is also referred to by other analysis as a 'development welfare' model (Ng, 2013, p. 207). It is developmental in that it matches Midgley's (1984) definition of social development (see Chapter 1), in that social welfare is planned and structured to support economic development. So not only were public programmes such as public education, health, housing and social care insurance implemented, but also these have incorporated social work provision in the form of child and family programmes, aged care and other social work services (cf. Conley, 2010).

Although it is an East Asian country, because it is also in the OECD Japan was included in Esping-Andersen's (1990) analytic model. There it is effectively seen as a form of the corporatist, conservative regime along with Germany and France (Aspalter, 2006). Social rights as the basis for welfare exist, tied to citizenship and employment contributions, with an emphasis on supporting the role of the family and the principle of 'subsidiarity' (i.e. that the role of government or major institutions is limited to that which cannot be done through family or community relationships) (Holliday, 2000; Soma *et al.*, 2011). Indeed, one of the frequent misapprehensions of European welfare models is that they remove the family from the mix, as opposed to being based on the contrasting goal of supporting families in care roles. In this respect, the parallel between Japan and countries such as Germany, France or Southern Europe may be stronger than Esping-Andersen's model allows (cf. Kim & Choi, 2010, p. 364). Japan's welfare system broadly supports access to education, health care and more recently long-term care for older people, within the context of support through employment and limited coverage when the employment market fails.

In South Korea, Aspalter argues (2006, p. 293), social welfare has become recognised more recently than Japan as part of the overall strategy for the development of the society as a whole. While it has aspects of a residual approach, it also combines some universal elements, including pensions and health care, alongside programmes aimed specifically to support employment, including various forms of job training. This is known as 'productive welfarism' and is linked to the idea of 'participatory welfare'. In the South African context, Hölscher (2008, p. 116) argues that the notion of participation used in this way is a smokescreen for policies that leave individuals and families to fend for themselves. In contrast, the South Korean model appears to have the goal of social inclusion. Yet unlike the South African system, it is not a rights-based approach. Rather it is targeted, while at the same time emphasising social harmony in a way that is consistent with an underlying Confucian ethos (Soma *et al.*, 2011).

Taiwan has created a social welfare system more recently than most East Asian countries. Historically, it has also been more limited than others until relatively recently (Li, 2012; Lue, 2014). The largest proportions of government spending on social welfare remain those of social insurance, which accounts for more than half the total, and welfare services, making up almost one third of the total. This latter category includes a variety of programmes aimed to buttress the central role of the family in providing for the well-being of vulnerable members, including children, people with disabilities and older people. This leads Lue (2014, p. 281) to suggest that it could be considered a softening of the 'productive welfarism' approach in the face of growing levels of social need. However, that still remains the main focus of the system and a gradual adaptation rather than a major shift of direction.

The other two states that tend to be included in discussion of the East Asia welfare model are Hong Kong and Singapore. Although in many ways they share important elements, especially the combination of a 'productivist' approach with the Confucian understanding of the centrality of the family in social welfare, there are also key differences with other countries arising from their particular histories. These were previously two major British colonies in the region (Singapore as part of what was then Malaya), and as a consequence the shape of their social welfare institutions that formed the foundations of present systems created unique opportunities for development. In that earlier era, both Singapore and Hong Kong had social welfare provision of the kind that has also been described in South Africa (Midgley, 1981; Patel, 2005). As Aspalter (2006, p. 295) notes, the motivation for the colonial administration in both cases was to support social order and to mitigate the potential for social problems to fuel social unrest and especially to limit support for communism.

In Singapore, the earlier independence from colonial rule and secession from Malaysia as a city state created the conditions for a social welfare approach that is more 'productivist' in the same mould as South Korea and Taiwan. Although, unlike these other countries, the government was not a military dictatorship, Singapore has been ruled by the same party for over 50 years, with very strong centralised control over the economy. From its early concerns to create rapid economic growth, the policies of the Singapore government have shifted over time to address the welfare needs of the population, both as a benefit of greater prosperity and as a strategy of human capital development that in itself contributes to the strength of the economy (Ng, 2013). The distinctive Singaporean welfare mix that has resulted is officially described as the 'Many Helping Hands' model, in that government policy overtly supports and encourages partnership between families and non-government service providers. Rozario and Rosetti (2012, p. 645) argue that this enables the government to maintain a residual, philanthropic stance towards people in need while promoting widespread social supports. They add that a communitarian gloss is also evident even though the logic of the system is in many ways as individualistic as many western systems. In particular, they point to the very low response to the housing policy of larger apartments that was intended to promote intergenerational family residence, noting that as economic prosperity increases a preference for nuclear family living appears to have grown among the emergent middle class (p. 647).

In the case of Hong Kong, the much later end to British colonial rule created the conditions for yet a further subtle variation in the meeting of Asian culture and the modern global economy. As with other East Asian countries, Hong Kong's policies are grounded in the Confucian assumptions about the role of the family (Aspalter, 2006). However, unlike Singapore, South Korea or Japan, the emphasis on the residual role of government is much stronger as the goal of social policy is to minimise the cost to government while also seeking to avoid what are seen as disincentives for people to engage with economic development (D. Lai & Chui, 2014). The main areas of government activity are in the structuring of income support measures on a very residual basis, and in subsidising education and health provision. However, D. Lai and Chui also identify that in Hong Kong the state is directly involved in the large-scale provision of housing, for rental as well as for sale at low cost (2014, pp. 265–6). Indeed, they assert that Hong Kong comes second only to Singapore in this respect on a global comparative basis (cf. Lee, 2013). The overall pattern is a welfare mix in which all four sectors (government, family, non-government and market) are strongly active in social welfare. For Mok and Hudson (2014) this appears to represent a shift from a strictly pro-growth position to one that has embraced global concern with a pro-poor focus. In that sense, it is a modified residualism in which both the poorest stratum of the society is targeted for more extensive support and particular types of welfare provisions are treated differently. So, the Hong Kong model in itself is complex and remains part of the very broad range of East Asian approaches, as opposed to being something entirely different.

Policy analysis is divided as to whether these different countries represent variations on an overarching model or simply different welfare mixes that share some general common cultural features. For example Holliday's (2000) concept of 'productivist' welfare regimes is questioned by Hudson *et al.* (2014), who claim that in a recent re-examination of OECD countries alongside East Asia the productivist model best described New Zealand and the USA, while the East Asian countries all exhibit much subtler variations that include major elements of social protection as underlying goals. Mok and Hudson (2014) suggest that the impact of the Asian financial crisis in the 1990s marked the beginning of a more integrative approach across the region, in which to different degrees countries recognised that as the market could not be relied on as it had been for several decades to ensure basic minimum levels of population well-being, more state involvement was necessary. This has been reinforced by the global financial crisis (GFC) of 2007. In that context, others, such as Rozario and Rosetti (2012), detect a continuing policy agenda to support economic growth as much as the maintenance of particular social values. In a study conducted not long after the GFC, in late 2009 to early 2010, Ng and Koh (2012) also found that among the Chinese community in Singapore there was increasing public sympathy for people living in poverty.

Others again, such as Soma and others (2011), Li (2012) and Chau and Sam (2013), argue that much of the debate ignores the ways in which assumptions about the centrality of the family in a 'Confucian' ethos are changing. This point raises questions about the absence of gender as a key issue in such debates, as by introducing this dimension Chau and Sam demonstrate that some East Asian countries appear quite progressive, such as in terms of female labour participation and maternity benefits. Using these parameters, they show that Australia and the USA can be said to have more residual approaches to maternity benefits than the East Asian countries (p. 363). There are similarities here also with the critiques of Esping-Andersen (1990) by Sainsbury (1994), among others, that the highly gendered area of social welfare that involves so many aspects of life that are centred on the family and the home cannot effectively be understood primarily through income protection policies used as a default measure of concern for human well-being.

The ascription of the term 'developmental welfare regimes' applied to East Asian systems suggests a possible comparison with countries such as South Africa, as discussed earlier. Both incorporate family-based and community-based provision, in which government is only one part of a welfare mix. Both are generalist in the way in which they connect micro-level with meso-level interventions and service delivery. However, at the same time there are two important differences between these approaches that must be made clear. First, development social welfare and the social work practices that support it are rights-based. In contrast, as observed by several analysts (Kam, 2012), the sense of a human rights framework is largely absent from the welfare systems in East Asia. With the exception of particular interpretations of the UN *Convention on the Rights of the Child* (1989), where rights exist they are seen as 'social rights' – that is as entitlements tied in some way to workforce participation and often very limited (Holliday, 2000; Aspalter, 2006). Second, any sense of community development being part of development social welfare is seen only in terms of support for the non-government not-for-profit sector in social welfare provision. To some extent there are also some parallels with the way in which South African communities seek to be empowered to respond effectively to social needs. What is markedly different is that the more politically engaged vision of community development that applies in the South Africa context is largely absent from social welfare in East Asia. As addressed in Chapter 9 in a discussion of ethics and values in social development, this may in part be explained by very different cultural traditions. These include differing expectations about the role of government to provide for social welfare, as well as concerning the ways in which social change might be achieved. However, it also reflects the different political contexts, such as the wide variations in the types of political systems as well as governance structures.

In summary, therefore, it can be said that although both South Africa and the countries of East Asia have been described as demonstrating developmental social welfare, they do so in ways that are quite distinct and have to be understood in their own terms. In each case there is a clear connection between social welfare and the goal of economic growth, in which the latter is supported by the former. This is certainly a different stance to that adopted by the neo-liberalism of the Washington Consensus in regarding social expenditures simply as a drain on productive capacity

(Stiglitz, 2002). Beyond this, however, there is also a question of the extent to which social welfare should be seen as valuable in its own right. That is, should it be valued only as a means to the end of a more productive population, or should it be regarded as a central means by which those populations achieve basic requirements of a good human life? Education, health and family well-being (where the notion of family is understood as inclusively as possible) are all goods in themselves as well as being key drivers of development. In recent years a new comparative concept has begun to emerge that provides a further basis from which to address the way in which a comparative analysis might provide this perspective: the 'social protection floor'. So it is to this concept that this chapter now turns.

The social protection floor: a global approach?

In 1952 the International Labour Organization (ILO) adopted a convention setting out minimum standards for social security (ILO, 1952). This convention established that signatory countries would develop social security mechanisms to ensure a basic level of well-being for their populations, with particular attention being paid to the needs of the most disadvantaged. Indeed, it could be taken as an implicit assumption that social security measures are required only in situations where people are unable to provide for themselves through socially and culturally normal means. While this approach provided the background to social welfare developments in the 1950s and 1960s, it remained aspirational in many parts of the world. So when the steady economic growth that had been experienced during those decades began to experience shocks in the 1970s, there were still many regions in which social welfare and social security remained aspirational. At the same time, in those countries where social welfare had become highly developed the fiscal crises that were generated provided the basis of legitimacy for dismantling welfare and social security systems (e.g. see Mishra, 1984). Thus by the 1990s the neo-liberal agenda was well established as a key ideological limitation on social welfare (Hugman, 1998).

As discussed in Chapter 3, in the mid-1990s the United Nations sponsored a global debate on social development which had behind it a concern to re-engage the commitment of governments to addressing the needs of the most disadvantaged members of their societies, with an emphasis on the particular issues faced by the most disadvantaged countries. The WSSD concluded with a commitment to eradicate poverty, including objectives to achieve gender equality, ensure universal access to primary education and to basic health care and change the approach of structural adjustment to make social development gains central (Correll, 2008, pp. 454–6). Yet by the end of the decade continued debate and negotiation led to a shift from these broad and ambitious objectives to the more modest, although still quite wide-reaching Millennium Development Goals (MDGs). Opinion is divided concerning the MDGs and their relationship to the WSSD. Most analysts who are concerned with social well-being are critical (e.g. see Saith, 2006; Deacon *et al.*, 2007; Correll, 2008, 2011). Correll concludes that since 2000 there has been a recognition that the MDGs do not provide the basis for social development that was set out in 1995, and an increasing number of major actors, including UN bodies, are beginning to work together on recalling the WSSD agenda, with particular emphasis on its vision of universal access to social supports for well-being and development.

It is in this context that the idea of the 'social protection floor' is being proposed. Drolet summarises the concept as 'nationally-defined sets of basic social security guarantees that secure protection aimed at preventing or alleviating poverty, vulnerability and social exclusion' (2014, p. 22). This embraces universal access to education, health care and basic income security that covers a whole population and which meets the minimum requirements of a human life within any given national context. These objectives, together with expanded definitions and more detailed discussion, are set out in *Recommendation No. 202* of the ILO (ILO, 2012). This proposal shifts the idea of social welfare as a 'safety net' – that is catching people as they fall below a stated level of social well-being – to a more positive idea that the system should seek to create the mechanisms that ensure people do not 'fall' in this way in the first place. To achieve this requires not only that the relevant technical policies and procedures are in place but also that appropriate values are reflected in other aspects of law and policy in each country. As Ortiz (2007, p. 6) notes, in order for this approach to be implemented there must be commitment to redistribution of resources and to goals of social justice. For Drolet (2014) this accords with key social work values of human rights, social justice and the promotion of social inclusion.

The international social work organisations have joined with the ILO to promote the concept of the social protection floor (IASSW/ICSW/IFSW, 2014). While acknowledging that there are many perspectives and debates in the fields of social development and social work (p. 4), the broad support for the concept of the social protection floor is seen as consistent with social work values in that it is concerned with the harm arising from social and economic inequalities (p. 5). Stiglitz (2012) has pointed to the way in which levels of inequality, as opposed to any particular measure of poverty, are the strongest indicator of a society's capacity to address human need. In particular, the more unequal a society is the more likely it is that there will be a section of the population whose basic needs are not adequately met. For Stiglitz, for example, this accounts for the reason that in otherwise very wealthy countries (defined in terms of GNI or of per capita wealth) there are strata of the population who remain in poverty irrespective of whether they have paid employment. It is a fallacy, Stiglitz argues, that poverty is necessarily the product of laziness or fecklessness, as evidenced by the large numbers of working poor in countries in North America, Northern Europe and Scandinavia. Although much of the 'social insecurity' arising from inequality and lack of access to social protection supports is concentrated in sub-Saharan Africa, South-East Asia and (to a slightly lesser extent) the Eastern Mediterranean, in global terms up to 80 per cent of people suffer degrees of social insecurity, while 20 per cent live in 'deep poverty' (Cichon & Hagemejer, 2007). Moves towards economic liberalisation and the promotion of free markets have often produced a rapid decline in the living standards of large parts of populations in these vulnerable countries (Habibov, 2010). However, perhaps counter-intuitively from an economic perspective, in a country-specific study of Azerbaijan support for access to higher education, along with wider social protection measures and social infrastructure projects, was seen to be a key factor in the population moving out of poverty (Habibov, 2010, p. 61; cf. Caminada & Goudeswaard, 2009; Salmina, 2014; Spolander *et al.*, 2014).

In a comprehensive comparative review of South-East Asia, Suharto (2009) identifies the wider range of permutations of a welfare mix in social protection, with state, market, community-based and family-based mechanisms all playing a part in a diversity of combinations. Across the region these countries have faced a series of challenges to social and economic stability from fiscal crises and price instability, environmental disasters and crop failures, and general problems of continuing low income levels. Nevertheless, with a welfare mix approach to social protection access to health care, disability support and aged care, as well as unemployment supports, the overall levels of social protection have improved. In countries as diverse as Singapore, the Philippines and Vietnam, inclusion of systems to improve the affordability of health, education and housing has been identified as 'best practice' (Suharto, 2009, pp. 19–21).

From a social work perspective, it should also be noted that in certain countries the inclusion of attention to the specific social protection issues faced by children, people with disabilities and older people is recognised as central to a social protection floor approach. For example in East Africa Mushunje and Mafico (2010) and Shibuya and Taylor (2013) have argued that the crisis of the number of orphans as a consequence of the HIV/AIDS pandemic must be regarded as a social protection issue. Quite simply, the number of orphans relative to the adult population means that the traditional family and community-based mechanisms of providing alternative care for children have collapsed (Mushunje & Mafico, 2010, p. 263). To deal with this situation, Mushunje and Mafico argue that direct cash transfers to child-headed households provide an effective mechanism to address poverty, declining school participation and other growing problems. They point out that such transfers do not need to be large to be effective and can involve regular payments for food and other routine necessities, as well as lump-sum grants for expenses such as education costs (p. 273). In Mozambique, Shibuya and Taylor (2013) note that children living in residential care homes are more likely to be adequately fed and to be supported in attending school. There appears to be little obvious difference between those cared for by a surviving parent, those cared for by grandparents and those cared for by younger responsible community members (p. 87). However, they do not advocate an increase in residential care but rather that governments might focus on 'comprehensive measures to address the physical, social, psychological and environmental well-being of children' (p. 90). In this sense, the concerns of social work for the person in his or her social environment add to the debate the psychosocial dimension of human need alongside the physical and material. Indeed, as IASSW/ICSW/IFSW (2014, p. 5, citing Davies, 1985) note, 'social work and social development practitioners are not normally involved in global macroeconomic decisions'. Yet they can add the perspective of the lives of people who are directly affected by such decisions to the global debates, through the United Nations and regional governance bodies, such as the European Union, the African Union, ASEAN, Mercosur and so on.

It is in this context that the strategy of creating the *Global Agenda for Social Work and Social Development* has been adopted by the international social work organisations (IASSW/ICSW/IFSW, 2014). Using the experiences and observations of social workers and other social development practitioners involved in work with those communities who experience need, the IASSW, ICSW and IFSW have added their shared voice to those of the more than 70 NGOs that are involved with the ILO in promotion of the social protection floor through discussion at various United Nations organisations and in other fora (pp. 4–5). In particular, this debate contributes to the development of the post-2015 agenda in reviewing the progress of the MDGs. A key rationale in this position is that social security and social protection policies and systems represent an investment in strong, stable societies rather than simply a cost at the expense of economic growth. In late 2014, post-MDG planning continues to be relatively undecided (see UN, 2015). The UN asserts that most goals either have been met or are close to being met. However, as these represented targets such as halving rates of poverty (as defined by a benchmark of 1990 figures) as opposed to the wider WSSD commitment to eradicating poverty altogether, critics remain concerned that insufficient attention will be given to the reduction of absolute numbers under each goal. As the UN's own figures show, while the rate of poverty measured as US$1 per day per capita has declined, at the same time the growth of inequality globally has increased by 11 per cent, not only in terms of incomes but also in terms of access to education, health care and other non-material dimensions of social development (UNDP, 2013).

The *Global Agenda,* social development and social work

Gray and Webb (2014) are highly sceptical of the *Global Agenda*. They find it to be flawed on four grounds, broadly considered. First, they argue that the field of social development is not the province of professional social work (cf. Gray & Crofts, 2008). They suggest that the vast majority of social workers are engaged in helping people to negotiate the problems of daily life, and in 'protecting and regulating aspects of clients' lives', 'encumbered by local context and experience' (p. 348, p. 350), rather than working to address social issues at the global level. Thus, they see in the *Global Agenda* an attempt for professional social work (or, at least, these three organisations) to insert itself into a domain in which there are already other players, such as the International Consortium on Social Development or the Association for Social Development. In short, they accuse these organisations of using the debate about post-MDG development priorities as a way of enhancing the standing of social work, rather than as a vehicle for achieving change for people in need, and of seeking to assimilate the field of social development as part of social work illegitimately.

Second, Gray and Webb argue that the *Global Agenda* represents a 'post-political' stance on issues that are inherently political. By this, they mean that it is couched in terms of implicit support for neo-liberal economic systems and consensus politics, which they read in '[its] refusal to name the historical causes of social and economic inequalities as neoliberal capitalism and to openly advocate a non-capitalist solution' (Gray & Webb, 2014, p. 354). Thus, they assert that the argument is at best seeking to advance normative statements about human rights and social justice, without actually placing this in context by addressing the concrete issues that people face in daily life.

This leads to a third criticism, of the very notion that a 'global' approach has a valid meaning. For Gray and Webb (2014, p. 350) social work ought to reject universalised perspectives and actions as this leads to professional imperialism (cf. Midgley, 1981; Gray, 2005). The alternative, that policies and practices are localised, indigenised and authentised, means that they can plausibly be addressed only to specific contexts and in particular ways.

Finally, their fourth criticism is that through the *Global Agenda*, the international social work organisations are positioning themselves as civil society organisations, existing in a 'third space' that is neither government nor market (Gray & Webb, 2014, p. 353). This, they suggest, is incompatible with the role occupied by most social workers as government employees providing services or acting to regulate people's lives.

Taken as a whole, the points raised by Gray and Webb challenge the nature and purpose of the *Global Agenda* process. Insofar as early statements in advocating for the adoption of the agenda as a shared strategy emphasised the gains for social work in participating in these international debates, the suggestion of professional self-promotion seems plausible. These beginning pronouncements were indeed also couched at a very general level and did not engage with particular political positions, such as that naming capitalism as a primary cause of social problems. However, at the same time, it also seems that Gray and Webb may be asking too much. They call for a clear political positioning, and at the same time they question whether the IASSW, ICSW and IFSW have established an open process that allows many voices to be heard. As the process has unfolded so far, in fact, both these aims are beginning to be fulfilled. Not only have the emerging 'regional observatory' structures enabled social workers from many specific contexts to make contributions, but also the first report (four years after the process began) has been more specifically committed to particular ways of addressing specific social development issues. Seen in a different way, the support given by the social work organisations to the social protection floor can be understood as advocacy. Another example is the recent study by Spolander *et al.* (2014) of the way in which neo-liberal economics and the related practices of 'new public management' have created particular challenges for social work, which has been published as a contribution to the *Global Agenda* debates.

The three organisations of IASSW, ICSW and IFSW have had reporting status at the United Nations for many decades. In that sense they already have a role as part of civil society. Whereas many individual social workers are employed by government or market-based organisations, the professional associations themselves are neither government nor market entities. Along with trade unions (in fact some function as both, such as in Scandinavia) national social work associations that are part of the three international bodies can provide spaces where social workers can use the experience they have in working with people who face poverty and other forms of disadvantage to achieve a collective voice in advocacy. This potential can then be contributed to forming an international voice. Moreover, engagement in social development practice and political activity is an aspect of social work that can be seen as a part of the profession's history and one which some seek to reclaim (as discussed in Chapter 2). As acknowledged elsewhere in this book, the International Consortium on Social Development, while not asserting a social work identity as such, largely comprises social workers and was founded in the USA as a vehicle to recapture the macro dimensions of social work practice (Midgley, 2014, p. 6). Indeed, some of the individual members of ICSD are also actively involved in the other organisations. The issue here may well be one of how the various organisations can seek common ground, or even to ask whether they should do so or if a multiplicity of voices may be both more effective and more open to diversity. In other words, the central issue is that IASSW, ICSW and IFSW should perhaps be more effectively seeking to create partnerships with ICSD and others in their pursuit of a social development agenda generally and the social protection floor specifically. As the *Global Agenda* process develops further, whether increased openness is matched with greater specific engagement with the concrete political issues in helping to achieve social development is a vital question.

To this conclusion can be added the observation that the *Global Agenda* has been formulated in the last six years, influenced by the restoration of historical working relationships between the ICSW and the other two bodies (IASSW and IFSW). The ICSW has a membership that is somewhat wider than that of the other two, as it includes the social welfare sector as well as professional social work; it also has a strong membership base in the global South. It is through this voice joining the conversation that attention to social development issues has become more central to the combined activity of the organisations, as well as a refocusing on macro-level questions about social policy and welfare systems. Given the history of social work in the formulation of social welfare policy, within countries and internationally (see Chapter 1), and in the creation of parts of the UN system, such as the World Health Organisation (WHO), UNICEF and the UN Research Institute for Social Development (UNRISD) (Eilers, 2008, p. 65; Healy, 2008, p. 152; Riga, 2008, pp. 77–8), this move can be regarded potentially as the *re*-engagement with the foundations of professional social work. To that extent it is less surprising than critics of the *Global Agenda* suggest. Gray and Webb (2014) provide an important caution that social workers need to avoid being lost in rhetoric but rather to find ways of working with colleagues, service users and others in creating policies and practices that address the social dimensions of development. If this can be achieved, then a more explicit focus on social development and social policy questions may be realised in macro-level action that is able to draw on the micro and meso knowledge and experience of individual and organisational members of the different bodies.

6

SOCIAL DEVELOPMENT AS INTERNATIONAL SOCIAL WORK

International social work

Healy (2008) identifies the origins of international social work in the earliest days of professionalisation. In the late 1800s and early 1900s there was a considerable exchange of ideas and shared training between countries of the global North, such as Denmark, the Netherlands, the UK and the USA. This led to the establishment of the International Conference on Social Work, which was first held in Paris in 1928 (Healy, 2008, p. 170). At that stage it was entirely a global Northern meeting. Indeed, although at that time social work also began to become professionalised in other parts of the world, such as Argentina, China, Egypt and India, this was through the export of global Northern models of theory and practice in a process Midgley (1981) has termed 'professional imperialism'. That is the ways of thinking about human need, social disadvantage and the practices that are appropriate for assisting people to resolve the social problems that they face were all applied in ways that are now regarded by critical analysis as inherently colonial (e.g. Walton & El-Nasr, 1988; Osei-Hwedie, 1993; Tsang & Yan, 2001; Gray, 2005; Hugman, 2010; Heinonen & Drolet, 2012).

In her discussion of international social work, Healy identifies four specific areas of practice: 'internationally related domestic practice and advocacy'; 'professional exchange'; 'international practice'; and 'international policy development and advocacy' (2008, pp. 10–16). Significantly, Healy (2008, p. 7) states that 'international' relates to relationships between two or more countries (whereas 'global' concerns the whole word, and a 'comparative' focus examines the differences and similarities between countries). Elsewhere (Hugman, 2010) I have suggested that these differences can be explained in terms of who crosses borders and in what way (also see Hugman et al., 2010). These in turn are: 'service users have come from another country'; 'relationships are created between social workers in two or more countries' (they may each go to the other for periods of time); 'social workers work in countries other than that from which they originate'; and 'working with international organisations', where borders are crossed at the organisational level (regardless of whether in the social worker's country of origin) (Hugman, 2010, pp. 18–20). In addition, Dominelli (2007) has argued for recognition that increasingly social workers practice with communities that are impacted by international relations, such as when decisions concerning livelihoods in a community are made in another country (also see Lyons *et al.*, 2006). Although this latter concept clearly draws on an understanding of globalisation, it can be seen as international social work in that it is the issue that has 'crossed borders', while the practitioners and services users are local.

There are many ways in which social development practice in social work takes the form of international social work. In order to examine these ideas in more detail, this chapter looks at three particular areas: practice with refugees, asylum seekers and forced migrants; 'humanitarian' programmes and projects; and the growth of professional social work and social work education. These are not intended to be a summary of the totality of social work in international social work, but rather to provide ways in which the various elements of international social work (as described by Healy, Dominelli and others) contribute to understanding social development as part of social work (and vice versa). It is also clear from these three examples that the various elements are often combined differently between any given instances. For example as discussed in more depth ahead, working with refugee communities in one's own country involves the service users having crossed borders, practitioners may go to other countries as part of their work and this practice may involve international organisations. Similarly, humanitarian projects may involve practice in a country other than one's own, partnerships between countries and working in or with international organisations. As will be shown, these discussions also draw on issues that have been introduced in the preceding chapters and begin to integrate these into a more complex picture, for example with regard to economics, the environment and the ways in which different approaches to social work (macro, meso and micro) may be combined.

Refugees, asylum seekers and forced migrants

The United Nations High Commissioner for Refugees has estimated that at the end of 2013 there were 51.2 million forcibly displaced people worldwide (UNHCR, 2013). This includes 16.7 million refugees (as defined by the *Convention Relating to the Status of Refugees*; UNHCR, 1951), 1.2 million people seeking asylum and 33.3 million people displaced internally in their country of origin or citizenship (UNHCR, 2013, p. 2). Of these, more than half were from three countries – namely (in order of magnitude) Afghanistan, Syria and Somalia – while approximately half of the global total (not necessarily from these countries) were children under the age of 18 (p. 3). That year also saw the lowest number of people returning to their countries of origin in approximately 25 years. Among the 16.7 million refugees, 6.3 million people have been refugees for protracted periods (which is defined in terms of 25,000 or more people of the same nationality living in forced exile for more than five years) (p. 6). The ten countries in which the largest numbers of refugees have settled or are finding shelter are, in order of magnitude, Pakistan, Iran, Lebanon, Jordan, Turkey, Kenya, Chad, Ethiopia, China and the USA (p. 13). Of the OECD countries, other than the USA, only France and Germany are among the 20 countries hosting the largest numbers. Thus, to explain these figures another way, it is clear that the largest numbers of refugees, approximating 86 per cent of the total, are resident in 'developing countries' or countries 'in transition' (p. 17). As many as one quarter of the global total number of recognised refugees are resident in countries that are regarded by the UN as 'least developed'.

The issues faced by refugees vary according to the country in which they are able to find asylum. The greater the resources that are available, or the more developed a social welfare system, the more refugees have the possibility of meeting basic human needs, such as water, food and accommodation. However, along with these gains there are also costs, including the difficulty of reaching many of the highly developed countries or of having a claim to asylum accepted. In many of the less developed countries refugees live in camps that by their nature are established to provide 'temporary' shelter, even though for some refugees the meaning of 'temporary' is lost in the difficulties of moving on and the impossibility of going back. To distinguish between the social development issues faced in these different types of situations and the social work responses that are relevant in those situations, two case studies will be discussed. As in previous chapters, while these are hypothetical, they are based on a combination of evidence presented in relevant literature and the practice experience of the author and colleagues, as well as more widely in social work (e.g. Pittaway & Bartolomei, 2003; Pittaway *et al.*, 2003; Hugman *et al.*, 2011; also see Boateng, 2009; Haynes, 2014).

Case study: issues in refugee camps

Maryam is aged 28 and is living in a camp that is currently housing 180,000 people. She fled from her home in a neighbouring country when the civil war led to the destruction of large parts of her town. Maryam has four children under ten years old, including a baby and a toddler. She does not know where her husband, Mohammad, is or if he is alive, as he was working away from home when Maryam and her neighbours were forced to flee. She has heard reports that many younger men were killed as they tried to return home to be with their families. In the camp, Maryam and her children are provided with a tent. There is a daily ration of food, and water is available from a standpipe located about 200 metres away. Toilets are a short distance beyond the water tap. Much of the infrastructure is provided by UNHCR, but although they have sanctioned the camp it is run on a day-to-day basis by the district government of the country, using local staff. There are problems of safety, particularly for women and at night, with sexual assaults common.

Maryam has had two encounters with social workers. The first of these began two months ago, as her situation is being assessed by UNHCR to determine refugee status. The case officer is a social worker from a global

Northern country, and she has a particular concern for the health and well-being of Maryam's two younger children, as well as considering that Maryam fits the 'women-at-risk' programme. However, as she has explained to Maryam, even with these factors taken into account the likely time to have to wait for a decision will still be long. Maryam acknowledges this but privately hopes that questions about the children mean that the case officer understands her situation. Maryam has never heard of social work and does not know what this means for the role of the case officer.

More recently, a team of researchers came to the camp with the support of UNHCR. This was a group from a school of social work in a university, also in a global Northern country. Many of the refugees who have been in the camp longer than Maryam were sceptical about research as they feel that they have been let down before by researchers, but at the same time they agreed to participate in case it helped and because it seemed interesting that this project was different. It was based on group sessions in which the refugees told the researchers their stories and at the same time learned about human rights. Maryam had not heard about human rights before, but has been encouraged to continue to discuss the questions that were raised by this process with her neighbours in the camp. One result is that a group of women demanded to have greater safety in accessing the water and toilets and are negotiating this with the camp management. The research team has promised to come back and to do additional work with the group to see if their situation can improve further. She was told that this is called 'participatory action research', and although Maryam is surprised that people from such a country would be interested in her circumstances, she thinks that there has been an improvement in that the women have been able to present their argument to the camp management. Being able to play an active part has helped Maryam and other women to begin to gain more confidence.

This case study shows two distinct aspects of the social development work that social workers may undertake with refugees, as a caseworker for an INGO and as community workers. In both aspects the social workers are practising in a country other than that of their own citizenship; in the former this is also practice in an international organisation. In fact, although this is not apparent to Maryam, the work of the research team has also been shared with UNHCR and has been used to begin to review aspects of policy and practice, especially as these affect women and children, including by enabling refugee women to attend UNHCR meetings and to present their own arguments (cf. Pittaway et al., 2010, p. 237). Thus it is also engaged in 'international policy development and advocacy' (see earlier).

Both of these areas of social work practice contribute to social development for refugees such as Maryam. This is perhaps more obviously the case for human rights–based participatory action research, in which members of the camp community are enabled to advocate for themselves. In this work we can see elements of community development and advocacy, enabling people in this situation to gain greater agency in shaping their circumstances. Moreover, the actual group on which this example is modelled engages actively in the deliberations of the UNHCR (see http://www.crr.unsw.edu.au/advocacy-and-community-engagement/advocacy-at-unhcr/). However, it would not be adequate simply to regard the work of a UNHCR case officer only in terms of 'case management', which from some perspectives might be considered as a bureaucratic function as well as micro practice. In contrast, such a role can also be seen as providing the basis for practitioners to contribute to the improvement of policy, by using knowledge of refugees' situations to work towards policy and systems improvements, in addition to attending to the rights and needs of individual refugees and their families.

Whether these practices can be seen as aspects of social development in social work follows from the way in which different actions are undertaken – it is not endemic in the practices. By this I mean that a social development approach is not necessarily part of either case management or community-based participatory research in themselves. Rather, it is found in the goals of these practices and the ways in which they are accomplished. For example there are many applied research projects in this field in which refugees themselves are further disadvantaged and demoralised, and even placed at great risk (Pittaway et al., 2010; Hugman et al., 2011). A social development approach must be centred on the promotion of agency and developing capacity among participants.

Case study: refugees in resettlement

UNHCR states that in 2013 there were 1.1 million individual applications for refugee status, of which 19 per cent were accepted and offered asylum in countries of settlement (UNHCR, 2013, p. 3). The largest numbers were settled, in numerical order, in Germany, the USA and South Africa. Many other countries also provide asylum and grant visas to refugees. Once in a country of settlement, however, the refugee journey does not end on arrival. Settling is a process, not an event, and is one that can challenge refugees further as they struggle to make sense of their new home. This is illustrated by the experience of Pol Lu.

> Pol Lu is ethnically Karen and was granted refugee status four years ago, along with several members of his family. They had been living in a camp in western Thailand for several years and are very grateful to have had the opportunity to come to a third country. However, there have been many problems they have faced because at the time they arrived none of the family spoke the local language and they were not familiar with the way of life, such as styles of housing, the education, health and social security systems, and patterns of employment. As there were several families from their camp granted asylum at the same time, they have supported each other and now live in the same district.
>
> Amy is a social worker employed by an NGO to provide support services for refugees during the process of settlement. Her role includes assisting families and individuals to find accommodation, to manage their access to education, health and social security services, and to consider other needs. All

children are legally required to attend school, while for adults there are also education and training opportunities. Amy assisted Pol Lu to enrol in adult language classes, and he has now gained sufficient fluency to be able to find work with a local shop. His parents, however, have had less success at language classes, and although of working age have not been able to get jobs. They have heard that in another town older Karen refugees have been able to find work in which they do not need to be able to speak the local language, and Amy is working with the adult training and education service to talk to local employers about how such a scheme could be created.

Another aspect of the way in which Amy has provided support is that all the members of the family have been referred to a separate trauma service, run by another NGO. Not only did they experience violence from soldiers who destroyed their home township, but also in the camp there was sometimes violence and one of Pol Lu's female cousins was sexually assaulted. Pol Lu saw a counsellor for a short time, but has mixed views about how much it helped him. His parents were not comfortable with this service because they had to rely on an interpreter who was another member of their community. In addition, the family are members of the Karen Christian minority and they have been welcomed by the local faith community. Other families who are Buddhist have also been able to make links with their wider faith community and find further support there.

One challenge that Pol Lu was not expecting is that at times he experiences personal racism from people in the wider community. He finds this confusing as he is receiving government-funded help in settlement and he feels welcomed by professionals such as Amy, the people whom he works with and the members of his church community. So usually he talks about this only to his Karen friends. He thinks it would be disrespectful to talk with Amy about this as he worries she may feel it is a criticism of her in some way.

Through his experience of assistance from Amy, Pol Lu thinks that social work is a good profession, and he now thinks that if he is able to access the adult university entrance programme he might consider this as a future career so that he can help his own community as well as other refugees.

This case study describes the way in which social work contributes to refugee settlement in the country to which refugees have arrived. The key practitioner in the settlement service, Amy, combines case management with some community development practice, illustrating the generalist focus that has been spelled out in previous chapters. The trauma counsellors may well also be social workers, as well as psychologists or other allied health practitioners.

However, this illustrative example is a (relatively) positive one. It is important also to recognise that there are many problems and barriers faced by social workers in this field of practice. The stresses of acculturation are widely documented, and social workers have to be aware that unless all the complexities of the process and the many aspects of the identity and experience of the refugees themselves are taken into account, social work intervention can contribute to stress (Suárez et al.,

2008; Nawyn, 2010). For example it is important to recognise the multiple factors involved in any situation, drawing on the concept of intersectionality to consider gender/sex, age, ethnicity, dis/ability, sexuality and other structural elements of identity and experience. Nawyn (2010) argues that even in refugee support agencies, uncritical practice can contribute to further oppression and act as social control in buttressing discrimination, such as by reproducing existing inequalities in the labour market, where refugees are directed to low-skill work that is already structured along ethnic and gender lines. That Pol Lu in the forgoing case study might be supported to think of university education and a professional career is an alternative example, and it is crucial that Amy and her colleagues would also provide such support to his female cousin. Suárez et al. (2008) also point to the way in which personal practice skills matter for example in cultural humility and willingness to listen carefully and openly to refugees' accounts of their own experiences, including how they see their own culture.

Likewise, from experience in working with South Sudanese refugees in Australia, Westoby (2008) suggests that although trauma is a reality for most (if not all) refugees, the therapeutic focus of many global Northern social workers can lead to them diminishing the human agency of refugees. In contrast, Westoby argues for practice that is based on the goal of (re)building a social world. He finds that this can be achieved only by taking a community development approach. Insofar as he seeks to oppose the medicalisation of atrocities and grief, this argument has something to say beyond refugee experiences. However, in relation to refugees specifically the core issue that is revealed is that NGOs and practitioners often pay insufficient attention to culture, to the strengths that people bring with them through the refugee journey or to the differences between communities. However, as Westoby also acknowledges (p. 486) this can be done by 'community-oriented practitioners', and he argues for the possibility of culturally appropriate or genuinely trans-cultural interpersonal helping. The central point here is that social work must be attentive to and respectful of culture and how people see their own identity, otherwise attempts to be 'critical' can become distorted – for example in forms such as 'rescuing' women from patriarchal relationships (cf. Suárez et al., 2008, p. 415). When this happens, social work is reproducing neo-colonialism; we will return to this issue in Chapter 9, concerning values and ethics. What is required is to maintain a 'self-critical' awareness, to seek to avoid this retrogressive tendency.

One example of the importance of a self-critical perspective in practice can be seen in the discussion by Benson et al. (2012) of the centrality of religion in the lives of many refugees (also see Suárez et al., 2008). Whiting (2008) argues that in many global Northern countries the way in which religious difference is accommodated has been to erase it from public discourse altogether. Similarly, Asad (2003) has suggested that secularism is usually taken to mean the ascendancy of reason and atheistic humanism in the modern world, whereas an alternative understanding would be that secularism should mean that all positions on faith, reason and the relationship between them can be heard in the public sphere. Adopting the predominant view of secularism, that faith and belief are not discussed in professional interactions, can lead social workers to fail to address its importance in many people's lives and even implicitly to discriminate (against religion in general or particular forms of religious expression). This can especially be the case when any given religious belief is regarded by those from outside as the cause of particular problems. However, Benson *et al.* also caution that in some situations strong involvement in ethnic and religious communities that separate refugees from the wider society can exacerbate acculturation stress (2012, p. 547). This suggests that social workers in settlement services need to be very skilful in helping refugees to find appropriate external connections and supports as well as gaining help from within their own community. In this sense, the situation described in the forgoing case study is possibly unusual in that Pol Lu has been able to engage with a faith community that is part of the wider society, and this cannot be assumed.

As with work in refugee camps, social work in refugee settlement services combines various aspects of international social work. That service users have crossed borders, as well as the particular experiences they have encountered (compared with other migrants), in itself makes this 'international', and this is highlighted by questions of culture, (re)building social worlds and the risks of perpetuating neocolonialism in uncritical practice.

International 'humanitarian' practice

In previous chapters various areas of social work practice have been discussed, including economic development such as microfinance, responding to environmental issues as in disaster relief and in more general environmental programmes. At this point I will revisit certain aspects of such practice as international social work, but in doing so consider some areas of work that have not yet been discussed, in particular in the fields of education and health.

The notion of 'humanitarian' practice is ambiguous. On the negative side, it has connotations of charitable effort, of 'doing good' in ways that echo the oppressions of colonialism. (Of course, most social workers would not wish to 'do bad'; the point here is that in un-self-critical practice 'good' is defined by the practitioner, not the service user.) On the positive side, it can refer to an orientation in international social development to focus on issues of human development, in which human rights and dignity are the primary goals. Vander Zaag (2012, p. 47) argues that official aid and development policies of countries such as Canada, Denmark, the Netherlands and Sweden have embodied this approach, along with civil society organisations, such as the *Jubilee Debt Campaign* and *Make Poverty History*. It is this latter sense in which the concept is discussed here, although the former, negative implication of 'charitable' action continues to characterise a great deal of global Northern attention to countries of the South.

Education

Since the debates of the 1990s concerning the relationship between human, social and economic development (that were introduced in Chapter 3), the importance of factors such as education and health have become more central questions in development policy and practice (e.g. see Summers, 1994, on education). Since 2000 UNICEF has made education and health key objectives. One example of this is the *UN Girls Education Initiative* (UNGEI), which is a set of policies and programmes to promote education for girls and young women. UNGEI programmes have been established in Africa, the Arabic countries, Asia, Central and South America and the Pacific Islands. These variously include public awareness campaigns, advocating for the idea of educating girls, support for schools and community education projects, and targeted assistance to communities and families to enable girls and young women to access education.

The involvement of social work in these processes is not always apparent (Claiborne, 2004; Hugman, 2010). However, a recent report on the way in which these policies are being implemented notes that civil society organisations have a large role in helping communities to engage with educational developments. Aspects of this include promoting awareness, advocacy, capacity building and evaluation of impact, all of which are practices that social work contributes in the civil society sector (UNICEF/UNESCO, 2013). In addition, development practitioners in both UNICEF and UNESCO, as well as in major INGOs, include social workers in policy, advocacy, programme director and project management roles. In addition, George (2011) argues that social workers must also be involved with the consequences of increased women's access to education in the wider impact of social change. From her home state of Kerala, in India, she states that one of the outcomes of greater access to education is a willingness of women to challenge entrenched gender inequalities, including a growing incidence of family and gender-related violence. This must be understood alongside other evidence – for example from Nepal (Acharya *et al.*, 2007) – that girls and women's education can equip women to play more active and empowered roles in their communities. Some of these issues are illustrated in the following case study, which, although hypothetical, is constructed from my own observations and reports from colleagues, as well as from published research (e.g. see Sommers, 2010).

Case study: promoting girls' education

Emma is an Australian social worker who is very keen to be involved in promoting gender equality. For the last two years, she has worked in community development with a programme sponsored by UNGEI and supported by an Australian INGO in East Africa. As part of this role she has been working with a local colleague, Dambisa, to engage the members of several villages in increasing the participation rate of girls in primary and secondary education. From this experience, Emma has concluded that the main barriers to girls' participation is not so much cultural views about girls being educated but more to do with the roles that girls are needed to perform in everyday life, such as collecting water, caring for younger siblings and otherwise helping their mothers, as well as wider economic and social issues.

So using a community participation approach, Emma and Dambisa have brought members of the villages together to discuss why enabling girls to go to school will help everyone in the future and to address problems in the present that make this difficult. What they have learned from the process is that action in relation to other factors may well help them to achieve the project goals. In particular, most of the families are too poor to be able to meet even the basic costs of children attending school – so when this is combined with needing the girls to do other work, prioritising boys' education is not questioned. Furthermore, from a cultural perspective the biggest single issue is that at the school that serves the villages the toilet facilities are not separated for girls and boys. This raises questions of cultural appropriateness, especially at the junior high school level, when girls begin menstruation.

Using these insights, Emma and Dambisa have been advocating with the INGO that is managing the overall project that it needs to have additional elements, including attention to poverty alleviation. In addition, they used the INGO's support base in Australia to raise funds to build separate toilet facilities for the girls. This latter project has already seen the rate of girls attending school start to increase. The organisation is now developing an extension to the project to assist with a poverty reduction programme for the villages.

Health

In the health field, also, international social workers are often involved in ways that are not always immediately recognised as 'social work' practice. Nevertheless, as briefly discussed in Chapter 3, there are many ways in which social workers are involved in health developments. For example in the *Philani* nutrition programme in South Africa, social workers worked together with medical and other health colleagues in a programme in Crossroads Township near Cape Town, which was funded by Norway, Sweden, Switzerland and the USA (Austin & Mbewu, 2009). Although the main focus was intended to be on promoting children's health through better nutrition, the programme also has found that it is necessary to address HIV/AIDS, mental health and other public health concerns. Social work has a particular role to play in health awareness raising, as well as in assessing mental and emotional health needs.

In a poor community of this kind, poverty is also a major factor in health, and so Austin and Mbewu trace the underlying problems facing families to opportunities to gain a livelihood, as well as health knowledge (2009, p. 154). Projects to create employment opportunities for women in particular, especially as many are sole parents, were seen to be necessary. In addition, early childhood development has been enhanced through childcare centres, in which some mothers also have been trained as day care teachers. Moreover, the home-based nutrition education programme uses a community development approach, in which the role of professionals is to recruit and support members of the community to become community workers, taking on the role of providing health education and support for their neighbours. In conclusion, Austin and Mbewu argue that global North countries could learn from this type of integrated social development, in which social and economic goals are pursued together, through community-focused practice.

From a different part of Africa, Nigeria, Karger *et al.* (2007) argue that community-focused practice can provide wider benefits for health and other developmental outcomes. A study by one of the authors, Iyani, found that most programmes to respond to HIV/AIDS in Nigeria were run or supported by INGOs, using global Northern models of health intervention (individual testing and treatment) combined with some community education. The failures of many projects, in Nigeria and many other countries, suggest a need to consider alternative strategies. This conclusion points to the importance of working with the various sources of power in communities to influence people's beliefs, understanding and choices in action (Karger *et al.*, 2007, p. 81). Drawing on the evidence from studies of particular projects, Karger *et al.* point to a community development model in which a participative approach is used to bring together all the various 'stakeholders', including international donors, INGOs, national and local governments, and community members (p. 83). The role of social work in this approach is that of 'facilitator', 'coordinator' or 'broker', rather than in direct intervention.

Creating professional social work as social development

Part of the continuing agenda of international social work has been for those countries that already have a recognised profession of social work to provide support for the development of the profession in other parts of the world. As noted at the beginning of this chapter, this has been an aspect of social work's growth and professionalisation since the late 1800s. The history of this process in the earlier days led to forms of social work in some countries that were part of the wider colonial relations, with implications that continue to the present. Recognising this in the profession's history highlights two important questions for current international work to support the development of social work in new countries – namely how such work is to be undertaken and whether such relationships can avoid the pitfalls of neocolonialism.

Clearly, this area of practice is one of the main examples within Healy's (2008) category of 'professional exchange' (see earlier); it may also involve social workers practising in a country other than that from which they originate. However, there are many ways in which the idea of exchange can be understood in this context, in that it can be a mutual, two-way process of a relationship between equals or it can imply an unequal relationship, in which each person or group gives and receives something quite different from the other. This latter possibility then raises the question of whether an unequal exchange enables all participants to exercise agency or if it inevitably results in the uncritical exercise of power by some over others. It is such power imbalances that support the continuation of neocolonial relationships, regardless of whether the participants recognise and accept the situation in this way. Although often called 'partnerships', Wilson and Hernández (2012, p. 170), quoting Peggy Antrobus, argue that this implies equality in the relationships when, in fact, it rarely is the case; so with Antrobus they prefer to think of international relationships, which may or may not actually be partnerships, which they regard as relationships between equals.

In recent years there have been many countries where social work was not formerly professionalised, in which under conditions of economic and structural modernisation social work is now being created. This can be seen in the increase in membership of the International Federation of Social Workers (IFSW), which is by country, as well as of the International Association of Schools of Social Work (IASSW), where schools may be a member as well as individual educators (see http://ifsw.org/membership/our-members/; http://www.iassw-aiets.org/list-of-iassw-member-131219). Recent growth in both these associations has been particularly seen in Africa, East and South-East Asia, the Pacific Islands and in the new countries of Eastern Europe and Western Asia. There are many particular examples of inter-country relationships or projects to develop social work, in both practice and education. As illustrations, this discussion focuses on three specific examples, each of which draws on published literature (and one of which also draws on the current author's own practice).

The first of these is a project led by universities in Canada and Ukraine, supported by the Canadian International Development Agency (CIDA), which sought to strengthen Ukrainian social work in its pursuit of social justice through developments in community-based social services and disability organisations (Hayduk & McKenzie, 2012). This project continued over a 16-year period from 1995 to 2011. It has involved many stages, beginning with a lengthy period of community consultation with practitioners and educators in Ukraine, followed by a collaborative design of the project, creating a social work programme at the Lviv Polytechnic National University to prepare students to work on the principle of social justice, and then building from that to a research and development centre at the university, alongside the creation of partnerships with disability organisations in the community. The collaborative way of working between the Lviv Polytechnic National University and the University of Manitoba was extended to similar relationships between the university in Liviv and the disability organisations and community-based social service agencies. Social workers in these organisations received training and support to work with students on placement, and graduates have been able to work in this and other related areas.

This project is notable for the way in which from the start it sought to use a social development framework to guide thinking and action (Hayduk & McKenzie, 2012, pp. 156–61). In particular, Hayduk and McKenzie regard the promotion of social capital, building capacity among all those involved in social work, including service users, and collaborative working between practice and education as key elements. Underpinning all of this is the principle of social justice, which for Hayduk and McKenzie is the defining value of social development. From the initial stages they note that in addition to disability organisations, the university programme and various practitioners have also extended the framework to include social work with children and young people in institutions, homeless people and women who have escaped human trafficking (p. 159). Hayduk and McKenzie (pp. 165–7) conclude that there are identifiable lessons for achieving social development in the partnership between education and practice, supported by international relationships. These are in achieving a transfer of decision-making control to local organisations while continuing to provide support to ensure that capacity building is sustained. They also make the observation that small changes make a difference and are important to the longer-term process.

A similar experience of links between social work practice and professional education in China and Hong Kong is reported by Ku *et al.* (2005). In this project, students from the Hong Kong Polytechnic University (HKPU) undertook practicum (experiential, practice-based learning) in a community development project in rural western China, in Yunnan province. Although Hong Kong is now a special administrative region (SAR) of China, this can be regarded as international social work in that the model of social work that exists in Hong Kong has a long history of development out of many influences, including that of the British system under which it first developed. In addition, compared to rural Yunnan, Hong Kong has a relatively well-developed economy as well as a modern social welfare system. Moreover, the local dialect is quite different to the form of Chinese spoken by people from Hong Kong, which emphasised the 'foreignness' of the project team and created some barriers in communication.

The Yunnan project involved students from HKPU working with groups of local residents to identify problems faced by the community, using an oral history methodology to develop a participatory approach in considering various issues, within an action research framework. In forming community groups to address key problems that the 'oral histories' had uncovered, the students also shared with community members some social work techniques, such as group work (Ku *et al.*, 2005, p. 228). The range of specific projects that the community members themselves then decided to implement was also varied, including generating methane as a biofuel, adult education, a range of income-generating projects and a local social services centre.

In stating capacity building as a major aim of the project as a whole, Ku *et al.* argue that this is not something brought from outside and 'given' to members of the community, but rather is achieved by community members for themselves. There are two aspects to this. First, several local groups formed around shared experiences, such as youth groups, women's groups and groups of elders (Ku *et al.*, 2005, p. 225). Second, both the students and the lecturers from Hong Kong quickly realised that in such work they were 'co-learners', sharing in the development of expertise relevant to the context. This they refer to as 'triple capacity building', in which all the different actors in the process were participants: social development is not simply a technique for 'alleviating poverty' but a process to 'assist people to discover and develop [their] capacities and potential' (p. 230).

Vietnam provides a different example of how professional developments in social work contribute to social development. Professional social work existed in the South before reunification in 1975 and then was abandoned as unnecessary under socialism. As the country has moved towards a market economy since 1986, social problems have been revealed and in some respects are being exacerbated by

economic growth (Nguyen Thi Oanh, 2002). Consequently social work began to re-emerge and since the 1990s has gradually professionalised.

Many international social workers have played roles in this process alongside an increasing number of Vietnamese colleagues (e.g. see Forgery *et al.*, 2003; Hines *et al.*, 2010). From 2004 I have worked with UNICEF Vietnam to collaborate with the Ministry of Labour, Invalids and Social Affairs (MOLISA) in the development of a policy framework for professional social work (UNICEF Vietnam, 2005; Hugman *et al.*, 2007; Hugman *et al.*, 2009; Government of Vietnam, 2010; Nguyen Thi Thai Lan *et al.*, 2010). The overall project has involved several stages, including a national study of social needs and the current social welfare system, international comparative reviews of social work services and of social work law, and drafts of policy documents for the government. In addition, at times I have also undertaken work with other international colleagues to review and advise on professional education, including curriculum developments from Australia, Canada, the Philippines, South Korea, the UK and the USA. (Furthermore, groups from Vietnam have visited these countries, as well as Brazil, South Africa and Sweden, to explore various alternative systems.) Most recently MOLISA has implemented a long-term strategy to create a modernised social welfare system in which professional social work will play a central role (Hugman, 2014).

A central question to be asked here concerns the professionalisation of social work as an aspect of social development. The answer can be found in the extent to which social issues and problems are seen to be increasing with economic growth. Child and youth welfare, drug misuse, prostitution and the spread of HIV/AIDS have all become prevalent challenges in Vietnam along with a rapid shift weakening more traditional forms of family and community-based welfare (Nguyen Thi Oanh, 2002; Nguyen Thi Thai Lan *et al.*, 2010). The intention is that professionalisation of social work can contribute to enhancing the national capacity to respond more effectively to such issues. For this reason, creating a formal system of social service provision, officially recognising social work as a profession and enhancing the curriculum for social work at the university level and other levels of education are all regarded as key elements in the process.

A key factor in this work is that it has been undertaken under the direction of local professionals and officials. The contribution of international social workers is managed by Vietnamese participants, in government ministries and universities, as well as in UNICEF Vietnam, where the officers directly supervising the relationship are Vietnamese social workers. Part of my own experience in this process has been in learning that as an international social worker my role is to ensure that decisions are as fully informed as they can be, rather than seeking to determine outcomes. The goal of developing Vietnamese social work means that it must be not only culturally relevant but also genuinely created from within the national community and not simply imported from elsewhere.

While it may be clear how international social work with refugees, education or health programmes can be regarded as social development, the creation of professional social work, often through higher education, is perhaps less obviously social development (although it is clearly international social work). However, I argue that it must be seen as such for two reasons. First, these programmes contribute directly and indirectly to creating and strengthening social welfare programmes. The examples described here include progressive disability services (Ukraine), community development (China) and various areas such as child and family welfare, community health and responses to human trafficking (Vietnam). Second, in each case these programmes contribute to the development of national capacity in the broad field of social welfare. Not only have many individuals now been educated for these roles, but in addition to national practitioners there are national educators who have been prepared to take on providing this type of education for future cohorts of students entering these fields. This 'train-the-trainer' approach is widely recognised by UN and INGO agencies as a vehicle for sustained social development (Kutcher *et al.*, 2005; Thorning *et al.*, 2013). What is crucial is that the principles of social development are embodied in the ways in which international relationships support and inform such practice.

The struggle for 'decolonisation' and 'indigenisation'

In the earlier examples of international social work practice, whether in working with refugees, in humanitarian assistance or in developing social work, there are some common themes that emerge. First, in all cases the underlying principle of practice is that international social workers should approach their role from a position of valuing people's strengths in terms of their capacities in living and working in their own societies and cultures. While social workers may be invited to provide support to social development in other countries, or practice in their own country with people who have come from other parts of the world, all these examples demonstrate attempts to create practice that is participatory. We may agree with Wilson and Hernández (2012) concerning the difficulties of making partnership a reality – the same point appears again and again in the critical international social work literature (Razack, 2000; Haug, 2005; Wehbi, 2011). Too often, international social workers fall into the trap of thinking that their own national perspective on social work, or even on social issues and problems more generally, is the only correct view. Especially when such relationships are 'South/North', as so many are, there is a tendency to consider global Northern knowledge and skills to be superior, often exhibited by both sides of the relationship. While this is increasingly challenged by critical practice and scholarship, it can be perpetuated both in the innate beliefs of those who come from countries where social work is long-established and in the internalised colonialism of people in countries that are still working to throw off the legacies of colonisation.

Internalised ideologies of colonisation can take a number of forms. For those from colonising countries it can be a 'well-meant intention to do good', even (at its worst) that those in less-developed countries 'need saving' (Wehbi, 2011, p. 27). For those from countries that have been colonised, it can be found in an implicit but very strong belief that foreign knowledge and skill are superior (Nguyen Thi Thai Lan, 2015, p. 248). There are parallels here with relationships between Indigenous peoples and the 'mainstream' society (Yellow Bird, 1999; S. Green & Baldry, 2008).

Decolonisation is the process of both sides of this unequal and unjust relationship actively challenging it through reconsidering the knowledge, skills and values that make up social work theory and practice.

As examples of practice that seek to move beyond neocolonialism, and to engage with the struggle involved in decolonisation, the situations discussed earlier all show ways in which both international social workers and the countries, or cultures, in which they are guests can seek to work towards a more genuine partnership relationship. However, this cannot be achieved without those who have inherited the legacy of colonising rethinking that which they know and understanding themselves as strangers and learners, while those whose inheritance is in having been colonised are able to value their own knowledge, skills and values. Decolonised social work might be when those in the global North seek routinely to learn from colleagues in the South as much as the other way around, for example, and approach international practice as a genuine dialogue (i.e. a conversation between two people in which both actively listen as well as speak; cf. Hugman, 2005, p. 129).

A concept that has sought to assert the value of global Southern perspectives is that of 'indigenisation' (Walton & El Nasr, 1988; Yan & Cheung, 2006; Nguyen Thi Thai Lan, 2010). Walton and El Nasr draw on a United Nations (1971) study of social work that was critical of the importation of global Northern social work to the South and quote the definition of indigenisation as taking ideas from one location to another and adapting them so that they are culturally relevant (Walton & El Nasr, 1988, p. 148). Beyond this, they point to another perspective, which they call 'authentisation', in which a local model of social work is created on the basis of the local cultural and structural characteristics of a society (p. 149). Yan and Cheung (2006, p. 64) use the term 'authentication' for this latter concept, but they are more concerned with the process that they see as one of 'recontextualising' social work theory and practice through the creation of an authentic Chinese understanding of social work as profession in all its aspects. Nguyen Thi Thai Lan *et al.* (2010) describe a similar process occurring in Vietnam. In these situations there are local differences of view between the various actors in the processes, including local academics (many of whom may have trained internationally, if indeed they actually have social work qualifications) and the relevant government ministries who are responsible for creating modern mass social welfare provision for very large populations.

The way forward in these processes that appears to be developing is for social work to be 'recontextualised' through ongoing debates between practice and education and successive shifts of understanding on both sides. If it is seeking to engage with 'decolonisation', it is important that international social work maintains a self-critical role and resists the temptation to rush in with understandings of what social justice and human rights must look like that are grounded in another culture (and often, within that, in particular social class, gender or other positioning). To do otherwise is to replicate colonising practices, in which the professionalisation of social work is another form of development through which the dominance of the global North is entrenched.

7

SOCIAL DEVELOPMENT IN 'DEVELOPED' COUNTRIES

Social development and social need in the global North

Much of the discussion about social development and social work focuses on the global South, especially on those countries that are considered to be the 'least developed'. However, there are also ways in which this approach has much to inform social work in the 'developed' countries, as they are often called. Most of these are in the global North, where social work first professionalised and in which institutional social welfare systems began. Although some global Southern countries, such as Argentina, Chile, Japan, Korea and Singapore, have now reached levels of economic growth that place them among the more highly developed nations, as we have seen in previous chapters they may still be in the process of building modern social welfare systems that provide social protection floors of the kind that have existed for longer in Western Europe, North America and Australasia. This chapter examines the way in which even in these latter so-called developed contexts there are still developmental needs and, from this, the potential for a social development approach to inform contemporary social work in these countries. In doing so, it explores the ways in which these societies are unequal. Thus it also addresses the question of whether it is appropriate to treat such countries as single entities or if international inequalities must be considered also at a national level.

In his encyclopaedic review of social work theories, Payne (2014) locates social development specifically as a form of macro practice. In particular, he firmly identifies the approach as having been derived from 'resource-poor' (global Southern) countries, in which social development is seen always as involving a community or structural focus. Indeed, at one point Payne states that 'social development grew out of community development' (2014, p. 228). In several places he refers also to 'social and community development' as a singular approach. Furthermore, Payne's understanding of social development places it at the very edge of social work, if not actually 'outside' the profession (p. 215). In this sense he takes a particular position in relation to the debates that are summarised in detail in Chapter 2, at times also referring to social development along with community work and related practices as 'indirect'.

That Payne is writing from a global Northern perspective is important here, as it is in these countries that the 'professionalisation discourse' can be said to have gained precedence over social change as a priority for social work. It is also argued by some social workers that in these countries, as social welfare has become institutionalised and the overall level of economic well-being has increased, the 'demise of community work' has occurred (e.g. Olson, 2007). However, Midgley (2014) argues that community development is only one part of social development, although an important part, and that the relationship between these approaches must be seen as more complex, even at times problematic. For Midgley, community work occurs in communities, whereas social development practice can be focused at the community level or it can be directed to change across districts, regions or countries. Consequently, although community practice may have shifted in some respects in global Northern countries as a consequence of political, economic and social changes, social development can remain relevant in that part of the world.

Cox and Pawar (2013) largely focus their analysis of social development on international social work, as discussed in Chapter 6. Much of their attention is focused on countries of the global South, although they also briefly address social work with refugees settling in the global North. They assert that their model of practice is of relevance in the global North, but this is not taken further. Similarly, Pawar (2014b) addresses social development in connection with community development and focuses his attention on practice in South Asia. Although there are very good reasons for doing this, in that South Asia has often been ignored by global Northern social work scholarship, except as the location of practice by global Northern social workers, application to global Northern countries themselves remains unexplored.

Gray and Crofts (2008) are more specific in their critical examination of the relevance of social development to the global North. Looking particularly at Australia, they ask questions about the relationships between economics, state welfare and different levels of social work practice, as well as social work theories and values. In particular, they state from the same perspective as Olson (2007) that in the modern global North social work effectively means social casework and other individual-focused practices. Consequently, the questions they ask about the relationship between social development and social work are as follows:

- Does the pragmatic emphasis of social development fit with social work theory and values, especially in its more critical forms?
- Does the systems (structural and collective) focus of social development harmonise with professionalised social work?
- Can global Northern social workers grasp the importance of economic and material issues in social development?

This last point is particularly central, as they note that social work has become completely focused on individual and family functioning and either ignores economic and structural issues or else sees them as objects of change. In other words, when social work concern shifts to social structures it is to critique and seek to change them, not to engage them as they are as a vehicle for improving people's lives. In summary, they then pose an overarching question of whether social development is too conservative for social work, or whether, in fact, social work is too conservative for social development (Gray & Crofts, 2008, pp. 96–8).

The answers vary according to which models of social work and of social development are being considered, as we might expect. If we compare critical or progressive social work with the tendency of some social development practice simply to accept neo-liberal capitalism and work with it, then that creates one tension. However, if a comparison is made between conservative individually focused social work (noting that not all social work with individuals is conservative) and the critical perspective on the central role of the state in social development, then we may see a different conflict of ideas and values. In his recent discussion, Midgley (2014) considers that there are several stances within social development on these questions, from the conservative and individualistic to the radical and structural, as there are in social work. In the context of the ascendancy of neo-liberal capitalism it may be that in both social development and social work we see an emphasis on individual and family functioning and less on communities and other collective perspectives. However, this continues to be debated.

An example of the way in which a developmental approach might be promoted, according to Conley (2010), is in the field of child protection. Conley notes the well-established evidence that the vast majority of children at risk of maltreatment are in families living in or close to poverty (2010, p. 32). Similarly, children from Indigenous or ethnic minority backgrounds are also over-represented statistically in these services (p. 38). As an alternative either to systems that focus on risk assessment and crisis intervention or to those in which community organisations are left to undertake 'preventive' functions, Conley advocates a developmental approach in which the promotion of child well-being is linked to the well-being of the whole family. This requires connections to be made between poverty alleviation strategies, together with early childhood development programmes, family support and wider community involvement. Underlying this approach is the principle of child rights – for example as set out in the UN's *Convention on the Rights of the Child* (UN, 1989). This brings together macro-level interventions and micro-level practices. It also supports the goal of preserving family and community relationships. However, as Conley also notes, in the 'developed' countries the prevailing approach to child maltreatment issues is that of 'rescuing' children from individual situations of harm.

Given the conceptual arguments questioning the relevance of social development for social work in 'developed' countries and broad historical evidence suggesting that other approaches are dominant, there appear to be limitations to the way in which social development might be considered outside the context of 'developing countries'. So, to look further at whether there is any way in which the approach should be thought of as part of the range of social work practices in 'developed' countries, it is necessary to examine specific attempts to undertake social development in global Northern social work to explore whether a viable connection can be created.

Social development in rural communities

In Chapters 2 and 3, examples have already been given of social development in social work, in community work in an inner city and in the use of assets-based programmes to assist families with low incomes. A further example can be seen in rural social work, which, although not proportionately a large sector of the profession in global Northern countries, is a vital aspect, in no country more so than that of the present author, Australia.

Pawar and Torres (2011) describe a project in which social workers from the federal social security agency Centrelink engaged in community practice in a farming region of rural New South Wales (Cootamundra Shire, in the Northern Riverina region). That one of the social workers (Torres) had trained and worked as a social worker in El Salvador before migrating to Australia meant that he drew on a global Southern understanding of the potential in this approach, which is explicitly generalist. Indeed, Pawar and Torres (2011, p. 259) note that it 'integrates casework, group work and community organisation'. Moreover, it also explicitly uses the Freirian model of community education, which embraces participation, a capacity-building focus, flexibility, sustainability and an equal partnership between those who are involved (p. 256). That is quite specifically it is focused on the ideas, hopes, relationships and actions of people in their own context. Although it involves those from outside, the role of external actors is as a catalyst, working alongside local people without being authoritarian (p. 254). In fact, in this situation, Pawar and Torres note that two of the Centrelink social workers live in the area and so are community members themselves (pp. 259–60).

Cootamundra faces many of the issues common to rural areas in the global North, especially those that are primarily agricultural – increasing median age, climate change (in this case severe drought), economic decline and reduced levels of public infrastructure (cf. Alston, 2007, 2013). In an initial consultation, however, contradictory evidence was provided, such as of a lack of employment opportunities and at the same time difficulties for farms and small businesses in being able to hire workers (Pawar & Torres, 2011, pp. 262–3). This in turn generated concerns about available services, such as further education opportunities (i.e. post–high school), a declining sense of social capital in the form of networks of relationships between different parts of the community and increasing disparities of advantage and disadvantage. In response, the social workers brought together members of the community with other stakeholders, including business, government services (the local council, education, social services, police) and non-government bodies (including churches, youth groups and local community service groups).

This process of dialogue generated a specific project with a goal of 'capacity-building through education, training, employment and social protection', with particular emphasis on opportunities for young people and older people (both groups that were seen as relatively disadvantaged in the community) (Pawar & Torres, 2011, p. 264). This took the concrete form of a 'community café', through which young people in particular were provided with a vocational training programme, various existing community programmes were able to work together, voluntary work became available, especially in a community garden, and the whole community benefited from being able to use the café (in particular older people, for whom it became a meeting place).

The Cootamundra Community Café lasted two years and then encountered a crisis. Because its management had been sponsored by the Community Council, when that collapsed because of allegations about poor management necessary core funding for the café was lost. Despite agreement between the stakeholders that the project had succeeded in delivering many of its objectives, it appeared that each expected others to take the responsibility. As Pawar and Torres note (2011, p. 266), power and resources are not equally distributed between the different sectors, with business and government being advantaged. Although they do not state this, their discussion supports the conclusion that while business expected government agencies to step in, those agencies expected the community itself (including business) to provide the ongoing material support that was necessary (given that a not-for-profit model had been adopted, at least partly to satisfy business interests that this was not creating government-funded competition). At the time of their analysis, Pawar and Torres report that community groups and some smaller government agencies were discussing ways of restarting the project.

This project is small and, as Gray and Crofts (2008) suggest, it is located at the margins of professional social work practice in Australia. However, it points to several ways of considering social development in social work in the global North, especially as this is seen in rural and regional areas. Elsewhere in Australia, Mendes and Binns (2013) describe how neither a community development nor social development perspective is valued in most social work. Again, they note that many social workers tend to equate social work specifically with micro practices and community development with macro practices, although Mendes (2007) clearly locates the two as necessary to each other. Pugh and Cheers (2010) go further, asserting that social work in rural communities of necessity has to be developmental and generalist. However, Slovak et al. (2011) and Mendes and Binns (2013) are agreed that rural practice is largely absent from social work research and scholarship. Explanations for this include the urban location of most social work academic schools, with all the problems both of understanding the need to include rural practice in research and of access (Slovak et al., 2011, p. 436) and more generally the tendency to focus on micro practices in global Northern social work education (Mendes & Binns, 2013, p. 608).

Certainly, the social development character of rural social work in the global North can be seen in models discussed by Chipeniuk (2008), from Canada, and

Parrish *et al.* (2013), from the USA. Chipeniuk focuses on the recent phenomenon in the global North of older people migrating to rural areas in order to take
advantage of the non-urban lifestyle. This is technically known as 'amenity migration' (in Australia it is known as 'sea-change' or 'tree-change', according to how
close to the ocean or 'the bush' the community of settlement is located). Although
some people migrate in this way to employment, many do so to access leisure and
other non-economic activities. Chipeniuk (2008) describes how a participatory
community-based planning model was introduced in an area of British Columbia,
in order to make and evaluate planning decisions regarding infrastructural development, including housing and tourism (e.g. resorts and changes to wilderness
access). The outcome was that a high level of participation occurred and participants reached agreement more easily than might have been anticipated, given their
different backgrounds and interests (long-term residents, amenity migrants, indigenous people) (2008, p. 231). Indeed, Chipeniuk also notes that First Nations concerns were able to be integrated within this process, to the satisfaction of all sections
of the community (pp. 232–3).

Parrish *et al.* (2013) explore a project to enable integration of publicly and privately funded social services at the community level. This project was intended to
improve access to opportunities and services in a relatively poor and disadvantaged,
predominantly non-English-speaking rural community in California. As with other
projects discussed earlier, it was grounded on community development principles
of empowerment, participatory ('resident driven') and local focus (Parrish *et al.*,
2013, p. 356). It used a technique of 'self-study' as a vehicle for conducting a community survey, which combined qualitative research methods with a high level of
participant control in the process. One distinction of this project as against those
examined earlier is that the 'local participants' were actually the service providers
at the local level and not the members of the wider community. So, in this sense,
the extent to which it embodied community development principles is that it was
looking for these in the practices of service providers. Therefore as a study it relied
on the self-reports of the agencies about their practice in using these principles in
their work.

In the light of cautionary statements about the lack of attention to rural social
development in social work scholarship (Slovak *et al.*, 2011; Mendes & Binns, 2013),
Gray and Crofts's (2008) scepticism about the place of social development in global
Northern social work may well be substantiated. It is certainly the case that in these
countries the institutionalised social welfare regimes and the professionalisation
of social work (which some claim to be a goal of social development; cf. Elliott,
1993), along with higher levels of task specialisation between professions, often
appear to render concerns about social development obsolete. Yet, in these brief
reviews of examples of rural social work, it can be seen that social development is
not irrelevant in such countries, even if it is less central than therapeutic or case
management activities. One reason for this may be seen in the division between
urban and rural, in which the latter are often disadvantaged in terms of access to
social resources, including health and social welfare services. This is especially so in

countries such as Australian and Canada, where the divide is more accurately seen as one of metropolitan-rural, given the majority of population in these countries reside in a few very large cities that are a long way apart from each other. Yet at the same time, as demonstrated by the case study of 'Irene' in Chapter 2, the use of a social developmental approach within generalist social work practice may have something to contribute even in the centre of a major conurbation. For this reason, it is also possible to see Gray and Crofts's (2008) scepticism as arising from the disagreements within social work about its nature and purpose, combined with the barriers to a social developmental approach that stem from the global political and economic context of the early twenty-first century.

Indigenous and First Nations people in the global North

Several of the countries of the global North are founded on the invasion and settlement of the land through European colonisation (Bennett, 2013). Notably, Australia, Canada, New Zealand and the USA are settler societies in this sense. Other countries, such as Finland, Greenland, Norway and Sweden, contain regions where there are Indigenous people (Karlsson, 2012; Nicolai & Sauss, 2013), while across Europe there is a widely dispersed Romany minority (also known as Gypsies or Travellers) (Cemlyn, 2008a). In some cases, after long periods of loss of land, of way of life or both, rights have mostly been restored and on indicators such as life expectancy some Indigenous peoples, such as the Sami of northern Sweden, are now achieving the same levels of development as the rest of the society (Karlsson, 2012). For those people for whom the dispossession of land has not been very much redressed the situation is quite different (Bennett, 2013). Notably in those parts of the (now) global North that were invaded and colonised by the British Empire (Australia, Canada, New Zealand and the USA) the Aboriginal, Indigenous or First Nations peoples have largely not gained to the same extent from the economic and social developments of the last century.

Using the human development index (HDI) criteria, the gaps between the gains achieved by Indigenous peoples and the gains achieved by those who are descended from the colonisers can be seen as stark (Bennett, 2013, p. 19). In summary, when compared to the 'settler' populations, Indigenous people have lower life expectancy and higher rates of ill health and of poverty, and are more likely to self-harm, to be incarcerated in the criminal justice system, to misuse drugs or to be involved in domestic violence. That this is broadly similar across all colonised countries, in which Indigenous cultures and traditions are different, indicates that these disparities do not come from intrinsic cultural factors, nor do they arise only from 'cultural clashes' (although cultural issues are part of the problem). Rather they are primarily the product of several centuries of policies and practices that have led to subordination and oppression (Trocmé et al., 2004; Weaver, 2004; Ban, 2005; Bennett, 2013). Put simply, the current social circumstances of many Indigenous peoples are the product of a denial of human rights and social justice over very long periods of time.

For these reasons, the creation of appropriate social work and broader social welfare provision for Indigenous people can be accomplished only through the process of 'decolonisation' (S. Green & Baldry, 2013). S. Green and Baldry state,

> Decolonising our hearts and our minds refers to the way we (Indigenous and non-Indigenous Australians) think and feel about each other, recognising that this has been determined and shaped by the Australia colonising project that has continued since invasion. [. . .] In order to decolonise we must first identify and articulate how this colonisation has occurred, how it continues to occur and how it has affected each one of us.
>
> *(p. 171)*

Without such a process social work will continue to be part of the problem for Indigenous people, as it will continue to practise in ways that perpetuate colonising assumptions (albeit, for many social workers, unintentionally).

This way of seeing the root causes of the frequent failure by social work to work effectively with Indigenous people points to two particular aspects that can be addressed. The first of these is the development of responses to the needs and rights of Indigenous people that are appropriate and relevant; the second is in the reconsideration of social work itself, in terms of theories and practices, not only in relation to Indigenous people as service users but in all aspects, including the increasing presence of Indigenous people *within* the profession as well as the impact of this process on non-Indigenous social workers.

Some of the ways that social work can take a more social developmental approach to working with Indigenous people have been discussed elsewhere in this book, with regard to economic and environmental approaches (Chapters 3 and 4). However, other areas of social work also have been the site of forming practices that incorporate Indigenous world views and traditions. A significant example of learning from Indigenous communities to create more effective practices is in the use of family-based and communal decision making for situations affecting the care of children, responses to young people in conflict with the community and the law, and also older people who require care and support (Mafile'o, 2004; Trocmé *et al.*, 2004; Weaver, 2004; Ban, 2005; Cheers *et al.*, 2006; Worrall, 2006; Holkup *et al.*, 2007).

These more collective ways of making decisions are based on a relational view of a person. Distinct from the tendency of modernist approaches to regard the person in isolation (biologically and psychologically), this is a view that constructs identity within the network of relationships. It is only in relation to others that a person's identity is formed and developed, and so it is only in relation to others that problems of living can be addressed. Using this world view, more communal responses have been developed in many areas of social work practice that are not widely associated with the idea of social development. These include family group conferencing in childcare and child protection (Trocmé *et al.*, 2004; Ban, 2005; Worrall, 2006), circle sentencing (Coates *et al.*, 2003; Androff, 2012) and family care conferencing in situations of elder abuse and neglect (Holkup *et al.*, 2007).

In each of these different areas, the central principle is that by bringing together members of families and communities that have a relationship with the person or people about whom there is primary concern, decisions take into account all aspects of the social context affecting the situation. In instances of offending behaviour, people who have suffered harm may also be involved (Coates *et al.*, 2003). In each type of communal decision making the importance of each person or group who are part of the situation being heard by others and being able to hear others' contributions is a key factor. In addition, in most situations it is these people who must also act to resolve the problem that has been identified, so for them to be part of the consideration of potential responses is vital culturally as well as being more effective. Such responses may include the provision of childcare by grandparents or other family members, reparation and reconciliation in situations of offending and shared care for vulnerable elders.

Also central to these practices is a refocusing of attention from blaming perpetrators to achieving the restoration of relationships. As against the modernist legal emphasis on individual guilt, the Indigenous approach seeks to restore harmony among family and community. Thus the main focus is on people taking responsibility as a constructive basis for finding solutions. In situations where harm has been done, for those who have caused the harm to feel shame is often seen as helpful because it forms part of the process of taking responsibility and can lead to a sense of healing, for perpetrators as well as victims. The difference between guilt and shame in this sense is that between seeing a person's character as flawed and regarding actions and the choices leading to them as harmful to the well-being of the society. Restorative outcomes cannot be achieved without acknowledgement of responsibility for mistakes; those outcomes aim to achieve the strengthening of family and community relationships rather than blame or punishment. This leads Androff (2012) to draw comparisons between such processes and the *Truth and Reconciliation Commission* in post-apartheid South Africa (cf. Patel, 2005). Although the origins of family and community conferencing predate that particular approach, this parallel highlights the social developmental nature of conferencing, or circle decision making, as a social work practice.

In the understanding of social development that is spelled out by Gray and Crofts (2008) the economic and material dimension is a central feature. So the restorative model of decision making in social work and social welfare described here could be regarded as part of institutional practice. However, because it changes the distribution of power and authority within decision-making processes and places the social worker within a network of community relationships rather than as an external actor, it contributes to a social developmental approach. In this sense it is part of social development in social work in the ways described by Elliott (1993) and Patel (2005).

Learning from Indigenous people contributes a great deal to rethinking social work more generally. Not only is this seen in the ways that the profession in 'developed' countries responds to Indigenous people, and recognises its own Indigenous members, but also it can be found in the wider impact of Indigenous ways of understanding the world in social work for all communities (which, in Australia, may be referred to as 'mainstreaming') (Walter et al., 2013). However, there is an inherent challenge in this process. While the shaping of relevant and appropriate practices out of Indigenous world views in 'developed' countries could possibly be compared with 'indigenisation' of social work in other parts of the world (e.g. see the discussion in Chapter 6), there is a crucial difference. In learning from Indigenous social work in 'developed' countries, the background of colonisation means that all social workers, especially those who are non-Indigenous, must guard against this being exploitative. For example circle sentencing has impacted in non-Indigenous communities (e.g. social work in the Scottish youth justice system), but in the settler countries if this happens it can represent 'taking from' rather than 'learning from', when in contrast the latter must start by asking critically about one's own ideas and actions.

So, where Indigenous lessons for social work enter the mainstream, it is necessary that their origins and character remain explicit. This has led several social workers to advocate that the dominant communities, those that derive their historical roots from Europe, also address their own identities, through engaging with the concept of 'Whiteness' (Young, 2008; Christie, 2010; Todd, 2011; Jeyasingham, 2012; Walter et al., 2013; Briskman, 2014). This is not simply a matter of culture, as both Christie (2010) and Todd (2011) make clear; it also requires mainstream social workers to recognise the implicit (and sometimes explicit) racism in much of the theory and practice that constitute the profession in 'developed' countries. For example in relation to Indigenous people, this can be seen in the way in which theory and practice readily construct Indigenous cultures and communities as the source of problems faced by children, youth, women and older people (Briskman, 2014). Unless this is explicitly acknowledged and addressed, the understanding of family and community that is embedded in theory and practice is modelled on European norms (which themselves tend also to have particular assumptions about class, sex and gender, sexuality, disability and age embedded).

This critical perspective leads Walter et al. to assert that 'Australian social work is white' (Walter et al., 2013, p. 230). Whiteness in this sense is the (usually) unseen set of assumptions about the world that is based on the experience of the ethnic majority of 'developed' countries. However, it is unseen and largely unknown to that majority. It can be manifested in such ideas that 'difference' is a property of the minority communities, which sometimes takes the form of regarding minority cultures as the source of problems faced by individuals and families. Even among progressive practitioners, such as those who wish to promote the human rights and social justice of ethnic minorities, there is a trap that when members of such communities question human rights as a 'western construct' the problem can be reduced to an issue of cultural clash (cf. Asad, 2000).

One example of the way in which Whiteness can operate is that Aboriginal Australian social workers can be expected to practise with Euro-Australian service users as if this were not cross-cultural but simply 'normal' practice (Walter et al., 2013, p. 240). The same issue is experienced in Canada, New Zealand and the USA. Ironically, the converse is also the case, that Indigenous social workers may be expected to provide services for their 'own' communities, with a parallel assumption that it is not appropriate for people from other backgrounds to work in their communities, especially those from the mainstream (Weaver, 2004). However, addressing Whiteness does not mean that non-Indigenous social workers should seek to avoid practice with Indigenous people, but that non-Indigenous people must take responsibility for being capable of working with diverse service users, in the same way that Indigenous social workers inevitably do. As the many contributors to this debate argue, this includes micro as well as macro practice, education and training and social work management. In this sense, as noted earlier, positive and respectful engagement with Indigenous practices and ways of knowing is developmental for social work and at the same time supports the social development approach in social work.

Social work with migrants and other ethnic minorities

Issues of social development practice with refugees and asylum seekers are discussed in Chapter 6. However, social work in 'developed' countries must also address the needs and rights of other ethnic minority groups, those who have migrated without having to seek asylum. Not all migrants are members of ethnic minorities; conversely not all members of ethnic minorities are migrants (although they may be the descendants of people who migrated). For the purpose of this discussion, attention will be focused on those migrant groups that are not part of the mainstream ethnic majority. For example I am a migrant, but as a white Australian (born in England) I am located in the ethnic majority. What is at issue here is the way in which a person's ethnic identity is constructed around difference between any particular ethnic origin and the ethnic majority of the country. Members of ethnic minorities may be more or less visibly or audibly identifiable, but in each situation there are degrees to which migrants who demonstrate ethnic 'difference' from any dominant group can be treated as (and feel) 'other'.

As well as the important distinction between ethnic minority migrants and Indigenous people concerning relationship to the land and other aspects of identity, or between ethnic minority migrants and refugees in terms of the experiences of arriving in the 'new' country, as minority groups all are subjected to the same processes of subordination, exclusion and oppression. Anti-racist social work and related concepts of anti-oppressive practice can assist social workers to engage with many of the challenges that working across cultural expectations can create (Dominelli, 2008). Here too, the issue of Whiteness and the willingness of social work to address this also have an impact.

Some aspects of these concepts require careful consideration. To use Australia as an example again, in the last 60 years there have been successive waves of migration of people from countries other than those of Northern Europe. Greek and Italian migrants in the 1950s and 1960s experienced racism and exclusion for several decades, but after the arrival of Vietnamese refugees, and then increasing numbers of migrants from other parts of Asia, followed by more recent refugees from Africa and West Asia, the early arriving communities are now largely part of the mainstream. Thus the experience of 'otherness' shifts over time and in relation to different 'others'.

Social development practice with ethnic minority migrants can be similar to that undertaken with refugees and asylum seekers. Access to language education, to the housing and education systems, employment training and opportunities and similar settlement provision may all be relevant. However, unlike refugee communities, it may also be that such services are not required because newcomers are joining wider family and community networks, perhaps with at least one family member who already has employment opportunities. Where social development practice may become necessary is when migrants experience discrimination and exclusion. Support in claiming human rights and social justice is relevant in this context, often through community-based projects or through services that provide support for migrants that parallels provision for refugees. This is illustrated in the following brief practice vignette (which is hypothetical, although based on practice experience).

> Adem and his family have migrated from Turkey to a Northern European country. Adem is a qualified electronics technician and has been granted a visa to work as he has been offered a job. Adem and his family have found a rented apartment close to other Turkish families, and his oldest child is attending school. However, after they moved into the apartment the landlord demanded an increase in rent. Under the housing laws he is not entitled to do so, but Adem felt intimidated, especially when the landlord made threats about 'people like you' and 'having Adem sent back to where he came from'. On the advice of co-workers and friends in the community, Adem sought assistance from a migrant support centre, where he was able to get support from a social worker. This centre also provides access to a lawyer and can assist migrants to use the law to enforce their rights, through the courts if necessary. The social worker negotiated with the landlord so that the threats were withdrawn, making it clear that Adem had support from the centre to go to court. Adem is now more confident that he will not be evicted, so he and his family are feeling more settled.

Such services for migrants exist in varying forms in many 'developed' countries. While they are not always able to prevent discrimination and oppression, they support migrants settling in a new country.

Ethnic minority communities that have settled for longer periods of time may continue to face similar problems. Over time ethnic-specific community services can develop, either providing general support to a particular community or creating ethnic-specific provision relating to particular needs, such as day care for children, disability support services, aged care services and so on. Decisions about such services and the processes for their establishment often involve social workers and other professionals, especially in situations where services have to be registered with a government agency. Ethnic-specific services create a dilemma. In one respect they are able to be part of the community by structuring and delivering services in ways that are appropriate for a given community; they may also be owned by and employ professionals and others from those communities. At the same time, they also run a risk of reinforcing divisions within the wider society. Newman *et al.* (2008) describe projects in Toronto in which various ethnic-specific organisations, including religious, social and health organisations, were seen to be more appropriate in helping Black Canadians from low socio-economic backgrounds in responding to issues of HIV prevalence in their community. They conclude that ethnic-specific services are vital (p. 838). Similarly, Radermacher *et al.* (2011) review ethnic-specific aged care provision in Victoria (Australia). However, although the Australian study shows that for some communities separate services are valued, they cannot survive in the wider health and social welfare field without support from government and larger non-government agencies. What Radermacher *et al.* (2011, p. 558) describe as the 'structural *status quo*' (the neo-liberal policy environment) makes small NGOs, as such agencies tend to be, vulnerable to withdrawal of government funding and other social supports. While Newman *et al.* do not address this point explicitly, the range of ethnic-specific services they discuss was also part of a wider network supported by government agencies and larger NGOs.

As forms of social development, ethnic-specific services remain marginal to the wider practice and policy field, despite the benefits they provide for those who prefer to use their services. At the same time they provide a bridge between the dominant ethnic community and minorities, and they bring together macro and micro practices in social work within a developmental framework. So this chapter will proceed to address the links between levels of practice as part of a social development approach to the wider society.

Social development and wider social welfare

Using varied practices in a developmental approach can be broadened to the overall social welfare field. Services that have been regarded by some advocates of social development as 'residual' or 'institutional' can also be reformed as 'developmental' under particular conditions. This includes not only active engagement with issues of economic and material need but also changing the way in which social workers (and other social welfare or human services professionals) relate with service users and others who are part of these systems and structures.

While some social work in 'developed' countries may be appropriately directed towards short-term, focused interventions that can be remedied, there are also other areas of need in which longer-term supportive work is more relevant. These include various types of disabilities, including physical disability, intellectual disability and certain forms of mental ill-health. Some childcare and family support work, likewise, should be considered as longer-term – for example when a child is placed in out-of-home care (including in many contexts where this is family-based care). Along with others, I have long argued that one of the challenges in the professionalisation of social work is not just that micro practice comes to predominate over macro concerns, but also that a 'curative' orientation comes to displace the importance of longer-term realities for many service users (Hugman, 1991, 2005).

In that analysis I argued that concerns with the goal of 'care' are regarded as weaker professionally, so that longer-term needs and responses are then 'ditched' to paraprofessionals and ancillary colleagues. The idea of 'care' is problematic, as for some it implies a patronising and domineering stance, often associated with the ancient charitable orientation of the 1800s that social work has sought to shed (compare Bauman, 1993, with Hugman, 1991). However, in the sense that was intended, the notion of care here refers to a relational stance (Hugman, 2005; cf. Sevenhuijsen, 1998).

One way in which this critique of professionalisation can be seen in practice is in the notions of social work as human rights advocacy, in which social workers act alongside service users in partnership. In the UK, Beresford and various colleagues have developed this concept in the field of mental health (Beresford, 2000; Postle & Beresford, 2007). Postle and Beresford describe this approach as 'supporting service users in initiatives such as self-help, campaigning and community action in ways that [. . .] offer a new interpretation of community or citizen-based social work' (2007, p. 144). Similarly, in relation to services for people with physical disabilities, Shakespeare (2006) argues that in professional and wider social responses to physical disability the concern with needs must be balanced with attention to rights. The role of social workers, among others, is to work with people with disabilities to support them in pursuing their rights in relation to life choices and also seeking to extend such rights. Policy and service management work therefore is a key part of this, providing that it is done in partnership with people with disabilities and not 'done for' (or even 'done to'). As with discussions of social work with Indigenous people noted earlier, there is also a tendency to debate these issues in ways that assume people with disabilities of whatever kind are service users and not that they may be (or may also be) professionals, such as social workers. A developmental perspective must reorient this way of conceptualising social work.

This tendency for professionalisation to construct short-term, curative micro practice as 'real' social work has contributed to the marginalisation of other practices, such as community work, policy, research or management (as discussed in Chapter 2). Even individually focused social work that enables people with disabilities to access material resources may be seen in this way (i.e. case management as properly understood, where 'case' refers to the package of services that a person accesses and not to the person her- or himself). Indeed, to reiterate the understanding of social work as concerned with the person in the environment, the central point here is that while social development in social work retains sight of the person, it also has a clear focus on the environment, in this area as 'disabling' (DePoy & Gilson, 2012).

Access to rights, self-control of service use and self-advocacy may require professional support and, if so, are very likely to be long-term. What makes this part of a social development approach is the active determination by service users of their own needs and the most appropriate ways in which they may be met. As DePoy and Gilson (2012) note, such practice is first and foremost human rights practice, so for that reason it necessitates engagement at the levels of policy, system and structure, as well as in the relationships between individual people with disabilities, their wider relational network and professionals, such as social workers. It is also concerned with social justice, in that the denial of human rights for people with disabilities leads to their exclusion and marginalisation. (The connections between human rights and social justice as values and principles for practice are discussed in depth in Chapter 9.)

There are parallels between the different forms of social development practice in social work in 'developed' countries that have been explored in this chapter – a human rights and social justice focus, changed relationships between service users and professionals, attention to the environment side of 'person in the environment' and addressing material and resource needs. These all connect social development in social work in 'developed' countries with practice elsewhere in the world. So at this stage in the discussion it will be helpful to examine the skills, knowledge and theory for this practice, and it is to this task that the next chapter turns.

8

SKILLS, KNOWLEDGE AND THEORY FOR SOCIAL DEVELOPMENT PRACTICE IN SOCIAL WORK

Understanding social development practice in social work

Many discussions of social development from a social work perspective clearly identify it as a 'macro-level' practice. For example Payne's (2014) categorisation of social work theories places macro practice and social development together in a single discussion. Moreover, Payne (p. 213) suggests that very few discussions of social development address practice as such, so that there is often an implicit assumption that it is, effectively, a form of community development (or, in some countries, 'community organising'). He identifies Midgley's (1995) examination of social development practice as one exception to this and places it alongside Burghardt's (2014) work on macro practice.

There are many points of agreement between the theorists of social development (e.g. Elliott, 1993; Midgley, 1995, 2014) and those of community development (e.g. S. Kenny, 2010; Ife, 2013). For example there is a common concern with issues such as environmental sustainability, the connection of social and cultural issues with the economy and politics, and specific groups, such as refugees and asylum seekers, Indigenous peoples and others who are marginalised. There is a shared understanding that social issues and problems arise from social structures, systems and processes, and so have to be dealt with in these terms. Thus, both are identified as 'macro' approaches.

Furthermore, both social development and community development often take a critical stance in relation to social work. This can vary from ambivalence (as recorded in Elliott, 1993, or Ife, 2013) to overt attack (summarised in S. Kenny, 2010). In summary, these views tend to characterise social work in terms of a focus on individual psychological pathology and the provision of remedial social (welfare) services. As a consequence, such approaches are regarded as at best offering small-scale gains for individuals and families and at worst as forms of residual assistance or social control that mask both the underlying causes of human need and the possible alternative structures and systems that could be created. Thus, from these perspectives social work is often equated with micro-level and some meso-level practices.

There is a parallel tendency among many social work theorists to make a binary distinction between macro and micro approaches. In some cases this takes the form of a rejection of macro perspectives as 'not real social work' (as discussed in Chapter 2). More usually it can be seen in assumptions that macro and micro approaches are distinct, which is often conveyed in the terminology of 'direct' and 'indirect' practice. This has the effect of characterising both social development and community development with policy work, research, campaigning and other actions that have as their focus structures, systems and processes. In other words, they are concerned with people only as members of collectivities or as part of generalities or categorisations, rather than as individuals and members of families or other such groups.

However, a brief consideration of discussions of macro practice in social work suggests that this binary distinction is overstated. While it is certainly the case that macro practice is not concerned with promoting change at the level of individual people and their families as the primary goal, both social development and community development require that practitioners are capable of working with people and of assisting others to achieve change in their own understanding and actions (Burghardt, 2014). What is different is that where such micro-level interactions are intended to help people to change how they act, they are understood in terms of personal development that complements and contributes to collective development. The crucial point here is that the characterisation of approaches such as social development and community development as 'indirect' is misleading, as they require engagement with people in their environment and not simply with abstract aggregations or generalisations.

More broadly, there are also important limits to the ways in which social development may be compared with community development. Indeed, to conflate the two is simply misleading. For example although there are shared aspects of attention to macro issues and the link between social and cultural issues and economic and political questions, social development can be seen as much broader in its focus than community development. That is, through attention to policy, planning and large-scale research social development may incorporate community development, but as an overall approach it also draws on other skills, knowledge and theory to combine practices at various levels.

Although there have been many other contributions to debates about social development practice, Midgley's (1995) statement is a pivotal point in the field, so the following examination of practice begins with this argument. It then proceeds to explore in more detail a range of ideas about relevant skills, knowledge and theory. This discussion is then drawn together in a consideration of specific reports of practice that illustrate the core ideas about social work action in the field.

Midgley's model of social development practice

The underlying ethos of Midgley's (1995) model is explicitly pluralist. That is it does not seek to propose one level of practice but rather to bring together individual, group, organisational, community and social dimensions. It also mixes the theoretical bases of the types of actions that are used in social development. Midgley differentiates between 'individualist', 'community' and 'governmental' approaches to practice. These each have different dimensions that draw on particular theoretical models of developmental issues, although as Midgley (1995, p. 103) notes they share a core orientation to economic and material aspects of human need. Indeed, as noted in Chapter 1, Midgley's starting point was that social development is concerned with the integration of social dimensions into economic development (Midgley, 1995, p. 25). Although more recently the term 'economic' has disappeared from the definition (Midgley, 2014, p. 13), it remains grounded in a material conception of the ways in which the improvement of human life can be achieved.

First, the approach of achieving social development through work with individuals is one that has had less attention than the others. These are identified as: fostering a culture of enterprise in order to promote social progress, promoting small-scale enterprises and enhancing individual capacities to promote human well-being. Examples of the practices that follow from these notions include assisting in the establishment of microfinance schemes, community-based businesses and other grass-roots enterprises (as discussed in Chapter 3). Other instances, to which Midgley points without discussing them in detail (2014, p. 34), include the promotion of social institutions and services in fields such as health, education and personal welfare.

The specific actions that form social development practice at the individual level include advocacy, empowerment, groupwork, organising and administration, capacity building and community education, and grass-roots research and planning. However, Midgley is sceptical about some early attempts to use counselling and other 'therapeutic' techniques in working with people living in poverty as a means to address their material needs or social exclusion (1995, p. 114).

At the community level, Midgley argues that social development involves community development, social action and the promotion of participation. The range of skills and knowledge on which such practices draw is in many ways quite similar to those identified in relation to individual-level intervention. The main difference, in this respect, is that while individual-level work seeks change in opportunities and the capacities of individuals, families and small groups, community-level intervention addresses change that affects neighbourhoods or whole towns, or within their institutions, such as schools and hospitals (Midgley, 1995, p. 119). In this sense, actions such as advocacy, empowerment, groupwork, organising and administration, capacity building and community education, and grass-roots research and planning are undertaken in a different way from an orientation to individual action. Concepts such as animation, conscientisation or mobilisation are also relevant within this focus.

Midgley is conscious of limitations also in the community-level approach. Communities are not unitary, and particular issues may or may not be addressed according to the way in which local dynamics operate. For this reason, the notion of participation is problematic. Consequently Midgley (1995, pp. 121–5) identifies gender as a major site of action, in a discussion that largely predates the impact of 'gender mainstreaming' on social development thinking. This discussion points to the way in which women's participation cannot be taken for granted because of the marginalisation of women in many societies, so that particular attention is required to ensure that this is addressed in itself as a social development issue. Despite the impact of 'gender mainstreaming' policies, it may be said that this continues to be an issue in many communities (Midgley, 2014, pp. 222–3). In addition, there are many other ways in which people are marginalised or excluded that present a challenge to the notion of participation.

The third level of practice in Midgley's model is that of 'governmental' approaches to development. Here the broad practice areas are seen as planning, policy and research. Indeed, at this level it could be said that Midgley's discussion becomes very general and is concerned not so much with practice as with the goals of policy. Indeed, most of the discussion is focused on economics, politics and the need for sustainability. Thus the roles of practitioners within this framework are inevitably defined by these broad terms. The particular area that is of relevance to most social workers is that of 'social welfare and basic needs' (Midgley, 1995, pp. 132–5), which includes education, health, housing and social security. In particular, the concept of basic needs links with the notion of the 'social protection floor' (discussed in Chapter 5), in that it seeks to provide some strength to the claim that inequality is harmful to overall developmental goals. It also incorporates civil and political rights (p. 133).

Midgley's (1995, 2014) approach to social development is consistently and explicitly connected to social work in many ways. In this he has sought to encourage social workers to engage with economic and other material aspects of human need. As part of this, he notes various criticisms of the tendency of social workers in the field to produce 'abstract and nebulous' definitions that are 'aspirational', 'heuristic' and 'hortatory' (1995, p. 31). Midgley partially defends social work in that he identifies a number of ways in which social development has been seen either as a form of macro practice, drawing on the same skills and knowledge, or as a field in which social workers bring a range of practices that overlap with other professions and disciplines (p. 32). However, although he provides a much more in-depth discussion of the practice areas, knowledge and goals for social work in social development, Midgley's own analysis is also reluctant to be detailed and prescriptive (see 2014, pp. 64–71). This raises the question of whether it is possible or appropriate to seek the degree of specificity that is often sought in discussions of professional skills and practices. This question can be examined by exploring further two of the types of practices that feature in Midgley's model – namely community development and macro social work practice.

Community development practice and social development

In order to examine the area of community development practice, I want to begin with Ife's recent discussion of the difficulties of addressing practices (Ife, 2013). Ife challenges the idea that it is necessary or possible to be specific about the practice skills that are required in community development. This argument is constructed in opposition to the notion of 'competencies', in which very detailed prescriptions about the actions of practitioners are specified. For Ife, such a view makes no sense because the nature of community development is fluid and contingent on context. He claims that to reduce community development to a series of technical tasks ignores what is most important – namely 'flexibility, commitment, passion, groundedness, a holistic perspective and a theoretical base' (Ife, 2013, p. 303). At the core of this argument is a concern also that a competency approach will tend to exclude people who do not have access to formal education or who do not fit a prescribed model defined by 'experts' (which is contrary to key values, such as 'participation'). Community development is 'much more than "just doing it"' (p. 304).

However, this argument also runs the risk of avoiding the question of what community development practitioners actually do and what someone employed in a community development role might be expected to be able to do. The forgoing list of the characteristics of a community development worker is value-based and hortatory in the way that is criticised by Midgley. So, in a non-prescriptive fashion Ife suggests four roles that each include within them a range of more specific tasks or practices that may in different ways contribute to community development work. These are: facilitational, educational, representational and technical (Ife, 2013, p. 307). The tasks that make up these roles are summarised in Table 8.1.

It is not my purpose to go through each of these aspects of practice in detail. Rather, I want to comment on the type and range of these skills and the knowledge that supports them. First, and perhaps most importantly, they are a combination of what might be termed 'direct' and 'indirect' practices. That is some concern the interaction of practitioners with the end users of their interventions. Moreover, these tend to rest on interpersonal capacities. Examples include interpersonal communication, advocacy, group facilitation, mediation and negotiation, networking, management and training. Such capacities run across the range of roles. Similarly, the knowledge-based capacities, such as research, computers, finance, resource finding and information, also cross over the role groups. In this understanding, Ife suggests that all of these role and skill areas might reasonably be anticipated, but that none is a universal requirement. It may also be that someone who is regarded by community members and others as a good practitioner is stronger in some and weaker in others.

Others who address community development (or community work, or community organising) practice point to similar expectations about the range of roles and skills that might be required (Popple, 2002; Netting *et al.*, 2004; S. Kenny, 2010). One element that is shared not only between the different discussions of community

TABLE 8.1 Roles and skills in community development work (after Ife, 2013, p. 307, adapted) (alphabetical order of elements – no hierarchy implied)

Roles	Skills
Educational	Confronting
	Consciousness-raising
	Informing
	Training
Facilitative	Consensus
	Group facilitation
	Mediation and negotiation
	Organising
	Personal communication
	Skills and resources
	Social animation and mobilisation
	Support
Representational	Advocacy
	Media
	Networking
	Public relations
	Resource finding
	Sharing knowledge and experience
Technical	Computers
	Financial control
	Management
	Presentation
	Research

practice but also between this overall approach and individualistic approaches is that of the capacity for interpersonal communication. However, an important difference between community practices and those that can be seen as clinical or therapeutic is that such communication is not regarded from the community perspective as a technique, as such, but rather as a capacity for clear thinking and expression, as well as the capacity to listen carefully to others.

The 'macro-practice' approach and generalist practice

The definition of social development, as discussed in Chapter 1, includes the following elements:

- planned social change;
- promotion of the well-being of the population as a whole;
- dynamic, multifaceted process.

(Midgley, 2014, p. 13)

This emphasises the large-scale focus that is usually regarded as requiring macro-practice approaches. Discussions of 'macro practice' in social work often tend to assume a distinction between 'macro' and 'micro' in relation to whether the practitioner focuses on intervention and change with individual people or groups, including families, or on collectivities or population categories. Thus, community work (or community development or community organising) is often regarded as macro practice, because it involves intervention in organisations, systems and structures, seeking change in those aspects of human life. It may be said that in relation to the orientation of social work to the 'person-in-environment' micro practice emphasises the person while macro practice emphasises the (social) environment, although both would normally be regarded as attending to the implications of the other side of the equation.

As a consequence of this emphasis the terms 'direct' and 'indirect' practice are also widely used (e.g. Allen-Meares & Garvin, 2000). These terms highlight the way in which the micro/macro distinction presupposes the former involves working directly with the human beings who benefit from social work and, in contrast, the latter affects those people indirectly, through changes in policy, systems, structures and so on. This can then lead to further assumptions that the practices and associated skills that are required differ in the same way and can be separated. One example of this is that discussions of direct practice and the associated micro skills do not frequently consider the actions of social workers in effecting organisational or structural change. Similarly, discussions of community development or structural practice do not often address micro-level skills and practices. So this suggests that skills, knowledge and theories for social development might draw on macro or indirect approaches in social work but not require any attention to those elements that are considered as micro or direct practices.

However, as seen ahead in concrete examples, there are many ways in which this binary distinction does not hold. If we consider some of the elements in Ife's model (see Table 8.1), for instance, the list of roles with implied skill requirements includes 'group facilitation', 'mediation and negotiation' and 'personal communication'. These same practices occur throughout discussions of micro or direct practice, not only because they are necessary aspects of that approach but also because, to put this at its simplest, they concern the skills of being able to communicate and relate with people either as individuals or as members of groups. Indeed, it is unlikely that a social worker in research or policy practice would not also be required to be able to exercise these capacities.

In recent analysis, the theme of connecting macro-level skills and knowledge with meso and micro levels is becoming more explicit in the contemporary literature on macro or indirect practice in social work (Weil, 2000; Netting *et al.*, 2004; Burghardt, 2014). While this is still a minority perspective, and largely seen in social work practice theory from the USA, it provides an opportunity to reconsider the way in which divisions of social work in terms of micro/macro and direct/indirect are helpful only in relation to considerations of the details of a specific practice or service. The extent to which these discussions argue for the integration of approaches differs, from those who see them as separate but linked

(Netting *et al.*, 2004), through those who regard them as a continuum (Poulin, 2005), to those who suggest that helping people to achieve change in themselves or their families, in their communities or in the policies and systems that affect their lives is a matter of considering what is required in any given situation (Weil, 2000; Burghardt, 2014).

The concept of 'generalist' social work practice is useful here to identify that way in which many areas of skill and knowledge can be seen as shared across different types of practices and services. Examples include the strengths perspective (which is discussed also in Chapter 2), collaboration and participation as a basis of practice, and critical reflection in practice, especially as this almost always involves working with disadvantaged and oppressed groups (Poulin, 2005; Franco *et al.*, 2007; Cox & Pawar, 2013; Burghardt, 2014). Generalism may refer either to a service, in which different social workers perform different roles in a multi-role team, or to a practitioner who combines different approaches in her or his practice according to the nature of the issues with which she or he is working. Burghardt (2014) in particular continually highlights the way in which critically reflective practice requires the integration of macro and micro, and of indirect and direct skills and knowledge. However, Burghardt recognises generalism in both an individual's practice and in agencies and in that sense also allows for a continuum of skills and knowledge.

In the social development field it is usually the case that practitioners are required to work across this range of practices, in various contexts. Many roles require social workers to be able to work with individuals and families as part of wider community development or policy-related projects (Franco *et al.*, 2007; Cox & Pawar, 2013). It is not that generalist practice includes therapeutic work, especially in social development roles, but rather that other types of individually focused interventions might be part of educative or training activities, for example. Flexibility is recognised as a quality of social development practice at all levels (Cox & Pawar, 2013; Burghardt, 2014), in which the capacity to work with individuals and groups is as important as working with administrative and political processes. This suggests that a generalist understanding of social work skills, knowledge and theory is a more constructive grounding than the binary divisions of macro/micro and indirect/direct practices.

Social work skills, knowledge and theory for social development practice

As shown in the preceding chapters, social work in social development practice covers a wide range of issues and situations. Moreover, these areas engage with economic, political, environmental, social and cultural dimensions of human life. For this reason Ife's (2014) reluctance to be overly prescriptive about skills and knowledge seems reasonable. Yet, as we have also noted, it is important to be able to identify what it is that social workers can be expected actually to do and the ideas that support their practice. As a way of resolving the difference between these points, examining instances of social work in social development can provide an inductive insight that avoids the pitfalls of abstractions or a technocratic approach. The three examples cited here are taken from published studies and systematic reflection. They cover different parts of the world and a range of issues, so they also illustrate the diversity of practice in the field.

Practice example 1: wartime and post-conflict development in the Balkans

Maglajlic (2011) provides a critical reflection on developmental social work in the Balkans (also see Ramon & Maglajlic, 2012). In this account Maglajlic (2011) describes a series of quite distinct projects. First, during the war, Maglajlic worked with children in refugee camps. In particular, she identifies a local organisation, *Suncokret*, as a positive example of practice. This organisation helped families in the camps to organise activities for children, including children from the local areas as well as those living in the camps. The roles of the social workers and volunteers, therefore, were in bringing people together and helping them to create community activities. On the basis of that, wider assistance was obtained by linking community members to social work and health agencies. Maglajlic identifies the key characteristics as local leadership and grassroots participatory action (2011, p. 109).

Second, immediately post-conflict, Maglajlic worked in a community-based mental health programme that was based on psychosocial principles, with a multidisciplinary staff team. Central to this was the creation of survivor-run mental health responses. This project succeeded in establishing a network of local provision and assisting the relevant governments in creation of more effective services. However, the project was funded by international donors, whose 'priorities' shifted suddenly and without adequate planning; 'exits were quick and ill prepared' (Maglajlic, 2011, p. 110).

Third, moving into the next 'developmental' period, Maglajlic coordinated an assessment of child welfare reform across South-East Europe. This contributed to the processes through which children's rights and wider social protection strategies were promoted, although Maglajlic notes (2011, p. 111) that because funding came from the World Bank MDG-based poverty reduction strategies were also implemented. However, by this time the World Bank had begun to recognise that participatory approaches produced more sustainable outcomes because they were owned by national and local stakeholders.

The practices that Maglajlic describes are varied, ranging from individual and family work with children and their parents, through the creation of services, to research and policy formation. In addition to the community development skills and roles discussed earlier, we can add planning (which is addressed in more depth ahead). Moreover, the different projects in which Maglajlic was involved required flexibility, not only in the roles she had in relation to each one but also in shifting across the various projects.

Maglajlic is also very critical of the actions and impact of international organisations. Her accounts detail ways in which they can so often be separate from the local contexts and 'impose' solutions through their provision of much-needed funds. Not only can this lead to actions that perpetuate dependency or impose culturally and socially inappropriate actions, but also sudden shifts in priorities, set by other countries, can thus be destructive of their own effects as well as undermining the building of capacity by local communities, professions and governments.

Practice example 2: family-based HIV prevention and the CHAMP programme

Franco *et al.* describe CHAMP, a collaborative community-based project that sought to create a family-based HIV prevention programme that would be effective both in Chicago and New York, and in South Africa and Trinidad (Franco *et al.*, 2007, pp. 316–7). The acronym CHAMP stands for Collaborative HIV-prevention and Adolescent Mental Health Project. It brought together social workers from the university school based at the Mount Sinai Medical Center with young people, parents and other community members, which included school staff and other professionals, to create and conduct HIV awareness and education action. This project had been running for ten years at the time of the published report (p. 317). The central feature of the programme was a collaborative approach to community education, in which planning and management were undertaken by representative community boards. The workshops through which community education was undertaken involved, variously, groups of young people aged 9 to 11, family members and other community members. The objectives included not only to provide knowledge and understanding of HIV and associated health issues, but also to support parents and others more widely in assisting their children and young people in the personal and psychosocial challenges of growing up in inner-city and other resource-disadvantaged areas.

Towards the end of the ten-year period, CHAMP was being transferred from being a university-supported project to becoming a community programme located in a community agency. As part of this process a collaborative study was undertaken of the New York project and of the collaborative nature of community-based development practice. Ten out of the 28 community members of the board contributed to a qualitative study – all ten were from ethnic minority communities, characterised by low income levels and urban disadvantage. The key practice issues that were identified are:

1   learning about a community, including cultural issues, is essential before professionals come into a community;
2   trust must be earned (it takes time and involves getting to know people, as well as clear communication in plain language);
3   time must be spent in the community;
4   community members must have full participation;
5   recognition of community and individual strengths is necessary;

6   the community must be involved from the start;
7   compassion and understanding are vital with members of disadvantaged communities;
8   turn up on time (and keep appointments);
9   people who need assistance must also be involved actively in the process;
10 ensure that other agencies that have to be involved also work collaboratively.

(Franco et al., 2007, pp. 319–21)

These dimensions of effective and respectful practice closely match many of the theoretical discussions in social development, community work and other professional analyses (Popple, 2002; S. Kenny, 2010; Ife, 2013). The common feature across all these points is that while professionals have knowledge and expertise from which the community members can benefit, social development practice should be done *with* and not *to* a community. Indeed, although it may seem tautological, it has to be made explicit that the goals of empowerment and capacity building cannot be achieved if professionals do things for or to people.

From this description, again it can be seen that social development practice requires a range of skills and knowledge on the part of social workers. Moreover, it demands that they are capable of working flexibly. Roles such as planning, organisation, research and advocacy are combined with groupwork and interpersonal communication.

Ironically, as at the point of this analysis by the CHAMP board members of the requirements for effective social development practice the project was about to be transferred to a community agency as a programme, the tenth dimension ('ensure that other agencies who have to be involved also work collaboratively') was being seen as a major challenge (Franco *et al.*, 2007, pp. 327–8). The new host agency was not seen by board members as collaborative in this way, and an alternative of creating its own new NGO was also being considered.

Practice example 3: Kliptown Youth Program

The third example is somewhat different, as it is taken from a project designed to use a research approach as a tool for developing a community-based youth programme in the township of Kliptown, in Soweto, South Africa, which is highly disadvantaged socially as well as materially (Nel & Pretorius, 2012, p. 45). In 2007 Kliptown Youth Program (KYP) was formed to provide after-school education and cultural activities, including performing arts, a food programme, tutoring and sport, as well as providing laptop computers. This programme was supported by community outreach activities, marketing and fundraising. Outcomes include increased attendance rates in formal schooling and increased pass rates among those young people who stay. Moreover, their performing arts programme has given young people the opportunity to travel and to present their culture to audiences in China and France.

Although the management committee was made up of community members, they recognised that this was necessary but not sufficient, in that they also considered they needed to develop a more professional approach to become more effective (Nel & Pretorius, 2012, p. 46). The committee decided to use a research approach, appreciative inquiry (AI), in order to accomplish this goal. It was important for them that the approach is participatory, people-centred and incremental, involving mutuality, dialogue and collective action. AI originates in organisational development work and also emphasises the strengths and assets of an organisation; in addition, it is relationship-focused (Nel & Pretorius, 2012, p. 40). Although they do not address the point explicitly, AI should be regarded as a form of action research in that it operates through a successive series of actions and reflections in which participants build up and test their developing understanding of the issue or situation that is being studied, while creating new ways of acting (Wadsworth, 2011).

The challenges that the committee faced included lack of resources for some of the youth activities, but they were also very concerned about their own skills and capacities to manage the organisation effectively. Through the AI research process, the committee members analysed the current situation, rethought their goals for the programme, planned and designed new ways of working and then began to deliver the new projects. For the committee members, Nel and Pretorius record that there were gains in skill, and knowledge, as well as wider capacities in leadership through improved 'motivation, self-worth, creativity and positive energy' (2012, p. 52). They also observed improved cohesion and functioning in the day-to-day work of the committee. At the time of writing, Nel and Pretorius were not able to report on the substantive impact of these changes on the programmes for the young people, although this remains the key factor in whether the process was to be considered successful (2012, p. 53).

The role of the social workers from outside the community in this process was that of facilitation. Although the direction of the process came from the committee, the external facilitators possessed skills and knowledge. So in order for their practice to embody the values and objectives of both the programme and the methodology being used, it was necessary for them to work from the 'consciousness-raising' approach that is widely used in community education (Nel & Pretorius, 2012, p. 49). This emphasises the subjectivity of participants, utilising the strengths-based notion that people are expert in their own lives and contexts, even when seeking assistance to change.

As with the other two examples provided here, KYP represents one particular approach to social development practice. As with the others, too, it combines elements of micro and meso practice with an overall macro orientation, especially as this explains the involvement of the social workers who acted as facilitators. Thus, although their practice can be described as 'capacity building', it is also 'bottom up' both in theory and in action.

The 'problem' of participation

A shared feature of the practice examples that have been presented here is an emphasis on the importance of participation as a principle in social development.

Whether described as such by social workers (as in Maglajlic, 2011) or by community members (as in Franco *et al.*, 2007, and Nel & Pretorius, 2012), the active participation of people from within the society, community or locality who benefit from social development interventions is widely regarded as an important positive factor (cf. Popple, 2002; S. Kenny, 2010; Ife, 2013). From a social work perspective, at least, the capacity to work in such a way that all those who are involved in a project can contribute as fully as they wish is an important skill.

Yet, as Payne (2014, p. 227) notes, some critics have questioned whether participation represents a 'tyranny'. For example Cleaver (2001) argues that the idea of participation is ill defined and carries many problems that are insufficiently addressed; five of these are discussed here. First, it often ignores social divisions within communities, such as those based on gender, ethnicity, (dis)ability, sexuality and age. Thus, there may be people whose voices are silenced by established social relationships. Second, in practice it often appears to assume that organisations or agencies are at worst neutral or, better, either already are or are capable of being made participatory. This may or may not be the case – it cannot be assumed. Third, it quite simply masks the possible extent to which, all other things being equal, community members may reasonably have different and even conflicting interests. Fourth, it can focus on process to the exclusion of outcomes or material limitations, such as resources. If nothing changes, then it can be asked whether participation was futile. Fifth, it also can be used to undermine professionals in areas where their knowledge is more accurate or extensive than that of community members. Community members have different levels of understanding, and not all may be equally valid in relation to the objectives of any one particular programme or project.

In the practice examples summarised earlier it is clear that Cleaver's concerns can be answered, at least in some if not all situations. Of course, it is not possible to redress established inequalities in social relationships in communities simply by introducing a simplistic process of participation. However, social work skills and theory acknowledge this and emphasise ways of opening up possibilities for participation in how groups or meetings are conducted or agencies are managed (Larsen *et al.*, 2014). The evidence from the earlier examples is that not only do diverse members of communities find ways of being involved but also such changes take time. Similarly, where the interaction is perceived as non-threatening community members often value the knowledge and experience of professionals. To use examples of 'bad' practice to argue that 'good' practice principles are unrealistic or constraining, which is one way Cleaver's (2001) evidence can be read, is overstretching the point, to say the least.

Moreover, although arguments for participation as a key practice principle in social development are at times hortatory, they cannot simply be questioned as inappropriately vague sweeping moral claims. Morality, usually addressed in professional debates as values and ethics, is vital to any conception of good practice, including the principle of participation (Hugman & Bartolomei, 2014). However, the point here is that the arguments for participation in these examples are also both technical and political as well as ethical. The lack of participation and time spent making working relationships with local people is argued by Maglajlic as a serious weakness in some development practice of international organisations. Among other things, it resulted in claims being made for the success of a project that were not recognisable to those who were involved in the affected communities (Maglajlic, 2011, p. 108). Similarly, the demands for participation discussed in the report of CHAMP (Franco *et al.*, 2007) were expressed by the community members themselves. Likewise, the committee members of KYP sought to improve their own skills and knowledge, not simply to rely on external expertise – as adult learners this could be achieved only in a participative process (Nel & Pretorius, 2012). In each case these examples represent attempts by members of communities to reject the imposition of limited and inappropriate external controls being exerted over their lives. Seeking to open the possibility of participation as widely as possible is a challenge facing social work in social development, to be sure. Nevertheless, that it is hard to achieve does not invalidate the attempt. In this sense, Cleaver's criticisms may be more usefully read as cautions about the pitfalls involved in participatory practice. They are the exemplars of 'bad' practice against which ideas of what may be considered 'good' practice can be compared.

Planning as social development practice: a comment

An area of practice in social development that has not yet been addressed is that of planning. Midgley (1995, 2014) refers to planning as a rational activity through which resources are allocated in order to achieve social development objectives. In this sense, planning is the operationalising of policy. This view of planning sees it as fact-based, indeed often as statistical, and usually conducted by professionals. However, Midgley is largely referring to governmental planning. He acknowledges that when conducted by community organisations or in social welfare services it is unlikely to involve specialists of this kind, but rather is undertaken by community development workers, including social workers, who will normally seek to involve community members in formulating plans (Midgley, 2014, p. 199). Moreover, while social workers may be involved in all levels of social development planning, including in national and regional governments, the profession tends to be identified explicitly with programmes and projects, especially in the use of job titles (Claiborne, 2004).

Critical perspectives in community development regard planning of this kind, especially at the governmental level, as 'top-down'. This is effectively the same debate as that concerning participation. To that, it adds the claim that only goals and objectives defined by community members can be considered legitimate. Again, this can be a moral and political claim, although to it may be added the view that unless developmental objectives are determined by those whom they affect they are likely to be unsustainable. Again, it may be reasonably observed that moral and political claims are also relevant – it would seem implausible, for example, to argue that a practice should be seen as good because it is technically effective if at the same time it is morally or politically unacceptable. In this sense, developmental goals are ultimately moral and political. If rapid economic growth, which would benefit many people, is to be achieved at the cost of destruction of rare natural habitat or the forced migration of a minority community, these must be recognised as moral and political choices, not as technical judgements (Roy, 1999). In a field in which the promotion of human rights and social justice are important guiding values (see Chapter 9), to reduce planning to technique without locating it in the wider purposes of social development is self-contradictory.

For all of these reasons, planning is appropriately regarded as a mid-level operational practice that requires a range of the skills and knowledge that have already been identified, and not as a distinct skill in itself.

Skills, knowledge and theory: issues for social work education

A further common point among advocates of social development is that for social work to incorporate social development as practice there must be shifts in the education provided for both new entrants to the profession and existing practitioners. Although the *Global Standards for Education and Training in Social Work* (IASSW/ IFSW, 2004) includes reference in various places to the dimensions of social development practice, it does not actually name any one skill or practice method. Thus programmes and registration mechanisms can fulfil these standards without necessarily engaging directly with social development practice. Thus, whether any programme includes social development depends on the local decisions made by that programme in response to local and national expectations.

In this way it can be seen that, where it occurs, the problem of the exclusion of social development is circular. The combined pressures of professionalisation and neo-liberal policy create particular demands for micro- and some aspects of meso-level knowledge and skills. Graduates then enter social work with an understanding of the profession that reflects this emphasis, and such a view is reinforced by their continuing experience, in the predominance of positions in remedial or institutional practice (Elliott, 1993). In turn, this process then reinforces the sense that these are the areas on which social work programmes ought to focus. As noted in Chapter 2, micro practices do not of themselves have to be remedial. That micro practices contribute to social development in social work has been an explicit element of this discussion. What is necessary for social development to become more widely recognised within the mainstream of social work is not only that macro practices are specifically addressed (although that is necessary) but also that a developmental focus is taken in learning about all areas of practice.

Gray and Crofts (2008, pp. 100–1) point to another issue for the inclusion of social development in social work education, that an emphasis on critical social theory can lead to a disengagement with practices that are dismissed as 'reformist'. In contrast, Gray and Crofts argue for a critical but reflective engagement with the 'local sites of the possible' (p. 101). From this perspective, being able to assist students to gain skills and knowledge in 'how to' engage in action to assist people in addressing the problems and issues in their social environment is the core of professional education. Thus the social development curriculum must include the necessary elements for practitioners to learn how to analyse, understand and act, as well as a capacity to think ethically, so that they can 'boldly and creatively engage productively in the fray' (p. 101). This concerns not only education for the roles described by Ife (2014) and discussed earlier, as many of these are usually addressed in curricula designed around micro and meso perspectives, but also being able to integrate them in a social development framework.

Two examples of this approach to professional education are described in studies of practice learning. The first concerns the field education project in Yunnan Province, China, that is discussed in Chapter 6 (Ku *et al.*, 2005). To recap, this project in itself was part of the advancement of social work in China and took the form of 'capacity building' in a rural area. Underlying this approach is a concept of 'triple capacity building', in which the student practitioner is a learner, whose own capacity is extended through interaction with members of the community, who are assisted to realise their own strengths, and from this the educator also learns and gains new capacities (Ku *et al.*, 2005, p. 217). This project took an action research approach, similar to that in KYP in South Africa (Nel & Pretorius, 2012; see earlier), working directly with community members to identify and respond to their own sense of crucial issues. Through this an oral history of the village was produced that helped the community members to gain an increased sense of their own knowledge and experience. In turn, this process led to the identification of some concrete needs that the field education project was able to assist with, including the generation of methane gas (for power), adult education, income-generation schemes and a community service centre to provide opportunities for various groups, such as women, young people and older people (p. 228). Following the first project, members of the team assisted in obtaining funding and continued to work with the community members to implement some of these ideas. Thus the project not only enabled the community to achieve developmental goals but also was in itself the site of skill learning, enabling students and teachers to gain new ways of working that included participatory action alongside communication, planning, advocacy and other relevant practices.

An example from a global Northern context is provided by Maidment and Brook (2014) in their analysis of a group and community work field education placement in Christchurch, New Zealand. The city was severely affected by earthquakes in 2010 and 2011, with large areas destroyed. This placement consisted of four project groups, the city itself and in nearby towns; one was national. The content of these projects varied according to local need and included integrating a national basketball project at the local level, community café, food bank, budgeting support, personal counselling and community surveys (including one of housing needs and another of issues in a rural region). The national project was to work with the Aotearoa New Zealand Association of Social Workers (ANZASW) to examine the engagement of students and younger practitioners with the profession (Maidment & Brook, 2014, p. 80). Maidment and Brook conclude that by the end of the placement these students had been able to make 'a significant contribution to rebuilding the earthquake-devastated city of Christchurch and surrounding districts' (p. 83). That is they had learned about social development practice by undertaking social development work in their own broad community.

In both these cases there is a strong focus on students learning 'how to' think and act in a social development framework. It is, perhaps, significant that both examples concern field education projects, in which the students learned actively, although drawing on the skill and theory development of the taught programmes. At the same time, in both instances gaining the capacity to critique existing social systems is brought together with the core values of human rights and social justice, approached through practical skill development. Although only two examples of such educational practice, these instances suggest that assisting students and practitioners to gain an understanding of a social development approach can be achieved in different social contexts. Moreover, they show that practice learning in such situations can, indeed should, be generalist.

As Patel (2005), Osei-Hwedie *et al.* (2006), Mupedziswa (2008) and Lombard and Wairire (2010) all note, in the global South models of social work education have already begun to address this goal, in some programmes over at least two decades ago, even though further progress may be necessary (Hochfeld, 2010). What is required is that the dominant global Northern constructions of social work engage more explicitly with decolonisation (e.g. see Razack, 2009) and seek, perhaps, to learn from those countries where social work continues to balance both sides of the 'person-in-environment' understanding of the distinctive core of the profession. In doing so it would be reclaiming an important dimension of its history. At the same time, it must also be recognised that social work curricula reflect the demands of practice in their own national contexts. Changes in social work curricula in South Africa contributed to the shift towards a more developmental model of social work (Patel, 2005; Hochfeld, 2010). Although there is no reason to expect that this necessarily would happen from similar curriculum changes elsewhere, to recognise the social developmental nature of much of social work, at all levels of practice, might offer some opportunity to support a more questioning stance of mainstream practice, without running the risk of simply standing on the 'moral high ground' against which Gray and Crofts (2008) warn. It would at least emphasise the role of professional education in social as well as personal development.

9

VALUES AND ETHICS IN SOCIAL DEVELOPMENT PRACTICE

Social work values and ethics

All professional practices embody values, including those that can be regarded as personal or as shared in the sense of being social or political. Although, as Banks notes (2012, p. 8), the term values can mean many things, in general it refers to those things that are regarded as important by people, whether individually or collectively. Thus values represent human goals and ambitions, describing those things that people consider are worth pursuing in life. At their broadest, values are descriptions of the good human life (Hugman, 2005).

Values can be of different types: moral and non-moral. Put simply, moral values concern what is good or right in human thought and action, such as 'honesty', 'loyalty', 'fairness', 'harmony', 'courage', 'commitment', 'respect' and so on. In contrast, non-moral values can be considered as conditions of human life, which may include 'health', 'education', 'beauty', 'utility' and so on. To complicate matters, a very few values may have elements of both. The prime example of this is the value of 'justice', which has both moral and non-moral aspects; in one sense it can refer to the way in which people conduct relationships or exercise judgement, while in another it concerns the workings of social institutions or systems, such as in courts of law.

Koehn (1994) argues that it is useful to make a distinction between moral and non-moral values in considering ethics within the professions. She suggests that the practical focus of the professions is on non-moral values, such as those of education, health, legal or procedural justice, social order and welfare. In this sense the good professional is the practitioner who uses her or his skills and knowledge appropriately in the pursuit of these goals. However, the good professional is the practitioner who focuses on skills and knowledge not for their own sake but for the benefit of service users. Indeed, for Koehn moral values provide the basis for practitioners to place service users at the centre of their attention. In Sercombe's words, professionals seek to serve, not simply to provide a service (2010, p. 10). In this understanding, moral values concern the way in which practitioners conduct themselves in the pursuit of the non-moral values that describe the goals of their profession. It is in this context that we talk about ethics, which is the explicit way in which people think about moral (as opposed to non-moral) values (Hinman, 2012, p. 5). (At least in the modern world the area of non-moral values often tends to be regarded as the domain of 'politics', although as will be discussed ahead, the separation of ethics and politics is not always clear-cut.)

Banks also observes that there is a distinction between personal and professional values (2012, p. 7). In any society individuals hold different sets of values, even if this may be in the subtle variations in the balance between certain life objectives, such as a situation in which loyalty and fairness cannot coexist in equal measure. When people work together in large numbers there is a potential for such value differences to be multiplied. Thus, although it is likely that all members of a profession will share the non-moral core of the profession in a broad sense, when it comes to more specific understandings about choices between specific aspects of these goals, or how these values are to be pursued, then the possibility of disagreement increases. It is this dynamic that explains the strong debates within a profession such as social work about macro, meso and micro objectives and practices (as discussed in other chapters).

In order to ensure that there is a common value base for a profession, formal statements are created, which are usually called 'codes of ethics' (Hugman, 2005; Banks, 2012). In many cases these documents not only address the shared moral values of the professions but also provide foundational descriptions of the non-moral values on which they are based. In the case of social work the most encompassing document of this kind is the international statement of ethical principles agreed between the International Federation of Social Workers (IFSW) and the International Association of Schools of Social Work (IASSW) (IFSW/IASSW, 2004). As these two organisations together include membership from more than 90 countries, this statement of ethical principles has widespread support globally. Consequently, the document is deliberately general in its approach and sets out core principles, with a great amount of discretion left for each country as to the ways in which these principles are applied in practice.

The core ideas set out in the IFSW/IASSW international statement of ethical principles are 'human rights and human dignity' and 'social justice'. It argues that both of these principles are necessary to understand the values of social work and that they are equally important. In other words, the moral values that the social work profession pursues are clearly set out in this document. It is important to note that these values are claimed in the context of the agreements reached in United Nations declarations, conventions and related instruments (IFSW/IASSW, 2004, Section 2). So although values such as human rights and social justice underpin the purposes and functions of social work, they are also recognised by the larger international community and by other professions (e.g. allied health, law, medicine, nursing and teaching) (Hugman, 2005). Thus, these values are not arbitrary but are contextualised in the societies and social institutions of which social work is a part.

Beyond setting out this value framework, the international statement of ethical principles for social work also provides a general indication of what these might mean for practice. However, as already noted, it does so in general terms in order to allow for the social and cultural differences between countries to be expressed in national codes of ethics and other similar documents. Nevertheless, it is expected that all members of the international organisations (national social work associations in the case of IFSW and schools of social work in the case of IASSW) will promote and adhere to the principles set out in the statement. So for the purposes of considering the ethics and values of social development in social work the concepts of human rights and dignity and of social justice are taken here as the core framework. Each will be considered in turn before going on to look in more depth at particular issues raised by the practice of social development.

Human rights, human dignity and social development

The notion of human rights derives from the ethical claim that each human being is of absolute and inalienable moral value. In other words, to be human requires that each person is shown respect for her or his dignity as a moral being. As Ife points out (2012, p. 27) there are positive and negative aspects to this concept. First, the positive sense means that there are things that each person should be able to enjoy, without which life cannot be considered to be fully human. These include health, access to the knowledge possessed by a society (education), determination for oneself of key life decisions, expression of culture and the practice (or not) of religion. These are rights that must be promoted if they are to be achieved. Second, the negative sense of rights can be understood as things of which people should not be deprived, such as freedom or a fair trial. These are rights that must be protected to ensure that they are achieved. Whether positive or negative, these various objectives are seen as rights because they are things to which everyone can make a claim on society and on all other people who are part of it. They are things to which each person has an entitlement, simply and without qualification on the grounds of being human.

A further distinction drawn by Wronka (1998) is that of the three 'generations' of rights. Wronka uses the idea of generations to express the sequential way in which particular types of rights have been developed over time. The first to emerge were civil and political rights. These include the right to participate in choosing a government (e.g. through elections based on a universal franchise), the right to defend oneself fairly in a court of law if accused of a crime or civil offence and the right to hold property. Then, more recently, economic, social and cultural rights became defined. These include rights to receive health care, to receive education and to benefit from access to other provisions that a nation has established, such as social protection. Since the adoption of the *Universal Declaration of Human Rights* in 1948 there have been several UN conventions on rights, regarding women (1979), children (1989), disabled people (2006) and Indigenous peoples (2007). The notion of the third generation concerns community and environmental rights. As Ife (2012) notes, among others, this is the area in which there has been relatively little progress in practice, with theory and advocacy still developing among practitioners.

Wronka's (1998) model of 'generations' not only describes the chronological order of the development of concepts of rights, but also points to the possibility that each set of rights has its own character. Two important issues follow from this. First, even among those who defend human rights strongly there may be disagreement about whether each set of rights is equally important. For example Cemlyn (2008b, p. 233) points to the way in which some activists in the field of disability have come to question economic, social and cultural rights as having provided the basis for professionals to exercise power over service users. Against this, Cemlyn summarises arguments that civil and political rights may also depend on economic and social rights, using as an example the ways in which the interactions of disabled people with professionals and organisations can be empowering or disempowering and so need to be grounded in a rights framework to limit the capacity of professionals to disempower disabled people. In turn, legal and political rights can support economic, social and cultural rights by strengthening the claims that disabled people have for tangible provision that enables equal access and participation in the wider society. Thus the concept of 'generations' has some heuristic value, but it does not adequately describe the more nuanced way in which human rights are sites of struggle and achievement in day-to-day life.

One of the most common debates about the concept of human rights is that it ignores the importance of the value of 'responsibility' in human relationships (Yip, 2004; Hugman, 2013, pp. 62–3). In other words, focusing on rights can have the effect of obscuring the way in which each person has obligations towards others, whether as individuals or as members of families, communities or the wider society. However, as it has developed in the twentieth century, when understood fully the concept of human rights is balanced with the notion of responsibility. For example in the *Universal Declaration of Human Rights* there is a very clear assertion of the duties that each person has to her or his community (UN, 1948, Article 29(a)). This statement is grounded in the view that without the performance of such duties by every person no one will be able to achieve the rights that are described throughout the *Declaration*. So, in other words, human rights can be achieved only if everyone in a society recognises and acts on their obligations to every other person in that society.

Various social workers, such as Wronka (1998), Briskman and Cemlyn (2005), Ife (2010), Reichert (2013) and Staub-Bernasconi (2013), have argued that human rights should form the basis for social work practice. The focus of their concern lies in the way that the human dignity of many people is compromised through abuses of their rights, whether by governments or by others such as non-government organisations. This can occur in the form of failures in the protection of negative rights and also in the promotion of positive rights; it can also take the form of overt abuses of such rights – for example in the implementation of policies that actually cause harm to people (individually or collectively) to whom a duty of protection or provision is owed, or of acts by individual practitioners that undermine the rights of specific service users.

Examples of human rights practice of this kind provided in these discussions include refugees and asylum seekers, Indigenous people and people with disabilities, with particular attention to issues in the more 'developed' countries of the global North, as discussed in several earlier chapters. In each instance these are groups within the wider society that face exclusion, discrimination and oppression, and although some professional practices challenge this state of affairs, others may contribute to it. For this reason, the practice implications of an ethical commitment to human rights are that social workers should be working to protect and promote rights that are denied to these and other groups. However, as Cemlyn (2008b, p. 234) argues, there is a risk that at the same time as debates about human rights have become more prominent in social work theory and in ethics the complexities have often been ignored. This can have the effect of obscuring the contested nature of human rights, both in terms of what should be considered a right and also of the ways in which rights can be protected and promoted. In particular, the tendency within a neo-liberal political environment is that rights are seen only as the legal properties of individuals, with little regard for economic, social, cultural, community or environmental rights.

In terms of social work practice it is easier to consider the second- and third- 'generation' human rights at the meso and macro levels. That is, such rights can be realised only in social or collective contexts, such as in organisations or communities. While the denial or abuse of rights can be experienced by individuals, protecting or promoting human rights requires engagement with organisations and institutions, policies and laws. Such practice usually takes the form of advocacy, administration and management, research, community work and social action that, as discussed in Chapter 2, tend to be regarded by some social workers as 'indirect' or even as outside mainstream social work. Thus, recognising human rights as a key principle again highlights questions about the scope of social work.

One of the greatest challenges to the emphasis on human rights as a core principle for social work comes from the accusation that it is culturally relative (Yip, 2004; Akimoto, 2007). These are not arguments in favour of exclusion, abuse or oppression, but rather that the language of human rights does not have the same meaning in all situations. The concepts detailed in the international ethics statement do not have same meaning in all cultural contexts, especially that of 'self-determination' (IFSW/IASSW, 2004, Section 4.1.1). In cultural contexts that emphasise the family or the community over the individual, the meaning of this idea is often highly problematic. However, it may also be that there are gaps between the discourse of human rights in theory and in practice. Indeed, that is another side of the point noted earlier that there can be tensions between the different 'generations' of human rights. Protecting an individual's civil rights can at times appear to be at odds with promoting the cultural or community rights of a minority group, for example (Banks et al., 2008; Hugman, 2008, 2013). In particular, it must be recognised that human rights language has been forged in the public arena, and when introduced into the private sphere not only does it indicate that something has already gone seriously wrong but also it is dissonant with the way in which many people regard normal interpersonal relationships, in global Northern as well as global Southern cultures. For example if members of families have to use human rights language to address interpersonal disputes, then clearly there are major problems within that family. However, not every world view can accommodate this way of thinking about personal relationships, and while in some cultural situations a human rights approach to such issues may be accepted as necessary, in others it simply cannot be thought of.

One attempt to find a way around this challenge of cultural relativity is offered by Nussbaum's approach to the idea of 'human capabilities' (Nussbaum, 2000, 2011). In summary, Nussbaum argues that what is at stake is not an abstract set of legalistic principles but rather those aspects of the social world that enable each person to live a human life. For Nussbaum the central question is '[w]hat are people actually able to do and to be?' (2000, p. 100). Thus, for Nussbaum, the goal of human rights, that people are able to live with dignity as human beings, can be approached in a variety of ways. Her notion of 'capabilities' concerns the intersection between personal capacity and the way in which the social world enables (or disables) people with regard to achieving their goals. This connects family, community, cultural, social and political circumstances – so the achievement of a dignified human life requires that people are able to act as members of their society. This approach is intended to allow that the detail of what constitutes a decent human life differs widely between cultures, while at the same time underpinning this there are certain shared aspects of being human. Such common factors include enjoying bodily health and bodily integrity (e.g. not being subject to domestic or community violence), being able to form valued social relationships, being able to enjoy senses, thought, emotions and practical reason and so on. Although Nussbaum provides a definitive list, which she has defended, she allows that this is open to review and revision (compare Nussbaum, 2000, with Nussbaum, 2011).

Although part of Nussbaum's purpose was to spell out what development practice should seek to achieve (beyond ever increasing GNI), she also argues that the capabilities approach enables us to go past the debate about human rights as culturally relative (Nussbaum, 2000, p. 100). To the extent that this is the case it provides the basis for social development practice in social work to operate from the value of human rights without getting stuck in conflict over cultural interpretations of either the general idea of rights or the particular rights that are claimed in a document such as the *Universal Declaration*. In Nussbaum's discussion she brings together many of the issues that are of concern to social development, including the various dimensions of economic, social, cultural, community and environmental rights. This suggest that for social workers in social development the value of human rights can be thought through in ways that are contextually relevant, even when they challenge prevailing cultural factors, such as the subordination of women. Indeed, as I have noted elsewhere (Hugman, 2008; cf. Banks et al., 2008), gender equality has become a norm in the global North only relatively recently in human history and even in that context is culturally contested, so that from a human rights perspective it requires continued protection and promotion. Social development affects all societies, as argued in Chapter 7, so these are issues that are relevant to so-called developed countries as well as those that are 'developing'. For this reason, debates that set the global South and North apart from each other and imply that the North has an unquestionably superior position with regard to the achievement of rights are, at the very least, overstated (cf. Asad, 2000).

Social justice and social development

Although social justice has long been held to be a core value in social work, like human rights it is highly contested. The international statement of ethical principles explains social justice in terms of: challenging negative discrimination; recognising and respecting diversity; equitable distribution of resources; challenging unjust policies and practices; and working in solidarity (towards social inclusion) (IFSW/ IASSW, 2004, Section 4.2). Much of the substantive focus of social development is clearly relevant to this value, such as ensuring access to adequate housing, clean water, adequate nutrition, employment, education, health and so on. Social structures and relationships are unjust when they deny such access. This *social* injustice occurs because of discrimination and exclusion on grounds of socio-economic class, sex and gender, sexuality, age, (dis)ability, 'race' and ethnicity, caste, religion and culture. While in many cases these areas of difference may intersect, each is sufficient in some circumstances to form the basis for discrimination, inequity and exclusion. At its core social justice concerns the distribution of goods that enable people to achieve a decent human life.

The most basic contested issue in social justice lies in whether it is desirable or feasible to seek literal equality or to pursue a more complex notion of 'fairness' (e.g. see Reisch, 2002; Solas, 2008). One of the most influential approaches to this question in the last 50 years has been that of Rawls (1972). Rawls began with the assumption that all human beings are morally equal and have an equal claim on society's natural resources. (This claim also underpins the value of human rights.) Yet, given the different preferences and needs of each person, how can resources be distributed fairly? To answer this question Rawls proposed that some inequalities could be considered just under very strict conditions. These are: (1) that any inequalities must produce a benefit for those who are least advantaged, and (2) that the life opportunities provided by a society must be equally open to everyone. Conversely, for example, arrangements to promote strict equality but that reduced benefits for those who are least advantaged would not be just.

This theory has prompted widespread discussion and generated critique from every other possible position (e.g. feminism, Marxism and neo-liberalism). In summary, such critiques are largely focused on the way in which Rawls's theory does not address a particular ground of social injustice (e.g. gender or socio-economic class) or is either too strong or too weak in its defence of personal freedom. Yet precisely because it is grounded in the principle that all people have the same moral standing, and hence an equal claim to the basic resources of a society, while at the same time seeking to ensure that all people are able to pursue their own goals to the maximum possible extent, this theory still has something to offer social development practice.

Sen (2009) seeks to extend some of Rawls's argument, in particular his attention to the complexity of fairness in balancing equality with difference. At the same time, Sen considers that Rawls's formalistic approach gives too much regard to the way in which people actually attend to others on grounds of moral equality. The areas of exclusion, discrimination and oppression are seen by many people as 'natural', even if it can be shown that they are social and cultural constructions. Thus, the social worker in social development who is running a project based on the objective of gender empowerment (e.g. increasing girls' participation in education, or providing microfinance for women) may face opposition and even overt hostility. The issue often is that people choose to oppose such changes because they are convinced that the proper order of the world is one of inequality (e.g. that boys should be prioritised in education and that women should be concerned with domestic matters and not business), rather than because they overtly choose to harm others.

Many areas of social development are quite specifically focused on challenging inequality and promoting social justice. At one level practitioners may be involved in this work because they have personal commitments to the values of equality and justice, such as the view that all people are morally equal. So, in this sense, attention to social groups who are excluded, disadvantaged, discriminated against or oppressed may not require any further ethical justification. However, it is also increasingly being recognised that social inequality creates the very problems with which social development is concerned in a material sense (Stiglitz, 2012). Midgley (2014, p. 47) notes that acceptance of the evidence for this now runs across much of the political and philosophical spectrum. Only the most individualistic or traditionalistic positions appear to hold that maintenance of social inequalities is in itself a good thing because it perpetuates (or even strengthens) particular hierarchies (e.g. those of class, caste, sex and religion). For Midgley (2014, pp. 48–9), the use of material arguments provides a more effective basis for guiding social development practice than moral claims (at least on their own). Examples he gives include the way in which poverty reduction, literacy promotion and maternal mortality improvement programmes have been shown to have a positive effect on more general, material social development outcomes. Each of these is a good in itself, but when aggregated can indicate broader levels of the improvement in human life. For example families and communities are better off as a whole, economically as well as socially, if fewer women and children die in the process of childbirth, as well as this being good for the individuals involved.

Midgley (2014, p. 49) also argues that it is for these reasons that the Millennium Development Goals (MDGs) appropriately focus on particular objectives (of which women's education is a prime example) and do so in quantifiable terms. In this argument he is effectively countering Correll's (2008) critique that the MDGs are thin and limited in their vision and scope (discussed in Chapters 3 and 5). These two positions represent different ways in which the value of social justice can be seen to apply to social development. Yet the heart of such an apparent disagreement is not a matter of values but the question of whether the detailed quantifiable scope of the MDGs enables practical steps to be taken towards greater social justice or reduces the aims of the global effort for social development and so impedes its pursuit.

Such a disagreement seems unhelpful, because practice requires that both an end goal and steps to achieve it can be specified. On the one side, Midgley is pointing to the ways in which such benefits support and add to each other, while noting that in order to achieve them specific goals must be set. However, he is not arguing that the objectives of women's empowerment through increased access to education, poverty reduction or improvements in maternal mortality are not good in themselves. On the other side, Correll's critique of the MDGs identifies the way in which setting quantifiable targets of this kind to create achievable goals then also serves to create unintended limits on practical efforts. He is not denying the importance of being able to establish and pursue steps to achieve progress towards the wider values of social justice. This, then, is an argument about strategy, practice and the detailed interpretation of values, and not about the core values themselves. The value of social justice is a clear basis for each argument.

Unlike the value of human rights, social justice is not often debated as a culturally specific construct within social work. This is a value that has a very long history in many cultural traditions, whether expressed in religious teaching, philosophy or politics (Reisch, 2002). Yet, as many ancient as well as modern debates show, in reality not everyone accepts the idea of equity or fairness as a desirable state in society; some people consider that inequality is not just natural but also desirable (presumably, especially when they are in an advantaged position relative to others). Thus, throughout human history it appears that explicit arguments for social justice have been made as part of religious, philosophical or political debate. For this reason, it is plausible to regard the role of social work in social development as requiring protection and promotion of this value as well as that of human rights, in both concrete instances and as a general position. Insofar as the non-moral values of social work include social well-being and this in turn is interconnected practically and theoretically with the moral value of social justice, then it follows ethically that social work ought to pursue social justice both as a means and as an end in seeking to promote social well-being. Understood in this way, it is not possible to have one without the other.

Community as a value of social development

Beyond the core values set out in the international statement of ethical principles for social work (IFSW/IASSW, 2004), in some cultural contexts there is a third area of values that is regarded as important. This area includes values drawn from the spiritual traditions of Indigenous peoples (Yellow Bird, 1999; Rainbow Spirit Elders, 2007), from African traditions (Mbiti, 1990; Graham, 2002) and from Confucian philosophy (K. Lai, 2006). Although the details of each of these perspectives are different, they have a broadly shared characteristic of regarding 'community' as a primary value. This has several aspects. First, in these cultures the underlying focus of ethics is not on the individual self but rather on community relationships. As K. Lai (2006) put it, in this sense the self can be seen only as interdependent and contextualised. Second, these value perspectives do not lend themselves so easily to being formalised and codified, as do the traditions that derive from the Judaic-Christian-Muslim family of religions or western (i.e. Greek, Roman and modern European) philosophy. Rather, the central place of relationships and context in Indigenous, African and Asian ethics makes such specificity meaningless. Third, at least for Indigenous and to some extent African values, people and community are not separated from land. This is often expressed in terms such as 'we do not own the land, the land owns us'. Thus people are tied in moral bonds through kinship and locality.

If there is one shared value that can be formulated from these various contexts it is that of 'harmony' (Graham, 2002; K. Lai, 2006, p. 157; Hinman, 2012, p. 67). Within this notion relationships and community form non-moral values, although as has been noted earlier moral and non-moral values may often be intertwined, so that it is not possible to achieve one without the other. So for the community to be sustained through appropriate relationships it is necessary for each person to seek harmony in her or his thoughts and actions. Another aspect that is shared by these traditions is that of respect shown to elders, where this concept refers more to people who are regarded as custodians of community wisdom rather than to people in terms of their chronological age (although there may often be a connection between these two factors). Graham also links this value to other African values, such as 'ma'at' (rightness in the world) and 'ubuntu' (identity achieved in community) (2002, pp. 81–3).

One of the difficulties of understanding the value of harmony in social work ethics is that it is often regarded from a global Northern perspective as accepting of subordination and so, often, of oppression. Given the dominance of the global North in the development and modern institutions of professional social work this has caused debate within the profession over a long period of time (Gray, 2005; also see Hugman, 2010). The tendency in the global Northern view has been that human rights and social justice are undermined by an emphasis on harmony, especially when those who are disadvantaged or oppressed are expected to take responsibility for its achievement by acquiescing to the power and authority of others (e.g. professionals). However, K. Lai (2006, p. 168) argues that even within Daoism, in which 'acquiescence' is a value, this does not mean 'giving in to injustice'. Rather, she asserts, it concerns the acceptance of simplicity and diversity; in contrast, Daoism, like Confucianism, accepts conflict as necessary in the face of oppression for the achievement of justice and of human development, precisely because oppression represents disharmony.

In 2014 the international social work organisations adopted a revised definition of social work in which 'social cohesion' now figures along with the other non-moral goods that are regarded as the objectives of the profession (i.e. 'social change and development', 'the empowerment and liberation of people' and 'address life challenges and enhance well-being') (IFSW/IASSW, 2014). While it is debatable if this is quite the same concept as that understood as 'harmony' in Indigenous, African or Asian perspectives, it was nevertheless an important compromise in seeking to be more responsive to different ethical voices. In the extensive accompanying commentary reference is made to 'constructive confrontation and change' as being necessary to achieve a balance between social cohesion, human rights and social justice. At the time of writing, this is yet to be integrated with the statement of ethical principles.

In addition to this way of understanding 'community' as part of the social work value frame of reference, social development practice also has come to emphasise community as both an objective and a means of achieving development goals. This often takes the form of attention to participation as both a means and an end (M. Green, 2002, p. 67). That is the direct involvement of members of communities who are the prime beneficiaries of social development is now conventionally regarded as good in itself or as a good to be achieved as an outcome, as well as being the right way in which social development practice should be conducted. However, M. Green argues, such participation is at risk of being another externally imposed technique, even of replicating existing hierarchies of oppression and exclusion (cf. the discussion of participation as a skill in Chapter 8). It can also, ironically, create an environment in which poor communities become held accountable for their own poverty (M. Green, 2002, p. 68). As a concept, the idea of participation can become disconnected in this way from the complexities of practice and reduced to an ideological label that is used to justify actions that actually exclude the voices of the beneficiaries of social development (McGee, 2002).

In an analysis of community development practice, Ife (2013) considers participation in these terms, both as a means and as an end. Without this aspect, he states, development is externally imposed and that is self-contradictory in relation to values. Ife (2013, p. 172) sets out a range of problems that must be overcome in achieving participation. First, participation is contrary to individualism that predominates under neo-liberalism. In a world in which people are encouraged to consider their own needs and wishes as primary, the requirements of co-operation in participatory development are less easy for people to appreciate. Second, it is often tokenistic. That is people can be given the opportunity to express their opinions or to undertake particular tasks, but the overall agenda continues to be controlled from outside the community. Third, it can be subverted in the form of co-optation, in which the process of participation is used to persuade community members to accept goals that are to the benefit of dominant or external groups.

To overcome these problems, Ife (2013, pp. 173–4) argues that participation must be grounded in a balance between rights and responsibilities. To achieve this, he proposes five elements of practice that are both effective and consistent with community and participatory values. These are: (1) community members recognise an issue as important; (2) they think that their participation will make a difference; (3) different forms of participation are possible; (4) participation is enabled and supported, in ways that do not co-opt (especially important in highly disadvantaged and excluded communities); and (5) the structures and processes of development are not alienating. Each of these elements is consistent with the skills discussed in Chapter 8, connecting them to concepts of community, participation and harmony in practice.

For all of these reasons, M. Green (2002, p. 70) questions Midgley's (1995) assumption of the central role of states in social development and criticises this as being 'top-down'. Like Midgley and Ife (see earlier), M. Green asserts that the state has responsibilities to support and enable participatory development in the form of creating sufficient infrastructure, such as transportation networks, health and education systems and so on. However, like Ife, M. Green is also sceptical about the way in which the power of states tends to buttress existing advantage and domination. However, Midgley's (2014) more recent discussion makes clear that while he continues to regard the state as having a major role in creating helpful environments for social development, he also considers that an over-reliance on states has led to some major problems (e.g. the damage caused through the imposition of neo-liberal market policies). In its place Midgley argues for a pragmatic approach that he calls 'institutional structuralism', which is mediated through 'managed pluralism' (2014, p. 212). Drawing on the theories of Bourdieu (1994) and Hearn (2012), Midgley argues that the state is a contested site of struggle, in which members of various sectors of society act, including community members, business, the professions, local and regional politicians, and religious and cultural leaders. That some of these actors have greater potential to control state agendas in their own interests (cf. Hearn, 2012) for Midgley demonstrates the importance of open democratic political structures for the achievement of social development. Evidence for a shift towards this view in the wider debates about development, he suggests, is supported by the widespread acceptance that inequality and exclusion negatively affect everyone in a society (Midgley, 2014, p. 216).

In the same way as the other core values of human rights and social justice, the contribution of community values, including harmony and participation, to social development must be seen as complex and contested. Although for some social workers, such as Ife (2012, 2013), community and participation are central to understanding human rights, for others these are necessary components of social justice (Reisch & Jani, 2012), while for others again they stand alone as expressions of global Southern thought against global Northern hegemony (Graham, 2002). Nevertheless, insofar as social development practice in social work draws on all of these ideas in different ways, it is vital to see community alongside human rights and social justice as a core social work value, with the ethical implication that good practice requires attention, including key aspects such as harmony and participation insofar as these are relevant in particular contexts.

Human rights, social justice and community participation working together

From a theoretical perspective, the way in which social work ethics claims the values of human rights and social justice as its foundations can tend to gloss over the divergent grounds of the two ideas. On the one side, the concept of human rights is derived from an understanding of the human person as being of absolute moral worth. This is the source of the argument for inalienable human dignity, which forms the underlying right from which all other rights derive. In these stark terms, because all human beings are of absolute moral value all people owe each other an absolute moral duty to uphold each other's dignity. Philosophically, this approach is called 'deontology' – that is the 'ethics of duty' (Hugman, 2005; Banks, 2012). On the other side, the concept of social justice is derived from an approach to ethics that focuses on the moral consequences of decisions and actions. At an extreme this idea can be reduced to arguments that ends justify means, but the more sophisticated and influential interpretation is known as 'utilitarianism', in which what is good is defined in terms of the greatest benefit for the greatest number of people (Hugman, 2005; Banks, 2012). In this approach, although all people are regarded as having equal moral worth, the outcomes that are achieved may be unequal. For example a person who is among the lesser number may receive lesser benefit compared to a person who is among the majority.

The moral and political context in which social work has professionalised is characterised by debates, struggles and accommodations between these two broad approaches. For example the form of parliamentary democracy that has developed in the global North is based on the utilitarian principle that every person has one vote and all votes are equal, with the government formed around the votes of the greatest number. At the same time, the idea of human rights serves as a limitation on the power of the majority in that it asserts the claim of each person to be treated with dignity.

In explicitly claiming both approaches as foundational to its ethics, social work sets itself the challenge of finding ways to balance the competing claims that follow. One answer to this is suggested by Baldry (2010), who argues that social justice seeks to ensure that access to human rights is distributed equitably. A similar notion is proposed by Lundy (2006), who states that it is necessary to argue for a robust concept of rights in relation to those things that people require in order to live a human life, as categorising them as 'needs' opens up the possibility that they can be denied. The human rights perspective emphasises that human beings require certain things in order to live a human life, so there is a shared duty of all to ensure that everyone can attain these things. Unjust social structures, systems and practices can prevent people from achieving human rights, and so in this sense human rights work is also pursuing social justice.

This pluralist position (Hugman, 2013) provides the ethical basis for social development practice to focus on those gains that both 'promote the well-being of the population as a whole' (Midgley, 2014, p. 13) and, when necessary, prioritise the protection and promotion of the human rights of those who are disadvantaged, excluded or oppressed. It is this complex balancing of human rights and social justice that is characteristic of ethical pluralism (Hinman, 2012) that defines social work's commitments (Hugman, 2013). Indeed, it is this balance that Rawls (1972) sought in his attempt to bring together concerns with freedom and with equality, which continues to speak to social work ethics despite the many problems and limitations of his theory of justice. Similarly, Sen (2009), who begins from a utilitarian position, accommodates human rights as a foundational way of understanding what is good (in much the same way that Baldry does; see earlier). For Sen, human rights can be understood as freedoms, whether these are negative (the freedom not to be assaulted) or positive (the freedom to receive medical attention for serious health problems) (2009, p. 367). However, if the resources necessary to meet the latter type of rights (which are 'second-generation') are relatively scarce, then it may be necessary to ration access on the basis of social justice principles, an example of which might be differential contribution towards the cost of such care.

To illustrate this point, let us consider the situation of a social worker engaged in social development practice with a large INGO.

> Kagiso is the key worker on a project to promote girls' education in an East African country. She has been asked to develop a briefing paper to assist in starting a dialogue with various stakeholders in a particular region, including government education authorities, teachers and school principals, employers, village leaders, parents and students. Kagiso is aware that this is a diverse audience, not all of whom accept that educating girls is important. So she faces the challenge of finding a range of justifications for this development that are both coherent and cover the various concerns that each stakeholder group will bring to the discussion. Although Kagiso knows that some of those who will participate in this dialogue are opposed to girls' education, as a local person herself, as well as a woman, Kagiso is convinced that the right of girls to equality with boys in education is not a denial of her culture. She is also aware that there are great potential benefits for communities as well as for families and individuals in ensuring girls can access education. So Kagiso plans to focus much of her paper on these benefits, while also supporting the issue with reference to the country's commitment to human rights through the *Universal Declaration* and the UN's *Convention on the Rights of the Child*, to which it is a signatory. Her senior colleagues agree that she needs to address both these aspects.
>
> To fulfil the criteria for good participatory practice, Kagiso also has to consider how the dialogue might be conducted with different stakeholders. For example is it necessary to consider several different ways of involving various groups? Perhaps students' voices will not be heard in meetings that include government officers, employers and village leaders? Indeed, is this a context where it would be considered appropriate for school students to participate? So even though Kagiso can base her discussion paper on core social work values, implementing them in practice may still be contested. This is something she and her colleagues have to consider and advocate, perhaps even struggle for, in their day-to-day practice.

As Kagiso's practice demonstrates, it is not possible to separate questions of the 'good' in a moral sense from what is 'good' in a technical sense (Hugman, 2005).

In other words, it is not possible to think of practice as 'good' if it embodies core moral principles but is ineffective, nor if it is highly effective but morally deficient. Therefore, as social development is concerned with human rights, social justice and community, it is vital that social workers consciously consider the moral values of the profession and are able to integrate them with the skills and the knowledge in practice. As we have noted in this discussion, achieving this involves careful thought, debate and struggle. In such a contested field social workers have a responsibility to be clear and explicit to themselves and to others. So to achieve this it is vital that social workers integrate methods and objectives – in other words, means and ends – which is the heart of professional ethics.

10

ADVANCING SOCIAL DEVELOPMENT IN SOCIAL WORK

Social work in social development

This discussion began with the recognition that the approach of 'social development' grew out of a concern by social workers to strengthen macro perspectives in
practice. For example Midgley (2014, p. 6) notes the role of social workers in forming the International Consortium on Social Development (ICSD), which continues
to have an explicit association with social work, although its membership is now
much wider. Likewise, Payne (2014, p. 228) observes that one of the major forces
in the identification of social development as a distinct area of practice came from
postcolonial struggles in the global South between a legacy of micro practices in
social work that perpetuated a residual approach to social issues and problems and
a tendency to regard development only in economic terms (also see Osei-Hwedie,
1993; Patel, 2005; Gray, 2006). In this sense, social development was created out of
community-focused development programmes that sought to overcome the limitations of the residual model in social welfare (cf. Elliott, 1993).

As England observes (1986, p. 13), social work professionalised in the twentieth
century with the primary function of assisting those people who cannot resolve
their social problems unaided. So, insofar as it continues to have a connection with
social work, M. Green (2002, p. 53) is concerned that social development retains
a 'welfarist' tendency that should be better abandoned. For Green such a connection should be replaced by recognising that all areas of development have a social
dimension – in other words social aspects of development should be made explicit
across all sectors, including economic, political and technical areas. Furthermore, as
an extension of its affinity with what she calls 'welfarism', Green also argues social
development is weakened as a distinct field of development practice because it is
most often operationalised in the work of community groups, civil society organisations and NGOs that are concerned with 'marginal social categories' (p. 69).

Although this is not a new comment on social work (e.g. see my own previous discussion of 'judging a profession by the company it keeps' in Hugman, 1991, pp. 94–101), it does not necessarily fit well in a consideration of social development. As discussed in previous chapters, Ife (2012, p. 59) observes that social work tends to focus on those aspects of human life that relate to economic, social and cultural rights and needs – so too does social development. That Midgley (1995, 2014) and others have emphasised that the objectives of social development should promote the well-being of a population as a whole does not deny that at the operational level, at least, attention often needs to be paid to people in poverty and the exclusion and oppression of women, Indigenous people, disabled people or other disadvantaged parts of populations. While these areas of concern may be relevant in other professions and disciplines as well, they are clearly central to the broader focus of generalist social work that combines macro, meso and micro analysis and intervention. So at the structural and policy levels it is important to engage with a more universal perspective across a society or country, but at the level of practice and intervention not all development issues affect the whole of a population equally. All governments face the task of identifying priorities, at all levels of policy, so this can add to the tendency to be selective in focusing on particular issues. Nevertheless, a social development perspective begins from attention to population groups and not individual members of a society, so to that extent it avoids individualising problems even though it may necessarily be focused broadly on social problems.

As discussed in the previous chapter, there is not necessarily a contradiction between the focus of social work or social development on a whole of population perspective and the focus on groups of people who face particular challenges to the achievement of human rights or social justice. That human rights and social justice apply to all members of a society can be reconciled with attention being directed towards those who face particular obstacles in their realisation. Indeed, being able to hold together the broad vision of human rights and social justice and detailed attention to those who are least advantaged reinforces the importance of ensuring that assistance to achieve these goals is provided for those who require it. As an example, we might consider the provision of access for people with disabilities to public buildings as a social good in this sense. The human right lies in all members of a community being able to access such a building, and if some people are excluded because of its design, then this constitutes an injustice. Therefore, public expenditure on appropriate adaptations to ensure access to such a building is not unequal attention to a minority, and it is certainly not 'welfarist', if by this is meant it addresses subjective preferences regarding well-being as the defining value (Sen, 2009). This is a clear example of Rawls's (1972) principle that inequalities may be fair if they provide a benefit to those who otherwise are disadvantaged.

From this we may extend our understanding to include poverty alleviation, gender equity and women's empowerment, and issues of rights and justice for many other groups that are discriminated against, excluded and oppressed. In each case the central issue concerns the interrelationship of human rights and social justice. Social work brings a particular set of skills, knowledge and values to this field alongside other professions and academic disciplines in constructing and implementing policies and programmes that enable developmental goals to be achieved in ways that ensure human rights and social justice are realised (e.g. see Patel, 2005).

In many global Southern countries the creation of professional social work in itself is actually seen as a part of social development. In countries such as Vietnam (Hugman *et al.*, 2007, 2009; Hines *et al.*, 2010; Nguyen Thi Thai Lan *et al.*, 2010), China (Ku *et al.*, 2005; Yan & Cheung, 2006; Wang & Lum, 2013), Botswana (Osei-Hwedie *et al.*, 2006) and South Africa (Gray, 2006; Lombard, 2008; Lombard & Wairire, 2010) the creation of nationally authentic professional social work has been part of the social development strategy of governments. Although in some respects social work is expected to contribute to alleviation of the social issues created by rapid economic and structural change, so that for example in Vietnam and China there is often a focus on micro-level practice, the overall gains are intended to be developmental and in reality wider social development is also being promoted in culturally appropriate ways (Ku *et al.*, 2005; Nguyen Thi Thai Lan *et al.*, 2010).

Social work as social development is a perspective that could be said to have existed previously in global Northern countries but has been lost because of the high levels of social welfare that have subsequently been achieved. However, this view suggests that social development is a unidirectional process with an end point, rather than seeing it as dynamic and continually subject to challenges to social well-being that shift over time, and to which there is an ongoing need to respond. This understanding turns our attention from the place of social work in social development, seen as a practice relevant to the global South, to the role of social development as a practice in social work in all parts of the world.

Social development in social work

As well as addressing the role of social work in social development, we also need to consider the place of this practice in the wider profession. As has been discussed in the preceding chapters this is also highly contested. To summarise, while for some social workers attention to social development strengthens (even restores) an important dimension of practice and theory, for others it is either of relevance only to global Southern countries or no longer plausibly regarded as part of the profession at all. In these arguments the combined historical forces of professionalisation and the global dominance of neo-liberalism are seen often to have either marginalised the social developmental aspects of social work or pushed them off the agenda altogether, especially in the global North.

However, it is at precisely this current point in the history of social work that that the international social work organisations have renewed their commitment to a developmental perspective in the establishment of the programme of policy formation and advocacy (IASSW/ICSW/IFSW, 2014). It is not a coincidence that this programme is largely constructed in relation to the United Nations (UN) and its agencies and entities with which social work is associated, along with national governments and large NGOs. As discussed in Chapter 6, social work historically has had a major role in these areas, including in the founding of some parts of the UN network, and the three major organisations (IASSW, ICSW & IFSW) have long held 'reporting status' (which acknowledges their competence to be involved in UN proceedings) (Healy, 2008). It is also not coincidental that this shift has taken place at the time in which ICSW has renewed its relationship with IASSW and IFSW, which had been collaborating again for some years previously. ICSW has a longer association with social development, not only having wider reporting status at the UN than the other two organisations (Healy, 2008, p. 183), but also having co-ordinated the contribution of the non-government sector in the 1995 World Summit on Social Development. By renewing their shared active engagement in this sector, the social work organisations can work more effectively together to use their knowledge from practice and programmes to contribute to wider policy and planning.

That social work in Africa, Latin America and many parts of Asia often takes the form of social development is seen by some social workers as a reflection of prevailing economic conditions combined with the social issues faced by large parts of those populations (Patel, 2005). That such conditions are not 'prevailing' in the global North and are encountered as problems faced by specific minority subgroups may be taken to suggest that social development practice is not relevant in such 'highly developed' contexts (Gray & Crofts, 2008; Payne, 2014). However, both Midgley (2014) and Payne (2014) suggest that renewed attention to social development in social work in the global North represents the influence of the global South through a 'reverse transmission' that mirrors processes of 'indigenisation' (cf. Walton & El Nasr, 1988; Elliott, 1993). Indeed, there is some evidence that this may be the case. Concrete examples of ways in which social development can impact global Northern social work are examined in Chapter 7. The practice considered there suggests that to some extent these approaches were influenced by the experience of social work in global Southern countries, such as El Salvador (Pawar & Torres, 2011, p. 259), or else in areas of social work practice that can be considered as outside the 'mainstream' of the profession, such as rural social work, or practice with Indigenous communities or with refugees and asylum seekers. So to that extent, local global Northern practice is being influenced by the re-encounter with issues and responses that are outside the modern mainstream and a realisation that this practice remains relevant to many issues with which social work is concerned.

As in various ways social development is part of the legacy of social work in the global North, for example through the 'settlement house movement' (see Chapter 1), the shift towards a majority focus on clinical practice and institutional social services provision could be seen as a characteristic of professional evolution, suggesting that social development is required for a time but can be jettisoned when a society becomes 'developed'. However, there are three problems with such a view.

First, as noted earlier, it assumes that development is a one-way process and that there is a given point at which it can be said to have been achieved. While there are certainly arguments from the perspective of environmental sustainability (see Chapter 4) for considering whether a point of 'enough' development has been accomplished, there is also evidence that factors currently considered as important in development cannot be expected necessarily to be maintained unless the conditions that support them are also maintained or are achieved by marginalised and disadvantaged groups as well as the majority.

For example although across the global North the twentieth century was marked by increased real levels of GNI and this is positively associated with improved life expectancy and other health indices that apply to overall populations (Schell *et al.*, 2007), for some population subgroups continued poverty has had unanticipated consequences. This can be seen in the way that obesity has become a major health problem, with implications that gains in life expectancy might be compromised by the mid-twenty-first century. What is significant in this phenomenon is that although increased levels of obesity can be seen to some extent across the whole populations of 'highly developed' countries, significant differences tend to be associated with levels of income and education, and hence with types of employment, housing and so on (e.g. see NHPA, 2013). Thus obesity is associated with socio-economic class, poverty and so on. One explanation of this is the impact of processed foods on the human metabolism and the relative lower cost and ease of access to such foods. From a different perspective, while the Global Financial Crisis (GFC) of 2007–8 did not have an immediate impact on mortality rates, it did affect poverty levels in many countries 'in transition' where poverty alleviation measures had been having a positive influence. The consequence is that in some countries poverty levels have risen again, with many other developmental gains delayed or lost (ODI, 2009). The impact on the immediate future can also be seen in the reduced budgets for development organisations, both government and non-government (Mendoza, 2010). These two examples, obesity and the GFC, point to ways in which assumptions about constant development must be questioned.

Second, explanations about why the process of professionalisation has tended to favour clinical practice and institutional social services provision and to exclude social development and other generalist or macro practices remain contested. On the one side for example Mendes and Binns (2013) found that among rural social work practitioners there was a widespread use of community development ideas and skills, yet there was a reluctance to see their work as developmental. Their study found that community development practice is core to rural social work, because in such locations social work is generalist, but at the same time it is marginalised by funding mechanisms and other aspects of policy that emphasise individual- and family-focused practice (also see Pugh & Cheers, 2010). Thus a developmental approach is pushed out by the dominant neo-liberal political and economic ethos. On the other side, Gray and Crofts (2008) have argued that social development does not have traction in global Northern social work because of the dominance within the profession of theory that serves only to critique political, economic and social structures in conceptual terms but does not engage with how to work with these structures in the realities of day-to-day social life. Thus a developmental approach is pushed out by the critique of the dominant neo-liberal political and economic ethos. For Gray and Crofts, a social developmental perspective in social work requires skills, knowledge, theory and values that enable practitioners to engage in promoting change from within existing systems, rather than standing outside on the moral (and political) high ground. The central values of human rights and social justice provide a way in which practitioners may maintain their critical understanding and at the same time apply this in action.

Third, the ascription of social development as a practice specifically only for 'developing countries' is also questionable. The ideas described by both Gray and Crofts (2008) and Mendes and Binns (2013) have parallels with many aspects of the types of practices that characterise social development in countries such as South Africa and Botswana (Patel, 2005; Osei-Hwedie *et al.*, 2006). However, not only is it the case that its implementation in these countries has been obstructed by neo-liberal policy and the impact of the GFC (e.g. see Hölscher, 2008), but also the same effects of these forces can be seen in other parts of the world (Mathbor & Ferdinand, 2008; Midgley, 2014). This is not to suggest that there has been no progress in social development – for example poverty rates have declined in many countries and in most places the recent reversal of the trend has not returned them to their previous higher levels (C. Kenny, 2011). It is also important to recognise that what has been happening in the longer term, while poverty eradication goals were slowly being realised, is that there has been a widespread significant increase in inequality, and this too is destructive of developmental objectives. Setbacks in poverty eradication add to the human cost of such longer-term shifts and may even mask the way in which inequality is a major challenge to future development (Deacon & Cohen, 2011; Stiglitz, 2012).

For some commentators the increase in inequality is a consequence of globalisation. Not only has the creation of global markets increased levels of GNI in many countries, through the provision of jobs and trade, but also it has created the conditions that led to the GFC. At the same time these dynamics have contributed to policies that have put pressure on governments to reduce or even abandon gains in the social arena, such as in education, health and housing. While some economists, such as Stiglitz (2006, 2012), are highly critical of this new form of 'distorted development', the effects of these policies continue to have a negative impact. For social workers in social development the negative aspects of globalisation mean that there will continue to be a hostile political and economic environment. At the same time, the social issues and needs that are exacerbated by globalisation are part of social work's international span of concern, such as refugees and asylum seekers, and victims of human trafficking (Cemlyn, 2008b; Healy, 2008; Hugman, 2010). In addition, social work continues to have a major role to play in poverty alleviation, gender equality (e.g. access to education and health) and issues of social justice for disadvantaged and marginalised groups.

In summary, globalisation has been marked by the ideological dominance of neo-liberalism (Deacon, 2007). The logic that supported policies to deregulate financial markets that in turn led to the GFC is the same as that which promotes reductions in public funding for health, education and social services, as well as severe restrictions on asylum seekers. In such a political and social climate social work faces challenges not only in the implementation of particular programmes and projects but also in its very purpose. In some respects the neo-liberal value of individual freedom (that might be expressed in notions of choice, consent and so on) is congruent with the principle of participation and other aspects of social work. Yet the same value also has led to large-scale reductions in public expenditure on social welfare, because funding such activity through taxation is regarded both as a constraint on the liberty of those who own the means of wealth generation to decide how 'their' wealth will be used and as a drain on the capacity of the economy to produce ever larger economic output. So, if taken to the extreme, the provision of funding for the well-being of others is regarded as a personal choice by those who have wealth, and thus philanthropy is seen as the only valid way of making resources available for developmental programmes. There is a correlative belief, also, that public funding of social programmes undermines the human agency of the recipients and so encourages dependency. That principles such as participation point to the goal in social work of supporting and promoting human agency is effectively ignored by the neo-liberal critique. In an internal contradiction, this perspective also reduces the legitimacy of publicly funded social work to the social control dimensions of complex tasks, such as child protection or juvenile justice, limiting the extent to which a social developmental focus can be created and emphasising areas in which human agency is purposefully overridden (Parton, 2006; Conley, 2010).

Ironically, the same processes of globalisation that have presented challenges to social development in social work have also created new opportunities for social workers to form new partnerships with colleagues and with service users. Globalised communications mean that sharing knowledge and analysis is much easier than previously, which can create solidarity around responses to questions of human rights and social justice (Payne & Askeland, 2008). Globalisation has also enabled new opportunities for social workers themselves to move between countries, again to exchange ideas and practices so that local and global problems and issues can be understood both locally and globally (Payne & Askeland, 2008; Pullen-Sansfaçon et al., 2012; Spolander et al., 2014). While international social work is not a panacea in the face of the many negative consequences of globalisation, when used in this way it provides a basis for creative practice to be pursued.

As noted in Chapters 1 and 2, some advocates of social development practice, including Elliott (1993), Midgley (1995, 2014) and Burghardt (2014), tend to regard it specifically as macro-level practice, as likewise do commentators such as Payne (2014). However, the argument in this present analysis has been that in both global Southern and Northern contexts social development practice requires social work to be generalist, working flexibly across macro, meso and micro forms of intervention (Patel, 2005; Conley, 2010). A generalist frame of reference points instead to a renewed strengthening of the place of macro practice within social work, as well as and often more than, but not instead of, micro or meso concerns. Rather, the evidence from a range of projects, programmes and other sources has shown that it is the integration of these dimensions that contributed to the success of developmental practice. This is the case for countries not only in Africa, Asia, Latin America and the Pacific Islands but also in Australasia, Europe and North America. For example Patel (2005) makes clear that in South Africa working with individuals and families in interpersonal helping and service provision continues to be a major contribution of social work – what is different is the context and ethos of practice, alongside the use of macro interventions to promote wider structural change. The same use of a multi-level approach can also be seen in the examples reported in Australia (Pugh & Cheers, 2010; Pawar & Torres, 2011), Canada (Chipeniuk, 2008), Eastern Europe (Maglajlic, 2011), New Zealand (Mafile'o, 2004; Maidment & Brook, 2014), the UK (Cemlyn, 2008a) and the USA (Nawyn, 2010; Smith, 2012; Parrish *et al.*, 2013).

What is at issue, therefore, is not whether social development might reasonably have a role in social work, but whether the combined pressures of professionalisation and the neo-liberal global environment so restrict the space in which it has to operate that it continues to be marginalised. However, although these contextual factors are given, rather than chosen, the response of social work is open to debate and action. In this respect critical analysis shares common ground in seeing opportunities for social workers to engage with macro-level intervention and change, notwithstanding differences in the exact practices suggested to do so. Arguments range from the promotion of a specifically politically radical social action perspective (Lavalette & Ferguson, 2007) to suggestions for critical-reflective engagement with existing systems (Gray & Crofts, 2008), although, given the way in which social development is concerned with changes in structures and systems to address issues and problems, this could be seen as a difference of degree between acting 'within' and 'against' existing social relationships to achieve change, rather than diametrically opposed positions. Arguments also range across areas of cultural, economic, environmental, political and social problems and issues, with diverse and often competing positions on how issues and problems are to be understood and the most appropriate ways in which to address them. The point of agreement here is that social work must redress the loss of macro-level and structural understanding and practice in order to contribute effectively to the social issues with which it is concerned.

Social work in collaboration with other social development professions

Various contributors to the debates about social development make the point that it is multidisciplinary (M. Green, 2002; Gray & Crofts, 2008; Payne, 2014). Although, as discussed elsewhere in this book, social work has had a leading role in social development at various times and in various places (Midgley, 2014, p. 6), the field is also of concern to others, such as business people, economists, government administrators, politicians and political scientists, social anthropologists and other social scientists. Each group brings its own perspective on the definition of issues and how they should be addressed. Thus social workers who are committed to social development may face multiple marginality – that is while social development is not central to social work in the global North (which still dominates global conversations about the profession), social work is not necessarily central to social development as understood by other stakeholders.

However, to what extent is this lack of a distinctive claim to social development as a field of practice a unique challenge for social work? The debates that have been explored in the preceding chapters frequently assume that in the process of professionalisation micro-and some meso-level practices have become the defining features of the profession. Yet, it should be asked, to what extent are other practices, such as counselling, family therapy, case management or social groupwork, accepted by others as the exclusive domain of social work? In reality, these are all multidisciplinary. Similarly, fields of practice, such as childcare, child protection, mental health, disability, old age and so on, all benefit from social work contributions, while being complex sites of multi-professional practices. Some parts of these fields, like some micro practices, such as counselling and case management, can be said to have origins in social work, but over time they have been opened up to much wider contributions, just as social work has entered other areas. What matters more is whether social work can or should make a contribution in social development practice.

The answers indicated by the analysis of this discussion are that yes, it can, and yes, it should. Social work can make a contribution to social development programmes and practices in the ways that have been explored throughout this book. It retains versatility in its approach, which is generalist at the core (Patel, 2005; Gray & Crofts, 2008, p. 101). It fosters a capacity to work with uncertainty and the 'messiness' of the social world (Mason, 2011, p. 385; Maidment & Brook, 2014, p. 83). Moreover, the skills of social work in bringing people together, assisting them to question issues, negotiating between competing perspectives and interests and promoting resilience are all ways in which the various social development examples considered in this book have benefitted from social work skills and understanding. It is indicative, perhaps, that the 'strengths perspective' that has become highly influential in micro practices beyond social work originated in the work of a social development social worker (Saleebey, 1996, 2002, 2004).

It is also the case that for much of its history, professional social work has been practised in contexts that are defined or even dominated by other professions or disciplines. It shares this characteristic with other professions, such as nursing and allied health (Hugman, 1991, p. 104). For some critics, the lack of a widely accepted, exclusive field of skill and knowledge is regarded as a weakness for the professional claims of social work (a critique that has a history as long as the profession itself, dating back to the late 1800s; see e.g. Flexner, 1915). Social work also tends to be an organisation-based profession, even in a country such as the USA, where there is a large minority in private practice. Again, this can be seen as a limitation, in that it can be taken to imply that social workers have to be managed (unlike more established professions, it is claimed, which are capable of self-direction and direct public accountability) (Hugman, 1991, p. 79). However, precisely because these descriptions are partly correct, social workers are educated in subjects that provide them with a basis for acting in these contexts, including social policy, social administration, organisation theory and management practice. This inclines social workers more than other occupations to view organisational work as part of practice, rather than as a necessary but obstructive addition to 'real' work. For social workers, the meso and macro orientation can provide the basis for grasping organisational means, including conscious planned teamwork as a practice, the management and development of service provision, and research and policy development, in order to support and promote wider goals, such as those of social development (Conley, 2010; Wang & Lum, 2013).

In this respect, while the recommendations that to practise social development social workers need to be educated in economics, environmental science and other areas that have not always been part of the curriculum are reasonably founded, this may be more necessary in relation to some roles than in others (cf. Midgley, 1995; Gray & Crofts, 2008). While it is certainly vital that social workers in social development can work with the other professions and disciplines identified earlier in positive and productive ways, the argument presented here may suggest that what is required is a sufficient understanding of those fields rather than for social workers to become expert accountants, economists, environmentalists, political scientists or whatever. Here too, valuing a generalist approach is more likely to be helpful than the pursuit of new specialisations.

In conclusion: advancing social development in social work

A central theme throughout this book is that social development practice is an important dimension of social work. It formed part of the early stages of professionalisation, but while it became eclipsed by more individualised practices within residual and institutional approaches to social welfare, in many parts of the global South it has grown again in importance. For this reason, the adoption of social development as a core focus for the international social work organisations (IASSW, ICSW and IFSW) in *The Global Agenda for Social Work and Social Development: Commitment to Action* can possibly be seen as an expression of the emerging influence of global Southern practice and theory on global social work. At the same time, social development is becoming more widely recognised again in the global North through the renewed attention of social work to issues such as poverty, refugees and asylum seekers, Indigenous peoples and other groups who face disadvantage, exclusion and oppression. The examples of practice contained in the first report of this process (IASSW/ICSW/IFSW, 2014) demonstrate that in all parts of the world social work is addressing material and structural issues alongside giving attention to needs experienced by individuals and families. It is doing so through contributions to policy development, community action programmes, political lobbying, environmental programmes, humanitarian intervention and other practices that seek to promote social justice and human rights. As the explicit goal in this process is to contribute to debates about post–Millennium Development Goals (MDGs) policy and strategy formation, this work is planned to continue through the present decade.

This '*Global Agenda*' reaffirms the central place in social work of social development over the long term. It provides a possibility of rethinking the historical connections of social work with structural dimensions of the issues and problems with which social work is concerned. It also highlights the importance of attending to macro-focused as well as meso- and micro-level practices and theories. In this sense it re-emphasises that there are two elements in the notion of 'person-in-the-environment' (as discussed in Chapter 1 and throughout). Both elements must be recognised and addressed.

The practices that follow from this understanding have a variety of labels: advocacy; empowerment; animation; mobilisation; conscientisation; community development; social action; policy formation; action research; capacity building. Although these are in some ways often quite different to each other, they share some common aspects. First, they all recognise that people are members of families, communities and the wider society, so that theory and practice must be founded on structural and collective understandings of human life. This is the case even in those parts of the world in which individualism is a dominant perspective. Second, these practices all begin from the realisation that every person and group have strengths and that effective practice therefore involves working *with* people and their capacities (Saleebey, 1996, 2002). Third, these practices place people who benefit from social work at the centre of practice, rather than the skills and knowledge of the professionals (cf. Koehn, 1994). It is not that skills and knowledge are irrelevant (this is what social workers bring to the process) but that these are a means to the ends of social and personal change and not ends in themselves for the benefit of the professionals.

Throughout this analysis and discussion the overall aim of social work has been understood as the promotion and protection of human rights and social justice. As a value statement this runs the risk of being an expression of high ideals that is divorced from the day-to-day realities of practice. Yet as the examples of practice identified throughout the preceding chapters demonstrate, as do those described in the *Global Agenda* report (IASSW/ICSW/IFSW, 2014), these values form the underlying goals of work in diverse areas of practice, such as social security, housing, employment programmes, services for older people, health care, children and family practice, and advocacy with disabled people's groups. Human rights and social justice are as important morally and as useful practically in counselling and case management as they are in policy formation, community development or social action. These values demand that all practitioners attend to the social contexts of peoples' lives even when their primary role concerns micro- or meso-level interactions (Reisch & Jani, 2012).

Given the sense that social development as a social work practice has been nurtured and promoted most recently in the global South and is being 'reimported' in various ways to the global North, it is possible to see it as having the potential to redress the historical legacy of 'professional imperialism' (Midgley, 1981; Osei-Hwedie, 1993; Patel, 2005; Hugman, 2010). However, in many ways it is as yet too early to tell. Although the *Global Agenda* (IASSW/ICSW/IFSW, 2014) suggests one tangible expression of a balance being found that is more congruent with the value of social justice (between global regions), it is also still the case that the global South is constructed as 'other' in much of the theory and the international debate of the profession (Hugman, 2010, p. 156). Recognition of social development as part of the mainstream of social work provides one potential contribution to challenging this imbalance.

A further way in which social development practice and theory can challenge the dominant global Northern perspective is in the construction of debates about values and ethics. As discussed in Chapter 9, the core values of human rights and social justice inform a social development approach as much as any other aspects of social work. However, the way in which these values are understood affects how they are expressed in action. Many of the challenges faced by contemporary social work derive from the strong individualism of the dominant global Northern value perspectives that underpin neo-liberalism. In those parts of the world where social development is more widely regarded as central to social work more communal values continue to be important, even though they may be under pressure from the ideological influences of globalisation. The more communal values encountered in Africa, Asia, the Pacific Islands and South America are more easily considered from a developmental perspective, because it integrates attention to wider social structures and relationships and the environment, emphasising the shared responsibilities for issues and problems as well as shared solutions and strategies (Patel, 2005).

Greater attention to social development in social work provides the basis for addressing these different issues. Not only does it contain the seeds of rebalancing relationships between global South and North, but also it opens up a wider vision of social work as a whole. Institutional and structural pressures continue to act against such a broader perspective in many ways, so the impact of social development in social work must be addressed explicitly. Moreover, as this book has argued, it remains a contentious approach. Yet at the same time it has also been shown that a social development approach contributes to the larger goals of social work that are often summarised in the core values of human rights and social justice; for this reason, advancing social development in social work, alongside the critical use of other skills, knowledge and theories, will contribute to the pursuit of a more just development of social work itself.

REFERENCES

Acharya, S., Yoshino, E., Jimba, M. & Wakai, S. (2007) 'Empowering rural women through a community development approach in Nepal', *Community Development Journal*, 42(1), pp. 34–46.

Ahmed, S. (2012) 'Development innovations through entrepreneurial microfinance and the attempt to achieve the United Nations Millennium Development Goals in Bangladesh', *Advances in Social Work*, 13(2), pp. 359–74.

Aideyan, O. (2011) 'Social theory and poverty reduction with special attention to Nigeria: Social institutional explanation of small-scale financial institutions', *Poverty & Public Policy*, 3(4), Article 4. Electronic document downloaded on 25 September 2014 from http://www.psocommons.org/ppp/vol3/iss4/art4

Akimoto, T. (2007) 'Requestioning international social work/welfare: Where are we now?', *Japanese Journal of Social Services*, 1(1), pp. 27–34.

Allen-Meares, P. & Garvin, C. (eds) (2000) *The Handbook of Social Work Direct Practice*. Thousand Oaks: SAGE.

Alston, M. (1990) 'Feminism and farm women', *Australian Social Work*, 43(1), pp. 23–9.

Alston, M. (2007) '"It's really not that easy to get help": Services to drought-affected families', *Australian Social Work*, 60(4), pp. 421–35.

Alston, M. (2013) 'Environmental social work: Accounting for gender in climate disasters', *Australian Social Work*, 66(2), pp. 218–33.

Alston, M. & Bowles, W. (2003) *Research for Social Workers: An Introduction to Methods*. 2nd edition. Crows Nest: Allen & Unwin.

Androff, D.K. (2012) 'Adaptations of truth and reconciliation commissions in the North American context: Local examples of a global restorative justice intervention', *Advances in Social Work*, 13(2), pp. 408–19.

Asad, T. (2000) 'What do human rights do? An anthropological inquiry', *Theory & Event*, 4(4). Electronic document accessed on 17 December 2014 at http:/www.muse.jhu.edu/Journals/theory_and_event/v004/4.4asad.html

Asad, T. (2003) *Formations of the Secular: Christianity, Islam, Modernity*. Stanford: Stanford University Press.

Askeland, G.A. (2007) 'Globalisation and a flood of travellers: Flooded travellers and social justice', in Dominelli, L. (ed.) *Revitalising Communities in a Globalising World*. Aldershot: Ashgate.

Aspalter, C. (2006) 'The East Asian welfare model', *International Journal of Social Welfare*, 15(4), pp. 290–301.

Austin, S.A. & Mbewu, N. (2009) 'Philani program: A case study of an integrative approach of empowerment and social and economic development', *Social Work in Public Health*, 24(1–2), pp. 148–60.

Australian Institute of Health and Welfare (AIHW) (2013) *Aboriginal and Torres Strait Islander Health Performance Framework 2012*. Canberra: AIHW.

Bagati, D. (2003) 'Microcredit and empowerment of women', *Journal of Social Work Research and Evaluation*, 4(1), pp. 19–35.

Baldry, E. (2010) 'Mental health disorders and cognitive disability in the criminal justice system', keynote paper presented at *Community Legal Centres NSW Conference*, Sydney, 6 May.

Bambra, C. (2007) 'Going beyond *The Three Worlds of Welfare Capitalism*: Regime theory and public health research', *Journal of Epidemiology & Community Health*, 61(12), pp. 1098–102.

Ban, P. (2005) 'Aboriginal child placement principle and family group conferences', *Australian Social Work*, 58(4), pp. 384–94.

Banks, S. (2012) *Ethics and Values in Social Work*. 4th edition. Basingstoke: Palgrave-Macmillan.

Banks, S., Hugman, R., Healy, L., Bozalek, V. & Orme, J. (2008) 'Global ethics for social work: Problems and possibilities', *Ethics & Social Welfare*, 2(3), pp. 276–90.

Barth, R.P., Landsverk, J., Chamberlain, P., Reid, J.B., Rolls, J.A., Hurlburt, M.S., Farmer, E.M.Z., James, S., McCabe, K.M. & Kohl, P.L. (2005) 'Parent-training programs in child welfare services: Planning for a more evidence-based approach to serving biological parents', *Research on Social Work Practice*, 15(5), pp. 353–71.

Bauman, Z. (1993) *Postmodern Ethics*. Oxford: Basil Blackwell.

Bay, U. & Macfarlane, S. (2011) 'Teaching critical reflection: A tool for transformative learning in social work?', *Social Work Education*, 30(7), pp. 745–58.

Beck, U. (1992) *Risk Society: Towards a New Modernity*. London: SAGE.

Benhabib, S. (1992) *Situating the Self: Gender, Community and Postmodernism in Contemporary Ethics*. Cambridge: Polity Press.

Bennett, B. (2013) 'The importance of Aboriginal and Torres Strait Islander history for social work students and graduates', in Bennett, B., Green, S., Gilbert, S. & Bessarab, D. (eds) *Our Voices: Aboriginal and Torres Strait Islander Social Work*. South Yarra: Palgrave-Macmillan.

Benson, G.O., Sun, F., Hodge, D.R. & Androff, D.K. (2012) 'Religious coping and acculturation stress among Hindu Bhutanese: A study of newly-resettled refugees in the United States', *International Social Work*, 55(4), pp. 538–53.

Beresford, P. (2000) 'Service users' knowledges and social work theory: Conflict or collaboration?', *British Journal of Social Work*, 30(4), pp. 489–503.

Besthorn, F.H. (2002) 'Radical environmentalism and the ecological self: Rethinking the concept of self-identity for social work practice', *Journal of Progressive Human Services*, 13(1), pp. 53–72.

Besthorn, F.H. (2003) 'Radical ecologisms: Insights for educating social workers in ecological activism and social justice', *Critical Social Work: An Interdisciplinary Journal Dedicated to Social Justice*, 3(1), pp. 66–106.

Besthorn, F.H. (2012) 'Deep Ecology's contribution to social work: A ten-year retrospective', *International Journal of Social Welfare*, 21(3), pp. 248–59.

Besthorn, F.H. & Saleebey, D. (2003) 'Nature, genetics and the Biophilia connection: Exploring linkages with social work values and practice', *Advances in Social Work*, 4(1), pp. 1–18.

Boateng, A. (2009) 'A mixed methods analysis of social capital of Liberian refugee women in Ghana', *Journal of Sociology & Social Welfare*, 36(3), pp. 59–81.

Bourdieu, P. (1994) 'Rethinking the state: Genesis and structure of the bureaucratic field', *Sociological Theory*, 12(1), pp. 1–18.

Bourdieu, P. (2005) *The Social Structures of the Economy*. Cambridge: Polity Press.

Brandt Commission [The Independent Commission on International Development] (1980) *North-South: A Program for Survival*. London: Pan Books.

Bransford, C. (2011) 'Reconciling paternalism and empowerment in clinical practice', *Social Work*, 56(1), pp. 33–41.

Briskman, L. (2014) *Social Work With Indigenous Communities*. 2nd edition. Annandale: Federation Press.

Briskman, L. & Cemlyn, S. (2005) 'Reclaiming humanity for asylum seekers: A social work response', *International Social Work*, 48(6), pp. 714–24.

Brotherhood of St Laurence (2014) *Submission to the Review of Australia's Welfare System*. Fitzroy: Brotherhood of St Laurence.

Burghardt, S. (2014) *Macro-Practice in Social Work for the 21st Century: Bridging the Macro-Micro Divide*. Thousand Oaks: SAGE.

Caminada, K. & Goudeswaard, K. (2009) 'Poverty reduction in the EU: A descriptive analysis', *Poverty & Public Policy*, 1(2), article 5. Electronic document accessed on 31 October 2014 at http://www.psocommons.org/ppp/vol1/iss2/art5

Campbell, C. (2005) 'Gendered microcredit programming in Nigeria: Questioning the bottom line', *Canadian Social Work Review/Revue Canadienne de Service Social*, 22(1), pp. 103–16.

Çelik, K. & Lüküslü, D. (2012) 'Spotlighting a silent category of young females: The life experiences of "house girls" in Turkey', *Youth & Society*, 44(1), pp. 28–48.

Cemlyn, S. (2008a) 'Human rights and Gypsies and Travellers', *British Journal of Social Work*, 38(1), pp. 153–73.

Cemlyn, S. (2008b) 'Human rights practice: Possibilities and pitfalls for developing emancipatory social work', *Ethics & Social Welfare*, 2(3), pp. 222–42.

Chambers, R. (1983) *Rural Development: Putting the Last First*. London: Longman.

Chau, R.C.M. & Sam, W.K.Y. (2013) 'Defamilisation of twenty-two countries: Its implications for the study of East Asian welfare regimes', *Social Policy and Society*, 12(3), pp. 355–67.

Cheers, B., Binell, M., Coleman, H., Gentle, I., Miller, G., Taylor, J. & Weetra, C. (2006) 'Family violence: An Indigenous community tells its story', *International Social Work*, 49(1), pp. 51–63.

Chipeniuk, R. (2008) 'Some tools for planning amenity migration in remote rural settlements: Lessons from participatory action', *Community Development Journal*, 43(2), pp. 222–38.

Chowa, G. & Ansong, D. (2010) 'Youth and savings in AssetsAfrica', *Children & Youth Services Review*, 32, pp. 1591–6.

Chowa, G., Ansong, D. & Despard, M.J. (2014) 'Financial capabilities: Multilevel modelling of the impact of internal and external capabilities of rural households', *Social Work Research*, 38(3), pp. 19–35.

Christie, A. (2010) 'Whiteness and the politics of "race" in child protection guidelines in Ireland', *European Journal of Social Work*, 13(2), pp. 199–215.

Cichon, M. & Hagemejer, K. (2007) 'Changing the development policy paradigm: Investing in a social security floor for all', *International Social Security Review*, 60(2–3), pp. 169–96.

Claiborne, N. (2004) 'Presence of social workers in non-governmental organizations', *Social Work*, 49(2), pp. 207–18.

Cleaveland, C. (2011) 'Borders, police and jobs: Viewing Latino immigration through a social spatial lens', *Families in Society*, 92(2), pp. 139–45.

Cleaver, F. (2001) 'Institutions, agency and the limitations of participatory approaches to development', in Cooke, B. & Kothari, U. (eds) *Participation: The New Tyranny?* London: Zed Books.

Coates, J. (2003) *Ecology and Social Work: Towards a New Paradigm*. Black Point: Fernwood.

Coates, J. (2005) 'The environmental crisis: Implications for social work', *Journal of Progressive Human Services*, 16(1), pp. 25–49.

Coates, R., Umbreit, M. & Vos, B. (2003) 'Restorative justice circles: An exploratory study', *Contemporary Justice Review*, 6(3), pp. 265–78.

Conley, A. (2010) 'Social development, social investment and child welfare', in Midgley, J. & Conley, A. (eds) *Social Work and Social Development: Theories and Skills for Developmental Social Work*. New York: Oxford University Press.

Correll, D. (2008) 'The politics of poverty and social development', *International Social Work*, 51(4), pp. 453–66.

Correll, D. (2011) 'News and views . . . from ICSW: Poverty eradication', *International Social Work*, 54(6), pp. 852–4.

Cox, D. & Pawar, M. (2013) *International Social Work: Issues, Strategies and Programs*. 2nd edition. Thousand Oaks: SAGE.

Cronin, M., Ryan, D. & Brier, D. (2007) 'Support for staff working in disaster situations: A social work perspective', *International Social Work*, 50(3), pp. 370–82.

Davies, M. (2011) 'Intercountry adoption, children's rights and the politics of rescue', *Adoption & Fostering*, 35(4), pp. 50–62.

Deacon, B. (2007) *Global Social Policy and Governance*. London: SAGE.

Deacon, B. & Cohen, S. (2011) 'From the global politics of poverty alleviation to the global politics of social solidarity', *Global Social Policy*, 11(2), pp. 233–49.

Deacon, B., Ortiz, I. & Zelenev, S. (2007) *Regional Social Policy*, DESA Working Paper no. 37. New York: UN Department of Economic and Social Affairs.

DePoy, E. & Gilson. (2012) 'Social work practice with disability: Moving from the perpetuation of a client category to local through global human rights and social justice', *Revista de Asistenta Sociala*, 9(1), pp. 11–22 (in English).

Dominelli, L. (2007) 'Globalising communities: Players and non-players', in Dominelli, L. (ed.) *Revitalising Communities in a Globalising World*. Aldershot: Ashgate.

Dominelli, L. (2008) *Anti-Racist Social Work*. 3rd edition. Basingstoke: Palgrave-Macmillan.

Dominelli, L. (2012) *Green Social Work*. Cambridge: Polity Press.

Dominelli, L. (2013) 'Empowering disaster-affected communities for long-term reconstruction: Intervening in Sri Lanka after the tsunami', *Journal of Social Work in Disability and Rehabilitation*, 12(1–2), pp. 48–66.

Drolet, J. (2009) 'Women and microcredit: Implications for social and economic development', *Social Development Issues*, 31(1), pp. 55–68.

Drolet, J. (2011a) 'Women, micro credit and empowerment in Cairo, Egypt', *International Social Work*, 54(5), pp. 629–45.

Drolet, J. (2011b) 'Women's micro credit loans and *Gami'yyaat* saving clubs in Cairo, Egypt', *Journal of Human Security*, 7(2), pp. 20–31.

Drolet, J. (2014) *Social Protection and Social Development*. Winnipeg: Fernwood.

Drolet, J. & Heinonen, T. (2012) 'An introduction to international social development', in Heinonen, T. & Drolet, J. (eds) *International Social Development: Social Work Experiences and Perspectives*. Halifax: Fernwood.

Eilers, K. (2008) 'René Sand (Belgium)', in Seibel, F. (ed.) *Global Leaders for Social Work Education. The IASSW Presidents 1928–2008*. Ostrava: ECSPRESS-edition.

Elliott, D. (1993) 'Social work and social development: Towards an integrative model of social work practice', *International Social Work*, 36(1), pp. 21–36.

Elliott, D. & Mayadas, N.S. (1996) 'Social development and clinical practice in social work', *International Social Work*, 21(1), pp. 61–8.

Elliott, D. & Mayadas, N.S. (2000) 'International perspectives on social work practice', in Allen-Meares, P. & Garvin, C. (eds) *The Handbook of Social Work Direct Practice*. Thousand Oaks: SAGE.

Elliott, D. & Mayadas, N.S. (2001) 'Psychosocial approaches, social work and social development', *Social Development Issues*, 23(1), pp. 5–13.

England, H. (1986) *Social Work as Art*. Hemel Hempstead: Allen & Uniwin.

Esping-Andersen, G. (1990) *The Three Worlds of Welfare Capitalism*. Cambridge: Polity Press.

Evers, A. & Svetlik, I. (eds) (1991) *New Welfare Mixes in Care for the Elderly* (vols. 1–3). Vienna: European Centre for Social Welfare Policy and Research.

Ferguson, I. (2007) 'Increasing user choice or privatising risk? The antinomies of personalization', *British Journal of Social Work*, 37(3), pp. 387–403.

Ferguson, I. & Lavalette, M. (2005) '"Another world is possible": Social work and the struggle for social justice', in Ferguson, I., Lavalette, M. & Whitmore, E. (eds) *Globalisation, Global Justice and Social Work*. London: Routledge.

Ferrera, M. (1996) 'The "southern model" of welfare in social Europe', *Journal of European Social Policy*, 6(1), pp. 17–37.

Flexner, A. (1915) 'Is social work a profession?', *Proceedings of the National Conference of Charities and Corrections*. London: Hildman.

Fook, J. (1993) *Radical Casework: A Theory of Practice*. St Leonards: Allen & Unwin.

Fook, J. (2002) *Social Work: Critical Theory and Practice*. London: SAGE.

Fook, J. & Gardner, F. (2007) *Critical Reflection in Practice*. Maidenhead: Open University Press.

Forgery, M.A., Cohen, C.S., Berger, S. & Chazin, R. (2003) 'Surviving translation: Teaching the essentials of social work practice in Vietnam', *Journal of Teaching in Social Work*, 23(1/2), pp. 147–66.

Fortescue Metals (2015) *A Billion Opportunities*. Electronic document accessed on 5 January 2015 at http://www.fmgl.com.au/Community/A_Billion_Opportunities

Francis, P. (2002) 'Social capital, civil society and social exclusion', in Kothari, U. & Minogue, M. (eds) *Development Theory and Practice: Critical Perspectives*. Basingstoke: Palgrave-Macmillan.

Franco, L.M., McKay, M., Miranda, A., Chambers, N., Paulino, A. & Lawrence, R. (2007) 'Voices from the community', *Social Work in Mental Health*, 5(3/4), pp. 313–31.

Furman, R., Downey, E.P. & Jackson, R.L. (2004) 'Exploring the ethics of treatment for depression: The ethics of care perspective', *Smith College Studies in Social Work*, 74(3), pp. 525–38.

Gapminder (2014) *The Wealth and Health of Nations*. Electronic document accessed on 25 May 2014 at http://www.gapminder.org/world

Gao, L.Z. & Hu, H.C. (2005) 'Overview of and reflections on Chinese practice of microcredit for poverty alleviation', *Social Development Issues*, 27(3), pp. 35–48.

Garnaut, R. (2008) *The Garnaut Climate Change Review: Final Report*. Melbourne: Cambridge University Press.

George, M. (2011) 'In the midst of a storm: Distress of Kerala women', *Affilia*, 26(3), pp. 304–13.

Girdwood, J. (2007) 'Reforming the World Bank: From social-liberalism to neo-liberalism', *Comparative Education*, 43(3) (Special Issue 34), pp. 413–31.

Gökavali, U. (2013) 'Everyone's own poverty: Gendering poverty alleviation in Turkey', *Women's Studies International Forum*, 41(1), pp. 65–75.

Gover, A. (2013) 'The right to health in the post-2015 development paradigm', *Reproductive Health Matters*, 21(42), pp. 41–2.

Government of Vietnam (2010) *Decision No 32/2010/QĐ-TTg: Decision on the Approval of the Social Work Profession Development Project 2010–2020*. Hanoi: Government of Vietnam [original in Vietnamese].

Graham, M. (2002) *Social Work and African-Centred World Views*. Birmingham: Venture Press.

Gray, M. (2005) 'Dilemmas of international social work: Paradoxical processes of indigenisation, universalism and imperialism', *International Journal of Social Welfare*, 14(3), pp. 231–8.

Gray, M. (2006) 'The progress of social development in South Africa', *International Journal of Social Welfare*, 19(supplement 1), pp. S53–64.

Gray, M. (2013) *Environmental Social Work*. London: Routledge.

Gray, M. & Crofts, P. (2008) 'Social development and its relevance to Australian social work', *Australian Social Work*, 61(1), pp. 88–103.

Gray, M. & Webb, S.A. (2014) 'The making of civil society politics in social work: Myth and misrepresentation with the Global Agenda', *International Social Work*, 57(4), pp. 346–59.

Green, D. & McDermott, F. (2010) 'Social work from inside and between complex systems: Perspectives on person-in-environment for today's social work', *British Journal of Social Work*, 40(8), pp. 2414–30.

Green, M. (2002) 'Social development: Issues and approaches' in Kothari, U. & Minogue, M. (eds) *Development Theory and Practice: Critical Perspectives*. Basingstoke: Palgrave Macmillan.

Green, S. & Baldry, E. (2008) 'Building Australian Indigenous social work', *Australian Social Work*, 61(4), pp. 389–402.

Green, S. & Baldry, E. (2013) 'Indigenous social work education in Australia', in Bennett, B., Green, S., Gilbert, S. & Bessarab, D. (eds) *Our Voices: Aboriginal and Torres Strait Islander Social Work*. South Yarra: Palgrave-Macmillan.

Gulcur, L., Tsembris, S., Stefancic, A. & Greenwood, R. (2007) 'Community integration of adults with psychiatric disabilities and histories of homelessness', *Community Mental Health Journal*, 43(3), pp. 211–28.

Habibov, N.N. (2010) 'Understanding the over-time evolution of living standard determinants in transitional countries: Evidence from Azerbaijan', *Journal of Comparative Social Welfare*, 26(1), pp. 43–63.

Han, C.K., Grinstein-Weiss, M. & Sherraden, M. (2009) 'Assets beyond savings in individual development accounts', *Social Service Review*, 83(2), pp. 221–44.

Hansen, J.E. (no date) *Settlement Houses: An Introduction*. Electronic document downloaded on 20 August 2014 from http://www.socialwelfarehistory.com/programs/settlement-houses

Haug, E. (2005) 'Critical reflections on the emerging discourse of international social work', *International Social Work*, 48(2), pp. 126–35.

Hayduk, N. & McKenzie, B. (2012) 'Developing a sustainable model of social work in the Ukraine', in Heinonen, T. & Drolet, J. (eds) *International Social Development: Social Work Experiences and Perspectives*. Halifax: Fernwood.

Haynes, J. (2008) *Development Studies*. Cambridge: Polity Press.

Haynes, J.M. (2014) 'Safe Third Country Agreement: Closing the doors on refugee women seeking protection', *Families in Society*, 95(2), pp. 140–8.

Healy, L.M. (2008) *International Social Work*. 2nd edition. New York: Oxford University Press.

Healy, L.M. & Wairire, G.G. (2014) 'Educating for the global agenda: Internationally relevant conceptual frameworks and knowledge for social work education', *International Social Work*, 57(3), pp. 235–47.

Hearn, J. (2012) *Theorizing Power*. Basingstoke: Palgrave-Macmillan.

Heidemann, G. & Ferguson, K.M. (2009) 'The girl child: A review of the empirical literature', *Affilia: Journal of Women and Social Work*, 24(2), pp. 165–85.

Helm, D. & Hepburn, C. (2009) (eds) *The Economics and Politics of Climate Change*. Oxford: Oxford University Press.

Hines, A., Cohen, E., Tran, T.D., Lee, P.A. & Le Van Phu (2010) 'The development of social work in Vietnam: The role of international collaboration', *Social Work Education*, 29(8), pp. 910–22.

Hinman, L.M. (2012) *Ethics: A Pluralistic Approach to Moral Theory*. 5th edition. Boston: Wadsworth.

Hochfeld, T. (2010) 'Social development and minimum standards in social work education in South Africa', *Social Work Education*, 29(4), pp. 356–71.

Holkup, P.A., Salois, E.M., Tripp-Reimer, T. & Weinert, C. (2007) 'Drawing on wisdom from the past: An elder abuse intervention with tribal communities' *The Gerontologist*, 47(2), pp. 248–54.

Holliday, I. (2000) 'Productivist welfare capitalism: Social policy in East Asia', *Political Studies*, 48(4), pp. 706–23.

Hölscher, D. (2008) 'The emperor's new clothes: South Africa's attempted transition to developmental social welfare and social work', *International Journal of Social Welfare*, 17(2), pp. 114–23.

Huang, J. (2010) 'Effects of individual development accounts (IDAs) on household wealth and savings tastes', *Research on Social Work Practice*, 20(6), pp. 582–90.

Hudson, J., Khüner, S. & Yang, N. (2014) 'Productive welfare, the East Asian "model" and beyond: Placing welfare types in Greater China into context', *Social Policy and Society*, 13(2), pp. 301–15.

Hugman, R. (1991) *Power in Caring Professions*. Basingstoke: Macmillan.

Hugman, R. (1998) *Social Welfare and Social Value*. Basingstoke: Macmillan.

Hugman, R. (2005) *New Approaches in Ethics for the Caring Professions*. Basingstoke: Palgrave-Macmillan.

Hugman, R. (2008) 'Ethics in a world of difference', *Ethics & Social Welfare*, 2(2), pp. 118–32.

Hugman, R. (2009) 'But is it social work? Some reflections on mistaken identities', *British Journal of Social Work*, 39(6), pp. 1138–53.

Hugman, R. (2010) *Understanding International Social Work: A Critical Inquiry*. Basingstoke: Palgrave-Macmillan.

Hugman, R. (2013) *Culture, Values and Ethics in Social Work*. London: Routledge.

Hugman, R. (2014) *Review of the Implementation of Decision 32/2010/QĐ-TTg Concerning National Plan 32 to Develop Professional Social Work*. (Unpublished report.) Hanoi, UNICEF Vietnam/MOLISA.

Hugman, R. & Bartolomei, L. (2014) 'The ethics of participation in community work practice', in Larsen, A.K., Sewpaul, V. & Hole, G.O. (eds) *Participation in Community Work*. London: Routledge.

Hugman, R., Durst, D., Nguyen Thi Thai Lan, Le Hong Loan & Nguyen Thuy Hong (2009) 'Developing social work in Vietnam: Issues in professional education', *Social Work Education*, 28(2), pp. 177–89.

Hugman, R., Nguyen Thi Thai Lan & Nguyen Thuy Hong (2007) 'Developing social work in Vietnam', *International Social Work*, 50(2), pp. 197–211.

Hugman, R., Pittaway, E. & Bartolomei, L. (2011) 'When "do no harm" is not enough: The ethics of research with refugees and other vulnerable groups', *British Journal of Social Work*, 41(7), pp. 1271–87.

Huston, L. (1991) *Shifts in the Welfare Mix: The Case of Care for the Elderly*. Vienna: European Centre for Social Welfare Policy and Research.

Ife, J. (2010) *Human Rights From Below: Achieving Rights Through Community Development*. Port Melbourne: Cambridge University Press.

Ife, J. (2012) *Human Rights and Social Work: Towards Rights-Based Practice*. 3rd edition. Port Melbourne: Cambridge University Press.

Ife, J. (2013) *Community Development in an Uncertain World*. Port Melbourne: Cambridge University Press.

International Association of Schools of Social Work (IASSW) (2010) *Policy Document on Disaster Interventions*. Electronic document accessed on 22 October 2014 at http://www.iassw-aiets.org/disaster-response-committee

International Association of Schools of Social Work/International Council on Social Welfare/International Federation of Social Workers (IASSW/ICSW/IFSW) (2014) 'Global agenda for social work and social development: First report 2014. Promoting social and economic equalities', in *International Social Work*, 57(Supplement), pp. 1–63.

International Association of Schools of Social Work/International Federation of Social Workers (IASSW/IFSW) (2004) *Global Standards for Education and Training in Social Work*. Electronic document accessed on 31 December 2014 at http://www.iassw-aiets.org/global-standards-for-social-work-education-and-training

International Federation of Social Workers (IFSW) (2012) *Globalization and the Environment*. Electronic document, accessed on 22 October 2014 at http://ifsw.org/policies/globalisation-and-the-environment

International Federation of Social Workers/International Association of Schools of Social Work (IFSW/IASSW) (2004) *Ethics in Social Work: Statement of Principles*. Electronic document accessed on 22 October 2014 at http://ifsw.org/policies/statement-of-ethical-principles

International Federation of Social Workers/International Association of Schools of Social Work (IFSW/IASSW) (2014) *Global Definition of Social Work*. Electronic document accessed on 31 December 2014 at http://ifsw.org/policies/definition-of-social-work

International Labour Organization (ILO) (1952) *Social Security (Minimum Standards) Convention (no. 102)*. Geneva: International Labour Organization.

International Labour Organization (ILO) (2012) *Social Protection Floors Recommendation* (no. 202). Geneva: International Labour Organization.

Jansen, G. & Pippard, J. (1998) 'The Grameen bank in Bangladesh: Helping poor women with credit for self-employment', *Journal of Community Practice*, 5(1/2), pp. 103–23.

Javadian, R. (2007) 'Social work responses to earthquake disasters: A social work intervention in Bam, Iran', *International Social Work*, 50(3), pp. 334–46.

Jeyasingham, D. (2012) 'White noise: A critical evaluation of social work education's engagement with Whiteness studies', *British Journal of Social Work*, 42(4), pp. 669–86.

Johnson, Y.M. (1999) 'Indirect work: Social work's uncelebrated strength', *Social Work*, 44(4), pp. 323–34.

Jorgenson, A.K. & Rice, J. (2010) 'Urban slum growth and human health: A panel study of infant and child mortality in less-develop countries, 1990–2005', *Journal of Poverty*, 14(4), pp. 382–402.

Juliá, M. & Kondrat, M.E. (2005) 'Health care in the social development context', *International Social Work*, 48(5), pp. 537–52.

Kabeer, N. (1991) 'Gender dimensions of rural poverty: Analysis from Bangladesh', *Journal of Peasant Studies*, 18(2), pp. 241–62.

Kabeer, N. (2001) 'Ideas, economics and the "sociology of supply": Explanations for fertility decline in Bangladesh', *Journal of Development Studies*, 38(1), pp. 29–70.

Kabeer, N. (2012) 'Empowerment, citizenship and gender justice: A contribution to locally grounded theories of change in women's lives', *Ethics & Social Welfare*, 6(3), pp. 216–32.

Kam, Y.W. (2012) 'The contributions of the health decommodification typologies to the study of the east Asian welfare regime', *Social Policy and Administration*, 46(1), pp. 108–28.

Karger, H., Iyani, C. & Shannon, P. (2007) 'The challenge of community work in the global economy', *Journal of Sociology & Social Welfare*, 34(2), pp. 69–85.

Karlsson, L. (2012) 'Demography of colonisation and the ageing population: Population profiles and mortality in Swedish Sápmi, 1750–1900', *Ageing & Society*, 32(5), pp. 812–32.

Kautto, M., Heikkilä, M., Hvinden, B., Marklund, S. & Ploug, N. (1999) 'The Nordic welfare states in the 1990s', in Kautto, M., Heikkilä, M., Hvinden, B., Marklund, S. & Ploug, N. (eds) *Nordic Social Policy: Changing Welfare States*. London: Routledge.

Kemp, S. (2001) 'Environment through a gendered lens: From person-in-environment to woman-in environment', *Journal of Women and Social Work*, 16(1), pp. 1–16.

Kenny, C. (2011) *Getting Better: Why Global Development Is Succeeding and How We Can Improve the World Even More*. New York: Basic Books.

Kenny, S. (2010) *Developing Communities for the Future*. 4th edition. South Melbourne: Thomson.

Khinduka, S. (1987) 'Development and peace: The complex nexus', *Social Development Issues*, 19(3), pp. 19–30.

Kim, J. (2010) 'Income inequality in China', *Journal of East Asian Affairs*, 24(2), pp. 29–50.

Kingsbury, D. (2008a) 'Globalization and development' in Kingsbury, D., McKay, J., Hunt, J., McGillivray, M. & Clarke, M. (eds) *International Development: Issues and Challenges*. Basingstoke: Palgrave Macmillan.

Kingsbury, D. (2008b) 'Environment and development' in Kingsbury, D., McKay, J., Hunt, J., McGillivray, M. & Clarke, M. (eds) *International Development: Issues and Challenges*. Basingstoke: Palgrave Macmillan.

Kirk, C., Lewis, R., Lee, F. & Stowell, D. (2011) 'The power of aspirations and expectations', *Journal of Prevention & Intervention in the Community*, 39(4), pp. 320–32.

Kirk, J. & Garrow, S. (2003) '"Girls in policy": Challenges for the education sector', *Agenda*, 17(56), pp. 4–15.

Koehn, D. (1994) *The Ground of Professional Ethics*. London: Routledge.

Kondrat, M.E. (2002) 'Actor-centered social work: Revisioning "person-in-environment" through a critical lens', *Social Work*, 47(4), pp. 435–48.

Kothari, U. (2002) 'Feminist and postcolonial challenges to development', in Kothari, U. & Minogue, M. (eds) *Development Theory and Practice: Critical Perspectives*. Basingstoke: Palgrave Macmillan.

Kothari, U. & Minogue, M. (2002) 'Critical perspective on development: An introduction' in Kothari, U. & Minogue, M. (eds) *Development Theory and Practice: Critical Perspectives*. Basingstoke: Palgrave Macmillan.

Ku, H.B., Yeung, S.C. & Sung-Chan, P. (2005) 'Searching for a capacity building model in social work education in China', *Social Work Education*, 24(2), pp. 213–33.

Kuruvilla, S. (2005) 'Social work and social development in India', in Ferguson, I., Lavalette, M. & Whitmore, E. (eds) *Globalisation, Global Justice and Social Work*. London: Routledge.

Kutcher, S., Chehil, S. & Roberts, T. (2005) 'An integrated program to train local health care providers to meet post-disaster mental health needs', *Pan-American Journal of Public Health*, 18(4/5), pp. 338–45.

Kvernflaten, B. (2013) 'Meeting targets or saving lives: Maternal health policy and Millennium Development Goal #5 in Nicaragua', *Reproductive Health Matters*, 21(42), pp. 32–40.

Lai, D.W.L. & Chui, E.W.T. (2014) 'A tale of two cities: A comparative study on the welfare regimes of Hong Kong and Macao', *Social Policy and Society*, 13(2), pp. 263–74.

Lai, K. (2006) *Learning From Chinese Philosophies: Ethics of Interdependent and Contextualised Self.* Aldershot: Ashgate.

Laird, S.E. (2008) 'Social work practices to support survival strategies in sub-Saharan Africa', *British Journal of Social Work*, 38(1), pp. 135–51.

Larance, L.Y. (2001) 'Fostering social capital through NGO design: Grameen Bank membership in Bangladesh', *International Social Work*, 44(1), pp. 7–18.

Larsen, A.K., Sewpaul, V. & Hole, G.O. (2014) 'Participation in community work: International perspectives', in Larsen, A.K., Sewpaul, V. & Hole, G.O. (eds) *Participation in Community Work*. London: Routledge.

Lavalette, M. & Ferguson, I. (eds) (2007) *International Social Work and the Radical Tradition.* Birmingham: Venture Press.

Lavitt, M. (2009) 'What is advanced generalist practice? A conceptual discussion', *Journal of Teaching in Social Work*, 29(4), pp. 461–73.

Lee, J. (2013) 'Housing policy and asset building: Exploring the role of home ownership in East Asian social policy', *China Journal of Social Work*, 6(2), pp. 104–17.

Lešnik, B. & Urek, M. (2010) 'Traps of humanitarian aid: Observations from a village community in Sri Lanka', *European Journal of Social Work*, 13(2), pp. 271–82.

Li, W.D.H. (2012) 'East Asian welfare model refocus? A case study on economic support for the elderly living alone in Taiwan', *International Journal of Social Welfare*, 22(3), pp. 260–8.

Lombard, A. (2008) 'Social change through integrated social and economic development in South Africa: A social welfare perspective', *Journal of Comparative Social Welfare*, 24(1), pp. 23–32.

Lombard, A. & Wairire, G. (2010) 'Developmental social work in South Africa and Kenya: Some lessons for Africa', *Social Work Practitioner-Researcher*, 22(special issue), pp. 98–111.

Lombe, M., Nebbitt, V.E. & Buerlien, J. (2007) 'Perceived effects of participation in an asset-building program on constructing future possibilities', *Families in Society: the Journal of Contemporary Social Services*, 88(3), pp. 463–71.

Lombe, M., Newransky, C. & Safadi, N.S. (2014) 'Assessing the effects of an asset-building program in resource-constrained households: The case of Sub-Saharan Africa', *Journal of Social Service Research*, 40(1), pp. 15–28.

Lombe, M. & Ssewamala, F.M. (2007) 'The role of social networks in micro-saving mobilization', *Journal of Sociology and Social Welfare*, 34(3), pp. 37–51.

Lordan, G., Tang, K.K. & Carmignani, F. (2011) 'Has HIV/AIDS displaced other health funding priorities? Evidence from a new dataset of development aid for health', *Social Science & Medicine*, 73(3), pp. 351–5.

Lue, J.-D. (2014) 'Globalisation, democratisation and the institutional transformation of Taiwan's welfare regime', *Social Policy and Society*, 13(2), pp. 275–84.

Lundy, C. (2004) *Social Work and Social Justice*. Calgary: Broadview Press.

Lundy, C. (2006) 'Social work's commitment to social and economic justice', in Hall, N. (ed.) *Social Work: Making a Difference*. Berne: IFSW/FAFO.

Lyons, K. (1999) *International Social Work: Themes and Perspective*. Aldershot: Ashgate.

Lyons, K., Manion, K. & Carlsen, M. (2006) *International Perspectives on Social Work*. Basingstoke: Palgrave-Macmillan.

Mafile'o, T. (2004) 'Exploring Tongan social work: Fakafekau'aki (Connecting) and Fakatokilalo (Humility)', *Qualitative Social Work*, 3(3), pp. 239–57.

Maglajlic, R.A. (2011) 'International organisations, social work and war: A "frog's perspective" reflection on the bird's eye view', in Lavalette, M. & Iakomidis, I. (eds) *Social Work in Extremis: Lessons for Social Work Internationally*. Bristol: Policy Press.

Maidment, J. & Brook, G. (2014) 'Teaching and learning groupwork using tutorial and community engagement', *Social Work With Groups*, 37(1), pp. 73–84.

Maslow, A. (1954) *Motivation and Personality*. New York: Harper & Row.

Mason, R. (2011) 'Confronting uncertainty: Lessons from rural social work', *Australian Social Work*, 64(3), pp. 377–94.

Mathbor, G.M. (2007) 'Enhancement of community preparedness for natural disasters', *International Social Work*, 50(3), pp. 357–69.

Mathbor, G.M. & Ferdinand, P.A. (2008) 'Progress or regress of the MDGs: South Asia perspective', *Journal of Comparative Social Welfare*, 24(1), pp. 49–64.

Mbiti, J.S. (1990) *African Religions and Philosophy*. 2nd edition. Oxford: Heinemann.

McGee, R. (2002) 'Participating in development', in Kothari, U. & Minogue, M. (eds) *Development Theory and Practice: Critical Perspectives*. Basingstoke: Palgrave Macmillan.

McGillivray, M. (2008) 'What is development?' in Kingsbury, D., McKay, J., Hunt, J., McGillivray, M. & Clarke, M. (eds) *International Development: Issues and Challenges*. Basingstoke: Palgrave Macmillan.

McKay, J. (2008) 'The economics of development', in Kingsbury, D., McKay, J., Hunt, J., McGillivray, M. & Clarke, M. (eds) *International Development: Issues and Challenges*. Basingstoke: Palgrave Macmillan.

McKinnon, J. (2008) 'Exploring the nexus between social work and the environment', *Australian Social Work*, 61(3), pp. 256–68.

Meinert, R. & Kohn, E. (1987) 'Towards operationalization of social development concepts', *Social Development Issues*, 8(1/2), pp. 70–88.

Mendes, P. (2007) 'Social workers and social activism in Victoria, Australia', in *Journal of Progressive Human Services*, 18(1), pp. 25–44.

Mendes, P. & Binns, P. (2013) 'The integration of community development values, skills and strategies within rural social work practices in Victoria, Australia', *Community Development Journal*, 48(4), pp. 605–22.

Mendoza, R. (2010) *Inclusive Crises, Exclusive Recoveries and Policies to Precent a Double Whammy for the Poor*. New York: UNICEF.

Midgley, J. (1981) *Professional Imperialism*. London: Heinemann.

Midgley, J. (1984) 'Social welfare implications of development paradigms', *Social Service Review*, 58(2), pp. 181–98.

Midgley, J. (1995) *Social Development: The Developmental Perspective in Social Welfare*. Thousand Oaks: SAGE.

Midgley, J. (1997) *Social Welfare in Global Context*. Thousand Oaks: SAGE.

Midgley, J. (2010) 'The theory and practice of developmental social work', in Midgley, J. & Conley, A. (eds) *Social Work and Social Development: Theories and Skills for Developmental Social Work*. New York: Oxford University Press.

Midgley, J. (2014) *Social Development: Theory and Practice*. Los Angeles: SAGE

Miller, S., Hayward, R. & Shaw, T. (2012) 'Environmental shifts for social work: A principles approach', *International Journal of Social Welfare*, 21(3), pp. 71–7.

Mishra, R. (1984) *The Welfare State in Crisis*. Brighton: Harvester-Wheatsheaf.

Mlama, P. (2005) 'Pressure from within: the Forum for African Women Educationalists', in Rao, N. & Smyth. I. (eds) *Partnerships for Girls' Education*. Oxford: Oxfam GB, pp. 49–63.

Mohan, B. (1988) *The Logic of Social Welfare: Conjectures and Formulations*. Hemel Hempstead: Harvester Wheatsheaf.

Mohan, B. (1992) *Global Development: Post-Material Values and Social Praxis*. New York: Praeger.

Mohan, B. (2007) 'Social exclusions: Challenges for new social development', *Journal of Comparative Social Welfare*, 23(1), pp. 69–79.

Mok, K.H. & Hudson, J. (2014) 'Managing social change and social policy in Greater China: Welfare regimes in transition?', *Social Policy and Society*, 13(2), pp. 235–8.

Moyo, O. & Moldovan, V. (2008) 'Lessons for social workers: Hurricane Katrina as a social disaster', *Social Development Issues*, 30(1), pp. 1–12.

Mullaly, B. (2003) *Structural Social Work: Ideology, Theory and Practice*. Ontario: Oxford University Press.

Mupedziswa, R. (2008) 'Twenty-two years of training social work practitioners: Reflections on strategies and techniques', *Journal of Teaching in Social Work*, 28(3/4), pp. 343–55.

Murdach, A. D. (2006) 'Rhetoric for direct practice', *Social Work*, 51(4), pp. 365–8.

Mushunje, M.T. & Mafico, M. (2010) 'Social protection for orphans and vulnerable children in Zimbabwe: The case for cash transfers', *International Social Work*, 53(2), pp. 261–75.

Mweru, M. (2008) 'Women, migration and HIV/AIDS in Kenya', *International Social Work*, 51(3), pp. 337–47.

Naess, A. (1989) *Ecology, Community and Lifestyle: Outline of an Ecosophy*. New York: Cambridge University Press.

National Health Performance Authority [NHPA] (2013) *Healthy Communities: Overweight and Obesity Rates Across Australia 2011–12 (In Focus)*. Canberra: Commonwealth of Australia.

Navarro, V. (2007) *Neoliberalism, Globalization and Inequalities: Consequences for Health and Quality of Life*. Amityville: Baywood.

Nawyn, S.J. (2010) 'Institutional structures of opportunity in refugee resettlement: Gender, race/ethnicity and refugee NGOs', in *Journal of Sociology & Social Welfare*, 37(1), pp. 149–67.

Nel, H. & Pretorius, E. (2012) 'Applying appreciate inquiry in building capacity in a non-governmental organization for youths: An example from Soweto, Gauteng, South Africa', *Social Development Issues*, 34(1), pp. 37–55.

Netting, F.E., Kettner, P.M. & McMurtry, S.L. (2004) *Social Work Macro Practice*. Boston: Pearson.

Newman, P., Williams, C.C., Massaquoi, N., Brown, M. & Logie, C. (2008) 'HIV prevention for Black women: Structural barriers and opportunities', *Journal of Health Care for the Poor and Underserved*, 19(3), pp. 829–41.

Ng, I.Y.H. (2013) 'The political economy of intergenerational income mobility in Singapore', *International Journal of Social Welfare*, 22(2), pp. 207–18.

Ng, I.Y.H. & Koh, G. (2012) 'Chinese Singaporean attitudes towards poverty and inequality: A comparative analysis', *International Journal of Social Welfare*, 21(2), pp. 149–59.

Nguyen Thi Oanh (2002) 'Historical development and characteristics of social work in today's Vietnam', *International Journal of Social Welfare*, 11(1), pp. 84–91.

Nguyen Thi Thai Lan (2015) *Social Work in Vietnam: International Organisations and Service Professionalisation for Disadvantaged Children*. Unpublished doctoral thesis. Sydney: University of New South Wales.

Nguyen Thi Thai Lan, Hugman, R. & Briscoe, C. (2010) 'Moving towards an "indigenous" social work education in Vietnam', *Social Work Education*, 29(8), pp. 843–54.

Nicolai, S.S. & Saus, M. (2013) 'Acknowledging the past while looking to the future: Conceptualising Indigenous child trauma', *Child Welfare*, 92(4), pp. 55–74.

Nilsson, D., Joubert, L., Holland, L. & Posenellli, S. (2013) 'The why of practice: Utilizing PIE to analyse social work practice in Australian hospitals', *Social Work in Health Care*, 52(2/3), pp. 280–95.

Nussbaum, M. (2000) *Women and Human Development*. New York: Oxford University Press.

Nussbaum, M. (2011) *Creating Capabilities: The Human Development Approach*. Cambridge: Belknap Press.

Nuttman-Schwarz, O., Dekel, R. & Tuval-Mashiach, R. (2011) 'Post-traumatic stress and growth following forced relocation', *British Journal of Social Work*, 41(3), pp. 486–501.

Ohmer, M. (2010) 'How theory and research inform citizen participation in poor communities', *Journal of Human Behavior in the Social Environment*, 20(1), pp. 1–19.

Olson, J. (2007) 'Social work's professional and social justice projects: Conflicts in discourse', *Journal of Progressive Human Services*, 18(1), pp. 45–69.

Ortiz, I. (2007) *Social Policy*. National Development Strategies, Social Policy Notes. New York: UN Department for Economic and Social Affairs.

Osei-Hwedie, K. (1993) 'The challenge of social work in Africa: Starting the indigenization process', *Journal of Social Development in Africa*, 8(1), pp. 19–30.

Osei-Hwedie, K., Ntsane, D. & Jaques, G. (2006) 'Searching for appropriateness in social work education in Botswana', *Social Work Education*, 25(6), pp. 569–90.

Overseas Development Institute [ODI] (2009) *The Global Financial Crisis: Poverty and Social Protection*. Discussion Paper 51. London: ODI.

Park, Y. & Miller, J. (2006) 'The social ecology of Hurricane Katrina: Rewriting the discourse of "natural" disasters', *Smith College Studies in Social Work*, 76(3), pp. 9–24.

Parrish, D.E., Harris, D. & Pritzker, S. (2013) 'Assessment of a service provider self-study method to promote interorganizational and community collaboration', *Social Work*, 58(4), pp. 354–64.

Parton, N. (2006) *Safeguarding Childhood: Early Intervention and Surveillance in a Late Modern Society*. Basingstoke: Palgrave Macmillan.

Parton, N., Thorpe, D. & Wattam, C. (1997) *Child Protection, Risk and the Moral Order*. Basingstoke: Macmillan.

Patel, L. (2005) *Social Welfare and Social Development in South Africa*. Cape Town: Oxford University Press.

Pawar, M. (2012) *Community Development in Asia and the Pacific*. London: Routledge.

Pawar, M. (2014a) *Water and Social Policy*. Basingstoke: Palgrave-Macmillan.

Pawar, M. (2014b) *Social and Community Development Practice*. New Delhi: SAGE.

Pawar, M. & Torres, R. (2011) 'Integrated community development through dialogue, capacity-building and partnership in an Australian town', *Journal of Comparative Social Welfare*, 27(3), pp. 253–68.

Payne, M. (2014) *Modern Social Work Theory*. 4th edition. Basingstoke: Palgrave-Macmillan.

Payne, M. & Askeland, G.A. (2008) *Globalisation and International Social Work: Postmodern Change and Challenge*. Aldershot: Ashgate.

Pease, B. & Fook, J. (1999) 'Postmodern critical theory and emancipatory social work practice', in Fook, J. & Pease, B. (eds) *Transforming Social Work Practice: Postmodern Critical Perspectives*. London: Routledge.

Pierre-Louis, F. (2011) 'Earthquakes, nongovernmental organizations and governance in Haiti', *Journal of Black Studies*, 42(2), pp. 186–202.

Pierson, J. (2011) *Understanding Social Work: History and Context*. Maidenhead: Open University Press.

Pittaway, E. & Bartolomei, L. (2003) *Seeking Hope, Seeking Safety*. Research Report. Sydney: UNSW Centre for Refugee Research.

Pittaway, E., Bartolomei, L. & Hugman, R. (2010) '"Stop stealing our stories": The ethics of research with vulnerable groups', *Journal of Human Rights Practice*, 2(2), pp. 229–51.

Pittaway, E., Bartolomei, L. & Pittaway, E. (2003) 'An examination of the role of identity and citizenship in the experiences of women in the Kakuma Refugee camp in northern Kenya', *Development*, 46(3), pp. 87–93.

Pittaway, E., Bartolomei, L. & Rees, S. (2007) 'Gendered dimensions of the 2004 tsunami and a potential social work response in disaster situations', *International Social Work*, 50(3), pp. 307–20.

Popple, K. (2002) 'Community work', in Adams, R., Dominelli, L. & Payne, M. (eds) *Critical Practice in Social Work*. Basingstoke: Palgrave.

Postle, K. & Beresford, P. (2007) 'Capacity building and the reconception of political participation: A role for social care workers?', *British Journal of Social Work*, 37(1), pp. 143–58.

Poulin, J. (2005) *Strengths-Based Generalist Practice: a Collaborative Approach*. 2nd edition. Southbank: Thomson.

Pugh, R. & Cheers, B. (2010) *Rural Social Work – An International Perspective*. Bristol: Policy Press.

Pullen-Sansfaçon, A., Spolander, G. & Englebrecht, L. (2012) 'Migration of professional social workers: Reflections on challenges and strategies for education', *Social Work Education*, 32(8), pp. 1032–45.

Pyles, L. (2006) 'Towards a post-Katrina framework: Social work as human rights and capabilities', *Journal of Comparative Social Welfare*, 22(1), pp. 79–88.

Pyles, L. (2007) 'Community organizing for post-disaster social development: Locating social work', *International Social Work*, 50(3), pp. 321–33.

Pyles, L. (2011) 'Towards sustainable post-Katrina recovery: Lessons learned from African American neighborhoods', *Families in Society: the Journal of Contemporary Social Services*, 92(3), pp. 344–9.

Radermacher, H., Karunarathna, Y., Grace, N. & Feldman, S. (2011) 'Partner or perish? Exploring inter-organizational partnerships in the multicultural community aged care sector', *Health and Social Care in the Community*, 19(5), pp. 550–60.

Rainbow Spirit Elders (2007) *Rainbow Spirit Theology: Towards an Australian Aboriginal Theology*. Hindmarsh: ATF Press.

Rajouria, A. (2008) *Micro-Finance and Empowerment of Women: Evidence from Nepal*. Doctoral thesis. UMI 3311899. Manoa: University of Hawai'i.

Ramon, S. & Maglajlic, R.A. (2012) 'Social work, political conflict and displacement', in Lyons, K., Hokenstad, T., Pawar, M., Hueglar, N. & Hall, N. (eds) The *SAGE Handbook of International Social Work*. London: SAGE.

Rawls, J. (1972) *A Theory of Justice*. Oxford: Clarendon Press.

Razack, N. (2000) 'North/South collaborations', *Journal of Progressive Human Services*, 11(1), pp. 71–91.

Razack, N. (2009) 'Decolonising the pedagogy and practice of international social work', *International Social Work*, 52(1), pp. 9–21.

Reichert, E. (2013) 'Human rights in the twenty-first century: creating a new paradigm for social work', in Reichert, E. (ed.) *Challenges in Human Rights: a Social Work Perspective*. 2nd edition. New York: Columbia University Press.

Reisch, M. (2002) 'Defining social justice in a socially unjust world', *Families in Society: the Journal of Contemporary Social Services*, 83(4), pp. 343–54.

Reisch, M. & Andrews, J. (2014) *The Road Not Taken: a History of Radical Social Work in the United States*. New York: Brunner-Routledge.

Reisch, M. & Jani, J. (2012) 'The new politics of social work: Understanding context to promote change', *British Journal of Social Work*, 42(5), pp. 1–19.

Riga, A. (2008) 'Jan Floris de Jongh (The Netherlands)', in Seibel, F. (ed.) *Global Leaders for Social Work Education. The IASSW Presidents 1928–2008*. Ostrava: ECSPRESS-Edition.

Rivera, D. & Miller, D.S. (2007) 'Continually neglected: Situating natural disasters in the African American experience', *Journal of Black Studies*, 37(4), pp. 502–22.

Robinson, L. (2007) 'Social work through the life course', in Adams, R., Dominelli, L. & Payne, M. (eds) *Social Work: Themes, Issues and Critical Debates*. London: Macmillan.

Rothwell, D.W. (2011) 'The case for asset-based interventions with indigenous peoples: Evidence from Hawai'i', *International Social Work*, 54(1), pp. 35–50.

Rothwell, D.W. & Sultana, N. (2013) 'Cash flow and savings practices of low-income households: Evidence from a follow-up study of IDA participants', *Journal of Social Service Research*, 39(2), pp. 281–92.

Rowlands, A. (2013) 'Disaster recovery management in Australia and the contribution of social work', *Journal of Social Work in Disability and Rehabilitation*, 12(1–2), pp. 19–38.

Rowlands, A. & Tan, N.T. (2007) 'Social development following the Indian Ocean tsunami', *Social Development Issues*, 30(1), pp. 47–58.

Roy, A. (1999) *The Cost of Living*. London: Flamingo.

Rozario, P.A. & Rosetti, A.L. (2012) '"Many helping hands": A review and analysis of long-term care policies, programs and practices in Singapore', *Journal of Gerontological Social Work*, 55(7), pp. 641–58.

Rush, M. & Keenan, M. (2014) 'The social politics of social work: Anti-oppressive social work dilemmas in twenty-first-century welfare regimes', *British Journal of Social Work*, 44(6), pp. 1436–1453.

Sainsbury, D. (ed.) (1994) *Gendering Welfare States*. London: SAGE.

Saith, A. (2006) 'From universal values to Millennium Development Goals: Lost in translation?', *Development and Change*, 37(6), pp. 1167–99.

Saleebey, D. (1996) 'The strengths perspective in social work: Extensions and cautions', *Social Work*, 41(3), pp. 296–305.

Saleebey, D. (ed.) (2002) *The Strengths Perspective in Social Work Practice*. 3rd edition. Boston: Allyn & Bacon.

Saleebey, D. (2004) 'The "power of place": Another look at the environment', *Families in Society: The Journal of Contemporary Social Services*, 85(1), pp. 7–16.

Saleebey, D. (2006) 'A paradigm shift in developmental perspective? The self in context', in Lightburn, A. & Sessions, P. (eds) *Handbook of Community-Based Clinical Practice*. New York: Oxford University Press.

Salmina, A. (2014) 'Social attitudes towards welfare policies in Russia and other European countries', *International Social Work*, 57(5), pp. 459–69.

Schell, C.O., Reilly, M., Rosling, H., Peterson, S. & Ekström, E.K. (2007) 'Socioeconomic determinants of child mortality: A worldwide study of 150 low-, middle- and high-income countries', *Scandinavian Journal of Public Health*, 35(3), pp. 288–97.

Schön, D. (1983) *The Reflective Practitioner: How Practitioners Think in Action*. London: Temple Smith.

Schulze-Boing, M. (2010) 'Inclusion and local development. Challenges for local and regional government', *Revista de Asisenta Sociala*, 9(4), pp. 147–51.

Selman, P. (2011) 'Intercountry adoption after the Haiti earthquake: rescue or robbery?', *Adoption & Fostering*, 35(4), pp. 411–49.

Sen, A. (2009) *The Idea of Justice*. Cambridge: Harvard University Press.

Sercombe, H. (2010) *Youth Work Ethics*. London: SAGE.

Sevenhuijsen, S. (1998) *Citizenship and the Ethics of Care: Feminist Considerations on Justice, Morality and Politics*. London: Routledge.

Shakespeare, T. (2006) *Disability Rights and Wrongs*. Abingdon: Routledge.

Sherraden, M. (1988) 'Rethinking social welfare: Towards assets', *Social Policy*, 18(3), pp. 37–43.

Sherraden, M. (1991) *Assets and the Poor*. New York: Sharpe.

Sherraden, M. & Sherraden, M.S. (2000) 'Asset building: Integrating research, education and practice', *Advances in Social Work*, 1(1), pp. 61–77.

Sherraden, M.S., Laux, S. & Kaufman, C. (2007) 'Financial education for social workers', *Journal of Community Practice*, 15(3), pp. 9–36.

Sherraden, M.S. & Ninacs, W.A. (1998) 'Community economic development and social work', *Journal of Community Practice*, 5(1–2), pp. 109.

Shibuya, T. & Taylor, V. (2013) 'Alternative care options and policy choices to support orphans: The case of Mozambique in the context of the SADC', *International Social Security Review*, 66(1), pp. 71–95.

Shobe, M.A. & Christy-McMullin, K. (2005) 'Savings experiences past and present: Narratives from low-income African American women', *Affilia*, 20(2), pp. 222–37.

Slovak, K., Sparks, A. & Hall, S. (2011) 'Attention to rural populations in social work's scholarly journals', *Journal of Social Services Research*, 37(4), pp. 428–38.

Smith, S.L. (2012) 'Coping with disaster: Lessons learned from executive directors of non-profit organizations (NPOs) in New Orleans following Hurricane Katrina', *Administration in Social Work*, 36(4), pp. 359–89.

Solas, J. (2008) 'Social work and social justice: What are we fighting for', *Australian Social Work*, 61(2), pp. 124–36.

Soma, N., Yamashita, J. & Chan, R.K.H. (2011) 'Comparative framework for care regime analysis in East Asia', *Journal of Comparative Social Welfare*, 27(2), pp. 111–21.

Sommer, M. (2010) 'Where the education system and women's bodies collide: The social and health impact on girls' experiences of menstruation and schooling in Tanzania', *Journal of Adolescence*, 33(4), pp. 521–9.

Spence, P.R., Lachlan, K.A. & Griffin, D.R. (2007) 'Crisis communication, race and natural disasters', *Journal of Black Studies*, 37(4), pp. 539–54.

Spolander, G., Englebrecht, L., Martin, L., Styrdom, M., Pervova, I., Marjanen, P., Sicora, A. & Adaikalam, F. (2014) 'The implications of neoliberalism for social work: Reflections from a six-country international research collaboration', *International Social Work*, 57(4), pp. 301–12.

Ssewamala, F.M., Karimli, L., Han, C. K & Isamyilova, L. (2010) 'Social capital, savings, and educational performance of orphaned adolescents in sub-Saharan Africa', *Children & Youth Services Review*, 32(12), pp. 1704–10.

Staub-Bernasconi, S. (2013) 'Economic and social rights', in Reichert, E. (ed.) *Challenges in Human Rights: a Social Work Perspective*. 2nd edition. New York: Columbia University Press.

Stern, N. (2007) *The Economics of Climate Change*. Cambridge: Cambridge University Press.

Stiglitz, J. (2002) *Globalization and its Discontents*. London: Penguin.

Stiglitz, J. (2006) *Making Globalization Work: The Next Steps in Global Justice*. London: Allen Lane.

Stiglitz, J. (2012) *The Price of Inequality*. New York: Norton.

Suárez, Z., Newman, P. & Reed, B. (2008) 'Critical consciousness and cross-cultural/intersectional social work practice: A case analysis', *Families in Society*, 89(3), pp. 407–17.

Suharto, E. (2009) 'Social protection systems in ASEAN: Social policy in a comparative analysis', *Social Development Issues*, 31(1), pp. 1–26.

Summers, L.H. (1994) *Investing in All the People: Educating Women in Developing Countries*. EDI Seminar Paper #45. Washington, DC: World Bank.

Swart, E. (2012) 'Gender-based violence in a Kenyan slum: Creating local, women centered interventions', *Journal of Social Service Research*, 38(4), pp. 427–38.

Tang, K.-L. & Cheung, C.-K. (2007) 'The competence of Hong Kong social work students in working with victims of the 2004 tsunami disaster', *International Social Work*, 50(3), pp. 405–18.

Taubman, A. & Weisz, A. (2011) 'Emerging concerns for international social work and disaster response: From relief to development and sustainability', *Columbia Social Work Review*, 2(1), pp. 37–48.

Terrazas, C., Schwartz, S.L. & Austin, M.J. (2011) 'Girls Incorporated of Alameda County at 50: A voice for girls (1958–2008)', *Journal of Evidence-Based Social Work*, 8(1–2), pp. 66–86.

Thane, P. (1996) *Foundations of the Welfare State*. 2nd edition. London: Longman.

Thompson, N. (1998) 'The ontology of ageing', *British Journal of Social Work*, 28(5), pp. 695–707.

Thorning, H., Shibusawa, T., Lukens, E. & Fang, L. (2013) 'Developing a train-the-trainer (TTT) model for social work education in Kazakhstan', *International Social Work*, 56(4), pp. 534–43.

Todd, S. (2011) '"That power and privilege thing": Securing whiteness in community work', *Journal of Progressive Human Services*, 22, pp. 117–34.

Tomaskovic-Devey, D. & Roscigno, V.J. (2007) 'Uneven development and local inequality in the U.S. South: The role of outside investment, landed elites and racial dynamics', *Sociological Forum*, 12(4), pp. 565–97.

Trocmé, N., Knoke, D. & Blackstock, C. (2004) 'Pathways to the overrepresentation of Aboriginal children in Canada's child welfare system', *Social Service Review*, 78(4), pp. 577–600.

Trudgen, R. (2000) *Djambatj Mala: Why Warriors Lie Down and Die*. Parap: Aboriginal Resource and Development Services.

Tsang, K.Y. & Yan, M.C. (2001) 'Chinese corpus, western application: The Chinese strategy of engagement with western social work discourse', *International Social Work*, 44(4), pp. 433–54.

UNICEF Haiti (2011) *Children in Haiti: One Year After – The Long Road From Relief to Recovery*. Port-au-Prince: UNICEF Haiti.

UNICEF Vietnam (2005) *A Study of the Human Resource and Training Needs for the Development of Social Work in Vietnam*. Hanoi: UNICEF Vietnam.

UNICEF/UNESCO (2013) *Making Education a Priority in the Post-2015 Development Agenda*. New York: UNICEF/UNESCO.

United Nations (1948) *The Universal Declaration of Human Rights*. Resolution 217 A(III). New York: United Nations.

United Nations (1971) *Training for Social Welfare: The Fifth International Survey*. New York: United Nations.

United Nations (1979) *Convention on the Elimination of All Forms of Discrimination Against Women*. Resolution 34/180. New York: United Nations.

United Nations (1989) *Convention on the Rights of the Child*. General Assembly Resolution 44/25. New York: United Nations.

United Nations (1995) *World Summit for Social Development, Copenhagen 1995*. Electronic document accessed on 25 May 2014 at http://www.un.org/esa/socdev/wssd

United Nations (2000) *Millennium Development Goals and Beyond 2015*. Electronic document accessed on 25 May 2014 at http://www.un.org/millenniumgoals

United Nations (2006) *Convention on the Rights of Disabled Persons*. Resolution 61/106. New York: United Nations.

United Nations (2007) *Convention on the Rights of Indigenous Peoples*. Resolution 61/295. New York: United Nations.

United Nations (2015) *Time for Global Action for People and Planet*. Electronic document accessed on 7 January 2015 at http://www.un.org/sustainabledevelopment

United Nations Development Programme (UNDP) (2013) *Humanity Divided: Confronting Inequality in Developing Countries*. New York: UNDP.

United Nations High Commission for Refugees (UNHCR) (1951) *Convention Relating to the Status of Refugees*. Geneva: UNHCR.

United Nations High Commission for Refugees (UNHCR) (2013) *War's Cost: UNHCR Global Trends 2013*. Geneva: UNHCR.

Vander Zaag, R. (2012) 'The ideals of international development assistance', in Heinonen, T. & Drolet, J. (eds) *International Social Development: Social Work Experiences and Perspectives*. Halifax: Fernwood.

Van Hout, M. (2010) 'The Irish Traveller community: Social capital and drug use', *Journal of Ethnicity in Substance Abuse*, 9(3), pp. 186–205.

Van Sluytman, L., Braine, N., Acker, C., Friedman, S. & DesJarlais, D. (2013) 'Migration narratives: Expanding methods to examine the interaction of person and environment among aging gay men', *Journal of Gerontological Social Work*, 56(3), pp. 219–36.

Vijayalakshmi, B., Prasad, D.B., Bhavani, V.P.S. & Haranath, S. (2010) 'Journey with communities: Engagement with SHGs from lower income neighbourhoods in Visakhapatam', *Indian Journal of Social Work*, 71(4), pp. 485–516.

Wadsworth, Y. (2011) *Do It Yourself Social Research*. 2nd edition. Crows Nest: Allen & Unwin.

Wærness, K. (1990) 'Informal and formal care in old age', in Ungerson, C. (ed.) *Gender and Caring: Work and Welfare in Britain and Scandinavia*. Hemel Hempstead: Harvester-Wheatsheaf.

Waker, A. & Wong, C. (eds.) (2005) *East-Asian Welfare Regimes in Transition: From Confucianism to Globalisation*. Bristol: Polity Press.

Walter, M., Taylor, S. & Habibis, D. (2013) 'Australian social work is white', in Bennett, B., Green, S., Gilbert, S. & Bessarab, D. (eds) *Our Voices: Aboriginal and Torres Strait Islander Social Work*. South Yarra: Palgrave-Macmillan.

Walton, R.G. & El Nasr, M.M. (1988) 'The indigenization and authentization of social work in Egypt', *Community Development Journal*, 23(3), pp. 148–55.

Wang, X. & Lum, T.Y. (2013) 'Role of the professional helper in disaster intervention: Examples from the Wenchuan earthquake in China', *Journal of Social Work in Disability and Rehabilitation*, 12(1–2), pp. 116–29.

Weaver, H. (2004) 'The elements of cultural competence', *Journal of Ethnic and Cultural Diversity in Social Work*, 13(1), pp. 19–35.

Wehbi, S. (2011) 'Key theoretical concepts for teaching international social work', *Revista Asistenta Sociala*, 10(4), pp. 23–9 [in English].

Weil, M. (2000) 'Social work in the social environment: Integrated practice – an empowerment/structural approach', in Allen-Meares, P. & Garvin, C. (eds) *The Handbook of Social Work Direct Practice*. Thousand Oaks: SAGE.

Weiss-Gal, I., Levin, L. & Krumer-Nevo, M. (2014) 'Applying critical social work in direct practice with families', *Child & Family Social Work*, 19, pp. 55–64.

Westoby, P. (2008) 'Developing a community development approach through engaging resettling Southern Sudanese refugees within Australia', *Community Development Journal*, 43(4), pp. 483–95.

Whiting, R. (2008) '"No room for religion or spirituality or cooking tips": Exploring practical atheism as an unspoken consensus in the development of social work values in England', *Ethics & Social Welfare*, 2(1), pp. 67–83.

Why Warriors (2005) *AHED – Arnhem Human Enterprise Development*. Electronic document accessed on 5 January 2015 at http://www.whywarriors.com.au/ahed-project/index.php

Wilensky, H.L. & Lebeaux, C.N. (1965) *Industrial Society and Social Welfare: The Impact of Industrialization on the Supply and Organization of Social Welfare Services in the United States*. Glencoe: Free Press.

Wilson, M.G. & Hernández, I.P. (2012) 'Solidarity, common cause, relationship', in Heinonen, T. & Drolet, J. (eds) *International Social Development: Social Work Experiences and Perspectives*. Halifax: Fernwood.

Woodhouse, P. (2002) 'Development policies and environmental agendas', in Kothari, U. & Minogue, M. (eds) *Development Theory and Practice*. London: Palgrave.

World Commission on Environment and Development [WCED] (1987) *Our Common Future* (The Brundtland Commission Report). Oxford: Oxford University Press.

Worrall, J. (2006) 'Challenges of grandparent custody of children at risk in New Zealand', *Families in Society: the Journal of Contemporary Social Services*, 87(4), pp. 546–54.

Wronka, J. (1998) *Human Rights and Social Policy in the 21st Century*. Revised edition. Lanham: University Press of America.

WWF (2014) *Living Planet Report 2014: Species and Spaces, People and Places*. Gland: World Wildlife Fund for Nature.

Yan, M.-C. & Cheung, K.-W. (2006) 'The politics of indigenization: A case study of the development of social work in China', *Journal of Sociology and Social Welfare*, 33(2), pp. 63–84.

Yellow Bird, M. (1999) 'Indian, American Indian and Native American: Counterfeit identities', *Winds of Change: A Magazine for American Indian Education and Opportunity*, 14(1). Electronic document accessed on 8 June 2011 at http://www.aistm.org/yellowbirdessay.htm

Yip, K.S. (2004) 'A Chinese cultural critique of the global qualifying standards for social work education', *Social Work Education*, 23(5), pp. 597–612.

Young, S.M. (2008) 'Indigenous child protection policy in Australia: Using whiteness theory for social work', *Sites*, 5(1), pp. 102–23.

Yunus, M. & Jolis, A. (1998) *Banker to the Poor: The Autobiography of Mohammed Yunus*. London: Aurum Books.

Zhan, M. & Sherraden, M. (2003) 'Assets, expectations and children's educational achievement in female headed households', *Social Service Review*, 77(2), pp. 191–211.

Zhan, M., Anderson, S.G. & Scott, J. (2006) 'Financial management knowledge of the low income population', *Journal of Social Service Research*, 33(10), pp. 93–106.

Zimmer, Z. (2008) 'Poverty, wealth inequality and health among older adults in rural Cambodia', *Social Science & Medicine*, 66(1), pp. 57–71.

INDEX